TEXAS SNAKES

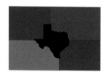

TEXAS NATURAL HISTORY GUIDES™

TEXAS SNAKES

A FIELD GUIDE

JAMES R. DIXON AND JOHN E. WERLER

Line drawings by Regina Levoy

UNIVERSITY OF TEXAS PRESS
Austin

Field guide edition of *Texas Snakes,*
by John E. Werler and James R. Dixon
(University of Texas Press, 2000)

Copyright © 2000, 2005 by the University of Texas Press
All rights reserved
Printed in China
Second field guide printing, 2007

Requests for permission
to reproduce material from this work
should be sent to
Permissions
University of Texas Press
Box 7819
Austin, TX 78713-7819
www.utexas.edu/utpress/about/bpermission.html

⊗ The paper used in this book meets
the minimum requirements of
ANSI/NISO Z39.48-1992 (R1997)
(Permanence of Paper).

LIBRARY OF CONGRESS CATALOGING-IN-PUBLICATION DATA

Dixon, James Ray.
Texas snakes : a field guide / James R. Dixon and John E. Werler.— 1st
field guide ed.
    p.   cm — (Texas natural history guides)
  Rev. ed. of: Texas snakes / John E. Werler and James R. Dixon. 1st ed.
2000.
  Summary: "Field guide to all snake species in Texas with a color photo,
range map, and information on identifying characteristics and behavior
for each snake"—Provided by publisher.
  Includes bibliographical references (p.   ) and index.
  ISBN-13: 978-0-292-70675-0 (pbk. : alk. paper)
  ISBN-10: 0-292-70675-8
1. Snakes—Texas. I. Werler, John E. II. Werler, John E. —Texas snakes.
III. Title. IV. Series.

QL666.O6D59 2005
597.96'09764—dc22   2004026120

We dedicate this book
to our wives,
Mary Dixon
and
the late Ingrid Werler,
and
to our children,
who participated in
nearly all of our field activities
throughout our careers.

CONTENTS

PREFACE

The notion to write a book about Texas snakes first surfaced in my mind during the early 1970s when I was serving as Chief Curator of the Texas Cooperative Wildlife Collection, Department of Wildlife and Fisheries Sciences, Texas A&M University. However, because of teaching duties, research, and other mundane tasks, the project began very slowly. In 1985 I was asked by John E. Werler, my fellow professional zoologist, to join him in an effort to complete the book he had envisioned as the Natural History of the Snakes of Texas. We joined forces and agreed to first complete the book on the natural history of the snakes of Texas, published in 2000, then follow with a field guide on Texas snakes. Before the latter effort could begin, John Werler died after a long and courageous battle with cancer. He is included as an author of this book because much of the wording is his, and I have drawn freely from *Texas Snakes.*

Although this book was written for a broad readership, it is directed primarily at the novice, the amateur naturalist, and the person who maintains live snakes as a hobby. It is expected, however, that the identification keys, general maps, and bits of new natural history information that it contains will be of interest to both the serious student and the professional herpetologist.

While a primary purpose of the book is to help the reader identify the various species and subspecies of Texas snakes, we have made a special effort to showcase their useful characteristics, distribution, and habitat. We believe such information will move the reader to see these creatures in a new light. This is the first step toward building an awareness of the need to conserve them, for with knowledge comes understanding. One other goal of the book is to encourage the serious amateur to submit significant and previously unreported natural history notes and range extensions for publication in appropriate journals or regional herpetological society newsletters. Even anecdotal observations may provide useful supplements to more formal, organized field studies. By reviewing the species and subspecies accounts in this book, the reader may readily detect the absence of some distributional information that may need further investigation.

JAMES R. DIXON, 2005

ACKNOWLEDGMENTS

To the many persons who assisted us in the preparation of this book we owe a profound debt of gratitude. Some, whose names are listed below, offered details of unreported personal observations. Others, whose published works on the taxonomy and natural history of serpents, particularly those in Texas, provided the major sources of information for this volume, are listed in the reference section at the back of the book together with the titles of their contributions. They are no less collaborators on this book than are those who offered us unpublished material.

To our wives, Mary Dixon and the late Ingrid Werler, who gave so generously of their time and understanding so that we could devote our own time to this project, there is no way to express adequately the measure of our gratitude. They also filed reprints, assisted with clerical work in general, and shared with us both the joys and tribulations of many field trips. Sincere thanks also to John Henry Werler, not only for his constant encouragement and companionship in the field but also for introducing his father to the world of computers. I thank LeeAnn Werler for devoting much of her time to the support and care of John E. Werler during his last few months of life. LeeAnn, John E. told me you were his angel on earth, and he said this with deep conviction. The late John E. and I appreciate your devotion.

David Johnson was particularly helpful in providing specimens and literature during virtually the entire time the book was in progress. He also served as our unofficial contact person with private reptile collectors throughout the state, whose cooperation he enlisted for the loan of live specimens to illustrate the book. To him we owe a special debt of gratitude.

Clay Touchstone and Kerry Touchstone, keen naturalists and longtime friends of the authors, also provided numerous live snakes for use as photographic models and over the years eagerly and unfailingly offered other assistance whenever it was needed.

We especially thank the late Dr. Sherman A. Minton, Jr., for reviewing the venomous snakes accounts and for suggesting improvements.

As would be expected, obtaining live photographic models of all the species and subspecies of snakes in a state as large and ecologically diverse as Texas, proved difficult—a task accomplished only with the help of the following herpetologists, both professional and amateur: Johnny Binder, Patrick M. Burchfield, William Degenhardt, the late Thomas Dieckow, James Dunlap, John Flury, Michael Forstner, Richard Funk, Ed Guidry, David Gyre, Gordon Henley, Charles Hoessle, Tim Jones, Tommy Jones, Jack Joy, Frank W. Judd, Stephen E. Labuda, Jr., Gerald Lentz, Rusty Martin, Greg Mengden, Hugh R. Quinn, Gus Rentfro, Buzz Ross, James Schwartz, Kelvin Scott, Norman Scott, Jr., Clay Touchstone, Kerry Touchstone, Bern Tryon, John Tveten, Robert G. Webb, Larry White, Richard Worthington, and Jim Yantis.

Most of the photographs in the book were made at the Houston Zoo by staff members Michael Bowerman, Andrew Odum (now curator of reptiles at the Toledo Zoo), and the late John E. Werler and are used here courtesy of the Houston Zoological Gardens and its former director, Donald G. Olson. To complete the list of illustrations, the following persons offered their own slides for use in the book: Dave Barker, Jonathan A. Campbell, Suzanne Collins, Paul Freed, Emmett Haddon, Toby J. Hibbitts, David Johnson, William W. Lamar, Andrew Odum, Wayne Van Devender, and Jim Yantis.

We are also grateful to the following individuals who offered their personal observations about the natural history of Texas snakes: Colette Adams, Ted Beimler, Patrick M. Burchfield, Roger Conant, Richard Etheridge, Michael Forstner, Gordon Henley, Tim Jones, Tommy Jones, Carl Lieb, John V. Rossi, Clay Touchstone, Kerry Touchstone, Larry White, Richard Worthington, and Jim Yantis.

We are pleased to acknowledge R. K. Vaughan for proofing the maps. Without her help several mistakes would have found their way into the literature.

Completing the maps for the field guide would have been impossible without the help of the many museum curators and their staffs who gave freely of their time and effort to provide the various Texas snake records. We thank them, one and all: Pere Alberch, the late Walter Auffenberg, Robert L. Bezy, Bryce C. Brown, Stephen D. Busak, Jonathan A. Campbell, David Canatella, Charles C. Carpenter, Alan H. Chaney, Charles J. Cole, Walter W. Dalquest, B. G. Davis, William G. Degenhardt, William E. Duellman, Harold A. Dundee, Robert R. Fleet, Neil B. Ford, M. Jack Fouquette, Jr., Thomas H. Fritts, Daniel A. Gallagher, Jimmy Green, Harry W. Greene, Stephen Hammack, Laurence M. Hardy, W. Ronald Heyer, Robert F. Inger, Sarah Kerr, Flavius C. Killebrew, Arnold G. Kluge, John M. Legler, David Lentz, Alan E. Leviton, Carl S. Lieb, Ernest A. Liner, Carol Malcom, Edmond V. Malnate, the late Robert F. Martin, Hymen Marx, Terry Maxwell, the late C. Jack McCoy, Roy W. McDiarmid, Ronald A. Nussbaum, William J. Pyburn, Fred Rainwater, Jose Rosado, Norman J. Scott, James F. Scudday Wayne Seifert, C. B. Smith, Hobart M. Smith, the late Philip W. Smith, Steve Smith, Fred Stangl, Thomas Uzzell, Jens V. Vindum, William J. Voss, David B. Wake, Robert G. Webb, Kenneth L. Williams, John W. Wright, George R. Zug, and Richard G. Zweifel.

Many colleagues and graduate students offered encouragement and provided records. A number of professionals and graduate students went out of their way to visit sites where we suspected certain species occurred, and either confirmed or denied their presence. For these and other courtesies we gratefully acknowledge the following persons: F. Andett, Ralph W. Axtell, David G. Barker, the late Richard J. Bauldauf, George Baumgardner, Patrick M. Burchfield, the late Roger Conant, Kurt Cornelison, Rob H. Dean, Curtis T. Eckerman, Carl H. Ernst, the late Edward Farmer, George W. Ferguson, Tony Gallucci, Brian D. Greene, Michael Haiduk, Chris Harrison, Fred S. Hendricks, Terry Hibbitts, Toby J. Hibbitts, Kelly J. Irwin, John B. Iverson, Jerry D. Johnson, Frank W. Judd, John P. Karges, Brian Keeley, Kenneth King, David Kizirian, Travis LaDuc, William W. Lamar, Harry Longstrom, John Malone, William L. McClure, Hugh McCrystal, Jenna McKnight, Edwin J. Michaud, Edward O. Moll, James Mueller, Roy Murray, Keith Nietman, William F. Parker, Ray Pawley, Karl Peterson, the late Floyd E. Potter, Andrew H. Price, Hugh R. Quinn, Gus Rentfro, Francis L. Rose, Michael E. Seidel, Jack W. Sites, Jerry R. Smith, Douglas Stine, Steve Stone, Robert A. Thomas, Okla W. Thornton, Thomas Vance, R. Kathryn Vaughan, Thomas G. Vermersch, Jack Ward, and Martin J. Whiting.

TEXAS SNAKES

INTRODUCTION

CONSERVATION

The loss of a single snake, or a dozen snakes, or even a hundred in one year will probably not seriously impact the balance of a particular ecosystem, at least not in the long term. Most natural changes occur slowly, over prolonged periods, like the rhythm of the seasons or the process of aging, so that their effects are usually not immediately apparent. But it is clear that over time the cumulative consequences of snake bashing, coupled with habitat destruction and environmental pollution, have taken a heavy toll of most native serpents, as probably has the insidious and sometimes equally devastating damage inflicted by the imported fire ant. Although habitat degradation and pollution are the chief causes of decline in local serpent populations statewide, it is not our intention to address these issues at length, since the resolution of such threats resides largely in the political arena and is therefore beyond the scope of this book. This is not to suggest, however, that interested persons should avoid becoming involved with local or national conservation groups to influence government policy makers in wildlife conservation matters. Indeed, doing so is often the best way to achieve significant and lasting results.

But to anyone with a clutching fear of snakes (which includes most of us), any idea of conserving these creatures will seem ludicrous or, at the very least, a misplaced priority. What is the compelling reason for this antiserpent bias? If we can accept that the great majority of snakes are incapable of causing us serious harm and that by reason of their feeding habits most of them are beneficial to our interests, by what logic do we feel obliged to destroy them on sight? The obvious answer is that a great majority of us lack even a basic understanding of these essentially timid and benign animals.

Our information about them often comes from those whose bias, like our own, is based primarily on the same myths and misconceptions that have confounded the subject since ancient times. Although erroneous, such implausible tales pique our interest, and their telling makes for lively after-dinner conversation. Unfortunately, however, by masking the truth they make more difficult the task of getting to the facts. The challenge then is to present the facts about these generally innocuous animals in such a way that even the snake haters among us will see these reptiles for what they really are—not vengeful creatures lurking in the brush to ambush the next human victim but another life form no more villainous than any of the others. Indeed, the life of a snake is basically not much different from that of other animal species. Like them it must find food, reproduce, protect itself from its enemies, and maintain a comfortable body temperature in the face of the changing seasons. How serpents fulfill these life functions can be as interesting as the bizarre snake stories we often hear and accept as fact. Only when we can cast aside such misinformation and replace it with an objective view of our subjects are we likely to entertain the idea of conserving snakes. That, it seems to us, is where the conservation ethic begins.

TEXAS THREATENED SNAKES

Texas snakes that are currently listed as threatened by the state of Texas and or the United States Fish and Wildlife Service are given below. The reason for this particular list of snakes involves human development of land, water, and timber resources. In addition, those snakes whose distribution barely enters Texas may easily be exploited by commercial and/or private collectors, as well as by the developers of natural resources mentioned above.

Cemophora coccinea copei (northern scarlet snake)
Cemophora coccinea lineri (Texas scarlet snake)
Coniophanes imperialis imperialis (black-striped snake)
Crotalus horridus atricaudatus (canebrake rattlesnake)
Drymarchon melanurus erebennus (Texas indigo snake)
Drymobius margaritiferus margaritiferus (speckled racer)
Leptodeira septentrionalis septentrionalis (northern cat-eyed snake)
Opheodrys vernalis blanchardi (smooth green snake)
Nerodia harteri harteri (Brazos water snake)
Nerodia harteri paucimaculata (Concho water snake)
Pituophis ruthveni (Louisiana pine snake)
Tantilla cucullata (Trans-Pecos black-headed snake)
Trimorphodon vilkinsoni (Texas lyre snake)

POISONOUS SNAKES, VENOM AND BITE

To a large extent, our fear of snakes is based on the knowledge that a few of them are venomous and capable of causing us serious bodily injury and sometimes even death. This fear, while logical enough when based on the facts of the matter, is usually so exaggerated that it can become unreasonable or, in the extreme, even grotesque, leaving little or no opportunity for rational dialogue. Some people have such an overwhelming fear of snakes that getting them to talk about the animals that cause them so much mental anguish may be impossible without professional help. Psychologists explain that ophidiophobia is among the more difficult fears to overcome. Such practitioners estimate that more than 50 percent of our population experience some anxiety in the presence of snakes, and another 20 percent are terrified by them. Extreme examples of the latter include those who become terror-stricken when they so much as see the picture of a snake in a magazine, a book, or on television, and others who avoid outdoor activities altogether for fear of encountering a snake, even a harmless one. Sadly, most of these people retain their morbid fear for life. But there are hopeful signs that the other 50-plus percent—those with only a moderate fear of serpents—are slowly but surely being reduced in number as both public and private institutions and organizations concerned with natural history education reach ever more people with their hands-on programs. Probably at the forefront in molding such attitudinal changes are the country's zoological parks (and aquariums), which, through live exhibits and informal teaching programs, annually expose their nearly 120 million visitors to wildlife conservation messages. Science museums, nature centers, and wildlife organizations are fulfilling a similar role. As a direct result of such efforts, one encouraging sign of the change taking place in our attitude about snakes is the phenomenal growth of the pet-snake hobby; having gained prominence only about 20 years ago, it continues to expand at an accelerated pace, with devotees nationwide numbering in the many thousands.

Despite such progress, a great deal of apprehension and misunderstanding still exist among Texans about their native serpents. In the minds of most persons, snakes are still the enemy. They are seen as mysterious and menacing, to be killed wherever and whenever they are encountered. The truth is that snakes—even the dangerous ones—are fundamentally shy and retiring, more than willing to avoid a confrontation with humans by fleeing when given the chance. Only as a last resort will they bite in self-defense.

Our native venomous serpents do not typically display overtly offensive behavior; they nevertheless pose a potential risk for those engaged in outdoor activities. This is, after all, a large state with a diverse snake fauna, consisting of 72 species (by our count), 11 of which are considered dangerous to humans.

Ranking the states by raw figures, Parrish (1964) estimated that Texas suffered more venomous snakebites in a single year than any other state nationwide, although when the number of such accidents was calculated per 100,000 residents, Texas ranked third, with an incidence rate of 14.70 percent, trailing behind North Carolina at 18.79 percent and Arkansas at 17.19 percent. Moreover, based on actual and projected snakebite incidents for 1958 and 1959, he estimated that approximately 1,408 snakebite victims were treated in Texas in each of those years, consisting of 784 inpatients and 624 outpatients. An average of only 2.4 fatalities occurred annually—a mortality rate of just one-fourth of 1 percent of those bitten. Even more encouraging are the mortality figures for the years 1978 through 1995, which according to the Texas Department of Health, Bureau of Vital Statistics, averaged only one death a year. These figures hardly classify venomous snakebite as a high-mortality occurrence, at least in the United States. Outdoor hazards more likely to cause human death in Texas are the stings and bites of insects and arachnids, lightning strikes, hunting accidents involving firearms, and drownings.

Among our dangerous snake species, two in particular are responsible for the greatest number of bites inflicted on humans. They are the copperhead and the western diamond-backed rattlesnake, both abundant and wide-ranging in the state. Although copperheads accounted for 22 percent of the bites reported by Parrish, they caused no fatalities, whereas the western diamondback, which was blamed for nearly all of the bites included in the rattlesnake category (47 percent of the bite total), was responsible for some human deaths. The cottonmouth ranked next in order of frequency but inflicted only 7 percent of the bites.

Reducing the risk of snakebite is largely a matter of learning to recognize the dangerous species in your part of the state, becoming familiar with their habits, and observing some commonsense safety practices, a few of which are listed here:

1. The first rule should be, never handle a venomous snake unless you are qualified by training or experience to do so. This admonition, while it may seem self-evident, deserves

emphasis, for an ever-increasing number of snakebites are being inflicted on inexperienced amateur herpetologists and reckless adventurers. Other bites are the result of mistaken identification. In one such incident, a Houston radio announcer encountered a coral snake on a city jogging trail. Believing the snake to be a harmless species, he picked it up and was promptly bitten on the hand, whereupon, momentarily startled by the reptile's reaction, he quickly dropped it to the ground. Still not convinced that the snake was dangerous, he handled it a second time and was bitten again. Also to be carefully avoided is a dead venomous snake, for such a creature often can bite reflexively for periods lasting up to an hour after death, as can its decapitated head, a reaction Klauber (1956) elicited many times from experimentally beheaded rattlesnakes. One of the most sobering examples of such an accident is the case reported by Kitchens and his colleagues (1987) in which a Florida man died after having been bitten by the severed head of a large canebrake rattlesnake.

2. Since nearly all snakebites occur on the arms or legs of human victims, avoid placing your hands in places where you cannot see, and wear protective footwear on the lower half of your legs when venturing into areas known to harbor venomous snakes. Be particularly alert when climbing rocky ledges or when walking near old logs and decaying tree stumps, places often favored by certain venomous species. It also makes sense when crossing a log to first step onto it in order to see what is behind it, then to step down on the other side when it appears safe to do so. Never reach into mammal burrows, especially in arid habitats where aboveground shelters are scarce, for such tunnels are frequently occupied by rattlesnakes. Since one of the leading causes of snakebite is the practice of lifting or turning surface objects with the bare hands, a sensible rule to follow is to move these items (rocks, boards, logs, brush, construction debris, etc.) with a long-handled tool such as a hoe, shovel, axe, or broomstick.

3. To discourage snakes from maintaining permanent residence close to a home or vacation cottage, it is advisable to keep the premises free of debris. Rock piles, trash piles, stacked lumber, and various forms of junk not only provide the serpents with shelter but also often harbor the rats and mice that constitute the principal food of most venomous species. Removing such debris helps to eliminate the snake's cover and that of its rodent prey.

4. If you must kill a venomous snake that is a threat to human safety, do so out of range of the snake's strike, which ordinarily is less than its own body length. To attack the reptile with a short-handled weapon such as a knife, hatchet, or hammer is simply to invite an accident. Although this word of caution may seem too obvious to bear mentioning, it is clear from our review of Texas snakebite cases that accidents from this cause happen with some frequency.

For most people, snakebite is a terrifying experience that finds the victim both emotionally and intellectually unprepared to deal with such an emergency. Usually fear and extreme apprehension result from such an accident, when what is most needed at this time is a sense of calm. Despite the rarity of human death from envenomation in the United States, convincing a fearful snakebite victim that he or she has an excellent chance to recover from such a mishap is difficult. Nevertheless, every attempt should be made to convey this information to the victim, since to do so may relieve his or her anxiety and thereby expedite their recovery.

Reaching medical aid as quickly as possible should be the first objective, but with a minimum amount of physical exertion on the part of the victim, who, if alone and on foot, should not run. If the bite is on an extremity, immobilize the bitten limb or at least avoid moving it, since muscular activity hastens the spread of venom through the lymphatic channels. Moreover, when the bite is on a hand or arm, take off any rings and tight bracelets before swelling makes their removal difficult.

Other, more aggressive first-aid measures—including incision and suction, with or without a constricting band or tourniquet; application of cold to the bite site; compression wrapping of the extremity; or stun gun electroshock—may or may not be used, depending on the knowledge and decision of the victim. However, such procedures, some of which are potentially harmful, have not been embraced with equal enthusiasm among the best-informed medical specialists, although the same experts agree that the several preliminary steps mentioned earlier (reassurance, prompt transport to medical aid without undue exertion, immobilization of the bitten limb, and removal of rings and tight bracelets) are beneficial. One expert, Dr. D. L. Hardy (1992), reviewed several commonly recommended first-aid methods for North American pit viper bites and presented his evaluation of their effectiveness. Anyone with a serious interest in snakebite first aid is encouraged to read this article.

The following is an account of Texas poisonous snakes, their behavior prior to and during a bite, and the effects of the venom on the human body.

TEXAS CORAL SNAKE. This seemingly inoffensive snake, which may not even attempt to bite if handled carefully, usually crawls away at the first sign of danger. It should never be touched, however, for an aroused specimen becomes unpredictable, and considering the high lethal toxicity of its venom, this serpent is potentially very dangerous to humans. Sometimes merely holding the snake gently causes it to turn its head, open its mouth, and without any apparent provocation, bite the hand that supports it. Some say that because the coral snake is unable to open its mouth widely, it can effectively bite only a highly curved surface of the human body such as a finger, toe, or the loose skin between these digits. That, unfortunately, is not the case. Just as a bit of epidermis can be pinched out with the fingers, so too can a coral snake gather up a fold of skin between its biting jaws, allowing its fangs to penetrate the skin. The serpent may use other defensive tactics as well. A coral snake that is approached too closely may lash out wildly at the oncoming target, though this is not considered typical *Micrurus* behavior.

The snake is far more likely to bite only when touched. Most coral snake bites occur when the snake is willfully handled, usually by someone who is attracted to the reptile's bright colors and, deceived by its small slender head, considers the snake harmless. The snake usually reacts to such familiarity by abruptly swinging its forebody sideways to seize the restraining hand. Then, seeming to sense that its biting apparatus is an imperfect one, the coral snake maintains its grip as long as it can, chewing on the hand to embed its short fangs as it tries to inject as much as possible of its meager venom supply. The minute, rigidly attached fangs, barely $1/8$-inch long, are incapable of deep penetration, and the primary muscles responsible for the ejection of venom from the venom glands are not well developed in this species and are unable to drive the venom forcefully from the gland, down the fang canal, and into the victim.

Despite the snake's somewhat primitive method of venom delivery, its neurotoxically active venom is undoubtedly one of the most lethally potent of any U.S. serpent. The dose needed to kill a person of average stature is estimated by Minton and Minton (1969) at only 4 or 5 mg of dry weight, which, incidentally, represents nearly the entire pool of venom contained in the glands of most specimens 20 to 24 inches long. Larger snakes, of course, can be expected to deliver a greater quantity of venom. This was demonstrated by Fix and Minton (1976), whose studies of coral snake venom extraction, using the eastern coral snake as a model, yielded 20 mg or more from each of two especially large individuals measuring between 33 $1/2$ and 35 $1/2$ inches long. (Such large coral snakes are seldom encountered in Texas.) According to Russell and Puffer (1971), the venom is nearly 11 times as lethal as that of the copperhead, 5.26 times as toxic as that of the cottonmouth, and nearly 4 times as virulent as western diamond-backed rattler venom. Because of the coral snake's highly toxic venom, it is often said that a victim bitten by this species has little or no chance to survive the experience. On the contrary, and in spite of frequently quoted mortality figures ranging anywhere from 10 to 75 percent, few human fatalities result from such poisoning. In the first place, not every bite is accompanied by the injection of venom. Although Russell (1980) found 17 human deaths among 82 published reports of coral snake bites nationwide, he could find no record of a fatality from such an accident since Wyeth coral snake antivenin was first developed and made available back in 1967. It is of particular interest to note that we are unable to find even one authentic record of a human fatality from coral snake envenomation in Texas since 2 deaths were mentioned by True in 1883, more than 120 years ago. These cases, incidentally, are the first published records of coral snake bite fatalities for the United States and, at least until now, the last for Texas.

The severity of a coral snake bite is not easy to assess. Unlike the venoms of North American pit vipers, which typically cause severe local tissue damage and extensive hemorrhaging, that of the coral snake produces only minimal early signs of envenomation or none at all. Consequently, the victim often has no reason to believe he or she has been poisoned. Pain, if present, is usually minimal at first and confined to the area of the fang punctures. In a serious bite it may be moderate to severe, depending on the amount of venom delivered. The fang punctures, so small that they may scarcely bleed, are separated from each other by $^1/_4$ to $^3/_8$ of an inch; the presence of only scratch marks usually indicates an imperfect bite and the probability that no venom was injected. Swelling at the bite area is usually absent as well or, if present, is hardly noticeable. It is evident that the lack of conspicuous signs or symptoms soon after a bite belies the potentially serious consequences that may follow. Unfortunately, this can give the victim a false sense of security, resulting in his or her unwillingness to seek medical aid.

In most cases of coral snake poisoning the first alarming manifestations do not appear until several hours after the bite, at which time it may be too late to save a severely envenomed patient by the administration of appropriate snakebite serum. Prognostic symptoms, when they finally appear, include apprehension, giddiness and euphoria, thickening of speech, increased salivation, and tongue tremors. Nausea and vomiting may also occur, as well as pinpoint pupils, blurred vision, and drooping eyelids. The victim may later experience weakness, drowsiness, and a feeling of impending unconsciousness. In many respects the symptoms produced by coral snake poisoning are not much different from those observed in a seriously intoxicated person. In advanced cases of envenomation there is hypertension, and the pulse weakens and becomes irregular. Convulsions may also occur. This is followed by the sudden onset of facial and bulbar-center paralysis, after which limb paralysis occurs. Finally, death comes as a result of respiratory and cardiac failure. Fatalities generally occur when the snake has been given the opportunity to inject a lethal dose of venom, either by maintaining its grip for more than just a few seconds (most when they have hung on for longer than a minute) or by inflicting multiple bites.

SOUTHERN COPPERHEAD. Although most abundant in wilderness areas, the southern copperhead is frequently encountered in certain suburban parks and woodlots of our largest East Texas cities. In such places, where it can find shelter under brush and human-made debris such as boards, rock piles, roofing paper, and other construction rubble, it is generally the most abundant local venomous snake and the one responsible for the vast majority of human envenomations in and around the cities of Houston, Beaumont, and Port Arthur. In Harris County alone the number of people bitten each year by this snake and treated in local hospitals and clinics is probably between 20 and 30, yet we can find no record of a human fatality resulting from such injuries. This is no doubt a result of the copperhead venom's relatively low lethal toxicity compared with that of most other native venomous snakes, together with the modest quantity of venom carried in its venom glands. The total amount of venom contained in both glands of a copperhead is usually 40 to 70 mg of dry weight, according to Minton and Minton (1969), and the same authors estimate the minimum lethal dose required to kill an adult human at 100 or more milligrams. Another mitigating factor is the small size of the copperhead's fangs, each of which seldom measures more than $^{15}/_{16}$-inch long, resulting in a shallow subcutaneous bite.

According to information assembled by Karant (in Wingert et al. 1980), only a single human death was discovered in his review of 2,000 cases of copperhead bite. He explained that this solitary fatality was probably not the direct result of copperhead poisoning but most likely was caused by certain side effects of envenomation that were never clearly defined. Despite these reassuring statistics, Amaral (1927) reported a human death from a copperhead bite involving a 14-year-old bitten on a finger. Likewise, P. Wilson (1908) recorded five deaths from copperhead envenomation, three of which he believed may have been exacerbated by the large amounts of whiskey consumed by the victims in their misguided attempts at treatment.

According to Sherman A. Minton, Jr. (pers. com.), who over the years has been involved as a physician with approximately 50 copperhead bite cases, generalized symptoms of envenomation by this species include local pain and swelling, nausea, vomiting, sweating, and thirst. In addition, the victims usually experience enlargement and tenderness of local lymph nodes, and the presence of blood- or serum-filled blisters is not unusual. In only one case, involving a five- or six-year-old girl, did he note hypotension and other evidence of shock. Minton commented that tissue necrosis can be severe but corrective skin grafting is rarely necessary.

BROAD-BANDED COPPERHEAD. Although the bite of a large broad-banded copperhead may cause serious medical consequences in humans, especially when the victim is a small child, records of human fatalities from copperhead envenomation are rare (even though the incidence of copperhead poisoning in Texas ranks second only to the number of snakebites inflicted on humans by the more wide-ranging western diamond-backed rattlesnake). Such a low mortality rate can be attributed to the snake's relatively short fangs, its modest venom supply (40–70 mg of dry weight per snake when extracted by milking, according the Minton and Minton [1969]), and the comparatively low lethal toxicity of its venom.

Symptoms of poisoning by this species are generally not dramatic, consisting primarily of pain and swelling. A typical case history was reported by Fitch (1960), who, after being bitten on the middle finger of his right hand, carefully observed and recorded the signs and symptoms produced by the bite. Early manifestations included twitching muscles and a dull ache at the bite location, followed in about 10 minutes by noticeable swelling and discoloration in the same area. The pain, which at first was not severe, soon became intense as the swelling moved steadily up the hand; in a short time it was followed by throbbing pain in the palm at the base of the middle finger and numbness of the skin. At this point, Fitch made a $1/2$-inch incision through one of the fang punctures, the one that was the primary source of venom injection. (The other fang struck a knuckle joint and apparently delivered little or no venom.) Two hours after the bite, the swelling had reached 4 inches above the wrist and the throbbing pain was still present in the palm of the hand, at which time Fitch took a quarter-grain of codeine. Approximately 15 minutes later, when respiratory congestion became evident, he took an antihistamine in an effort to relieve the symptoms. By 10:15 PM the pain had reached its peak, prompting Fitch to take a second quarter-grain of codeine. Between 30 and 45 minutes later, the victim became nauseated and subsequently regurgitated, but he experienced no further deterioration in his condition after 12:45 AM. The systemic manifestations experienced earlier were gone by morning, although the affected hand eventually swelled to almost twice its usual size, and it was nearly a month before Fitch regained full use of his hand.

WESTERN COTTONMOUTH. According to Parrish (1964), whose study provides the most recent survey of statewide snakebite statistics, only 7 percent of Texas' 461 hospitalizations for snake envenomation during 1958 and 1959 were caused by cottonmouths, despite the serpent's local abundance in many parts of southeastern Texas. The nationwide rate of approximately 10 percent was not much higher. Such a low incidence is not surprising, considering the snake's normally unaggressive behavior. Although very young cottonmouths often are quick to strike when approached, most adults of this subspecies we encountered in the field either tried to escape or simply pulled back their heads in a defensive stance without taking any aggressive action. Not only is the bite rate from this snake relatively low, but hospital records also show that few humans die from cottonmouth envenomation. Scarcely one human fatality a year can be attributed to this species nationwide.

Although not as lethally toxic as the venoms of most rattlesnake species, cottonmouth venom causes considerable local hemorrhaging, rupturing small blood vessels and allowing the blood to seep into the surrounding tissues, resulting in dark discoloration of the bite area and the oozing of bloody fluids from the injection site. Since the venom literally dissolves the affected tissues, the area at the site of the bite can become gangrenous, and in severe cases may even liquefy, complicating an already serious medical emergency. As evidence of the deleterious effects of cottonmouth venom, Allen and Swindell (1948) reported that in Florida approximately half of all bite victims suffered gangrene-crippled fingers or toes. In spite of the high incidence of tissue necrosis in such cases, Findlay Russell, one of the country's leading snakebite practitioners, believes this condition can be largely prevented by the prompt intravenous injection (by a physician) of adequate amounts of antivenin. Sherman A. Minton (pers. com.), another of the nation's eminent snakebite experts, takes a different view. Based on the results of animal experiments he conducted in the laboratory, together with clinical evidence, he found antivenin to be of little value in preventing necrosis from pit viper venoms. Other symptoms of cottonmouth envenomation may include pain in the bite area, swelling, weakness, giddiness, rapid or reduced pulse, drop in blood pressure, some breathing difficulty, and nausea and vomiting.

WESTERN DIAMOND-BACKED RATTLESNAKE. Most of the more than 1,400 estimated (Parrish 1964) venomous snakebites inflicted each year on Texas residents are caused by this species, as are the majority of serious envenomations and most of the fatalities. Several factors, among them a great striking distance, long fangs, and a large venom capacity, account for the negative impact this snake has made on the state's human population. Other elements contributing to the diamondback's ranking as the most dangerous of all Texas serpents include the snake's continued abundance over much of its present range and its inclination to defend itself vigorously when disturbed. In spite of its ability to injure or kill a human victim, the western diamond-backed rattlesnake, like all other snakes, venomous or not, prefers to avoid confrontation with humans.

Its venom is not as lethally toxic as that of the rock rattlers, prairie rattlesnake, Mohave rattlesnake, or coral snake, although it stores a much greater quantity of the toxic substance in its venom glands than do any of the others. Using a variety of extraction methods, from manually squeezing the glands to stimulating them electrically, the maximum yield per adult is reported to range from 600 mg to 1,145 mg of dry weight, the larger amount having been removed from a specimen measuring 5 feet, 4 inches (163 cm) long. Klauber (1956) suggests that under ideal conditions as much as 1,500 mg could be extracted from a large western diamond-backed rattlesnake. He also gives 277 mg as an average extraction for this species.

It seems logical to conclude that because of the greater quantity of venom ordinarily delivered by a large rattlesnake, its bite would produce more serious consequences in a human victim than the smaller dose administered by a shorter rattler, all other factors being equal. This, however, is not always the case.

Theakston and Reid (1978), after hearing of a human seriously poisoned by one of three two-year-old western diamond-backed rattlesnakes he kept as pets, were motivated to investigate how so small a snake could produce such dire medical consequences in a grown human. In assaying the qualitative chemical changes in the venom of these specimens over time, the researchers demonstrated that the lethal toxicity of their venom was actually greatest when the specimens were only 2 months old, declining gradually until it leveled off after the snakes reached 13 months of age. A similar result, incidentally, was noted by Minton (1957), who tested the virulence of a single western diamond-backed rattlesnake's venom over a span of 19 years and concluded that its lethal toxicity decreased by 2.4 times during this period. Theakston and Reid also found that the venom of very young *C. atrox,* because of its defibrinating action, can cause serious internal bleeding in a human victim. As a result, they strongly urge clinicians to monitor carefully the blood-clotting quality of patients bitten by such a snake, since nonclotting blood in this case is a good indication that the offending rattlesnake is less than a year old and, more important, that the victim probably has been injected with a potentially fatal or near-fatal amount of venom. Minton and Weinstein (1986) likewise found a clear disparity between the lethal toxicity of juvenile western diamond-backed rattlesnake venom and that of the adults. Two specimens they examined from North Texas, each less than a year old, had venoms 6.6 times as toxic as that of adults from the same area. Variability in venom lethality was also evident among adult snake populations throughout the species' range; the most toxic samples were found in adult diamond-backed rattlesnakes collected in the Big Bend region of Texas, especially those from the base of the Rosillos Mountains.

In a typical case of poisoning by this species, the victim experiences a variety of signs and symptoms, some of which appear immediately, others much later. The first to be noted is pain in the bite area, usually intense. Occasionally pain is absent. More often, a serious case of envenomation produces agonizing pain, which begins at the site of the bite and over several hours gradually follows the course of the swelling. Swelling usually appears within 10 or 15 minutes and progresses along the bitten limb, toward the body. The more venom injected, the more severe the swelling. In particularly serious cases, swelling may even reach the body cavity, and the lymph nodes nearest the bite area may become tender and painful to the touch. A bruiselike discoloration also appears at the site of the bite soon after the venom enters the tissues; it ultimately may involve the entire bitten limb. In most instances the pulse rate increases (sometimes doubling), blood pressure drops, and frequently the victim experiences weakness, sweating, faintness, and dizziness. He or she may also suffer nausea and vomiting.

Death, if it occurs, is preceded by the following scenario, as described by Russell (1980): hemoglobin drops during the first 6 to 72 hours after the bite, abdominal bleeding occurs, as well as hemorrhaging in the heart, lungs, kidneys, adrenals, and perhaps also in the brain. Finally, the victim succumbs to acute pulmonary edema. It should be mentioned that unlike the dramatic, sudden-death snakebite episodes usually depicted in motion pictures and on television, human fatalities from pit viper envenomation generally do not occur immediately. They typically take place from 6 to 24 hours after the encounter. There are, of course, reports of victims succumbing to western diamondbacked rattlesnake bites in less than an hour, but they are uncommon and often involve small children whose lesser body weight places them at greater risk than adults.

CANEBRAKE RATTLESNAKE. Because the canebrake rattlesnake generally lives in areas remote from centers of human population, is not abundant in our state, and is often reluctant to strike at sources of passive annoyance, it is seldom the cause of human envenomation in Texas. Nevertheless, its bite can be deadly. Several fatalities caused by this subspecies have been reported for southeastern Texas, including one documented by Guidry that involved a small child bitten near La Belle in Jefferson County. This snake's danger is in its considerable striking range, its relatively long fangs, and its substantial venom output—Glenn and Straight (1982) obtained 244 mg dry weight from one specimen—to say nothing of the unusually toxic venom of certain populations. There is, of course, a certain degree of variation in the venom toxicity within a given snake population, just as there is in venom obtained from the same snake at different times in its life, although the elevated toxicity measured by Glenn and Straight is not the result of such normal variation.

The venom of juvenile canebrakes, like that of some other pit viper young, can actually be more toxic than that of the adults. This was discovered in a study by Minton (1967), who tested the venom of several canebrakes from the time they were five days old until they reached a year of age. Although the venom of the five-day-old snakes was not even one-third as potent for mice as that of adults, its toxicity gradually increased until at six months of age it had become nearly three times as potent. When the snakes reached one year of age, their venom toxicity had dropped to 1.8 times that of the adults.

Envenomation by this subspecies produces symptoms generally similar to those observed in many other pit viper bites. The canebrake's strongly hemolytic venom, like that of most rattlesnakes, causes pain, hemorrhaging, swelling, ecchymosis, vesiculations, weakness, faintness or dizziness, weak pulse, nausea, and even paralysis. Signs and symptoms manifested in a patient bitten by one of these snakes was reported by Parrish and Thompson (1958). The victim, a 37-year-old male reptile handler working in a large Florida tourist attraction, was struck at the base of the right index finger by only one fang. Even though the offending snake had been milked of its venom only 24 hours earlier, the man experienced a moderately serious level of poisoning. Within just a few minutes there was a burning pain at the site of the bite and the beginning of local swelling. Thirty minutes later the swelling had reached the back of the hand, and in 24 hours it extended almost to the man's shoulder. Other symptoms included cold and clammy skin, facial numbness, and a blood pressure reading of 100 systolic and 76 diastolic; four days after entering the hospital the patient was discharged and suffered no further complications.

MOTTLED ROCK RATTLESNAKE. Although no human death has been attributed to rock rattlesnake venom, several reported bites by this species show that the snake is indeed dangerous to humans and probably capable of inflicting a fatal bite. Studies of banded rock rattlesnake venoms from several widely separated points in the snake's range have revealed the presence in some local populations of a dangerous component similar to Mohave toxin (in addition to the hemorrhagic elements found in most rattlesnake venoms) that produces neurological symptoms typically observed in victims of coral snake and some Mohave rattlesnake bites. Although such rock rattlesnakes have a distinct potential to cause a human fatality, the neurotoxic element responsible for their higher lethal toxicity has not yet been found in any Texas populations of *C. lepidus*. Nevertheless, the mottled rock rattlesnake has the capacity to cause serious consequences in humans, and a bite from one of these serpents should be treated at a medical facility with the utmost urgency.

In one of the few documented cases of envenomation by this subspecies, A. H. Wright, a renowned herpetologist of his time, reported that after having been bitten on the thumb by a specimen he was holding, he experienced considerable swelling of the affected arm, which also affected his lymph glands (Wright and Wright 1957).

BANDED ROCK RATTLESNAKE. Because this snake occupies rugged and usually inaccessible terrain, visited primarily by naturalists and a few adventurous backpackers, and since it is a timid creature that easily avoids large intruders, it is infrequently encountered in its mountain habitat and rarely bites humans. Such bites, when they do occur, nearly always happen to amateur or professional herpetologists who are deliberately handling live specimens at the time of the accident. We can find no record of a human fatality resulting from the bite of either this subspecies or the mottled rock rattlesnake, but there is good reason to believe that an accident involving a banded rock rattler could be life-threatening, at least when it involves certain isolated populations within the serpent's geographic range.

Although little is known about the precise biochemical nature of the snake's toxins, studies by Glenn and Straight (1982) reveal that significant variation occurs in the venom's lethal potency among several geographically isolated populations of this wide-ranging species. The biologists discovered, for example, that banded rock rattlesnakes from the Florida Mountains of New Mexico possess venom nearly 9 times more virulent than that of the same subspecies collected in Zacatecas, Mexico. Similar results were obtained by Rael and his coworkers (1992), whose experiments indicated the presence in the more lethal venoms of a neurotoxic component corresponding to the powerful Mohave toxin found in the venoms of some Mohave rattlesnakes. Using mice as laboratory animals, their studies revealed that the venoms of rock rattlesnakes from Chihuahua, Mexico, and some parts of Arizona and New Mexico had 3 to 100 times the lethal toxicity of those from Texas and were on average about 10 times as toxic as that of the western diamond-backed rattler.

Despite the high lethal toxicity of the more virulent venom samples, the individual dry-weight yield extracted mechanically from this species has typically ranged from only 5 to 33 mg. It may be assumed that the relatively small amount of venom ordinarily delivered in a single defensive strike is insufficient to kill a grown human. No doubt the severity of a bite would also be moderated by the smallness of the serpent's fangs, which are too short to penetrate the skin deeply. Scarcely ¼ inch (5 mm) long in the adult, they are clearly better adapted for subduing lizard prey than for inflicting a lethal bite on a large mammal such as a human. Among other native pit vipers, only the western pygmy rattlesnake has fangs so small.

Unlike Mohave rattlesnake type A venom, which causes serious neurological consequences in humans but creates only minimal hemorrhagic effects, banded rock rattlesnake venom with Mohave-like component produces both significant neurological symptoms and equally severe hemorrhagic degradation. In at least two well-documented cases of human envenomation by the banded rock rattlesnake, the victims experienced considerable swelling of the bitten extremity and suffered two of the classic neurological symptoms of coral snake poisoning: labored breathing and impaired vision. Bitten on the hand by a banded rock rattler, Robert Hubbard (pers. com.), then a reptile keeper at the Houston Zoological Gardens, was admitted to a local hospital in shock 30 minutes after the bite. His hand and forearm were significantly swollen, and his systolic blood pressure was perilously low (70 mm Hg). He also experienced nausea, chills, vomiting, and severe pain at the bite area, but he eventually recovered. Another case, reported by Klauber (1956), involved an experienced herpetologist who was struck on the middle finger of his right hand by one fang of a 16-inch-long banded rock rattlesnake. The day after the accident, the swelling extended to the forearm, and the following day it reached the shoulder. A severe and burning pain, which began at the site of the bite on the second day, became nearly unbearable the next day, but then moderated, although five weeks after the accident some swelling persisted, accompanied by numbness and tingling.

NORTHERN BLACK-TAILED RATTLESNAKE. Because it is a relatively shy, retiring serpent with a penchant for remote and rugged terrain, the usually mild-mannered black-tailed rattlesnake rarely bites humans. A black-tailed rattlesnake's fangs are proportionately the longest of any native rattlesnake; those of a 4-foot (122 cm) specimen measured more than $1/2$ inch (1.3 cm) along the curve, or about the same size as the fangs of a western diamond-backed rattlesnake a foot longer. Add to this the substantial amount of venom that the black-tailed rattlesnake's sizable venom glands are capable of producing, and it would seem logical to conclude that this is indeed a very dangerous snake. Yet that is not the case. In spite of the high venom yield produced by the adult of this subspecies—calculated by Klauber (1956) to average about 286 mg of dry weight per specimen), the lethal toxicity of the venom when injected into laboratory mice is less than that of most other Texas rattlesnakes, being only 79 percent as potent as the venom of the western diamond-backed rattlesnake. One reason for this is the venom's limited amount of chemical components responsible for severe tissue destruction. Because such components occur in higher percentages in timber, diamond-backed, and prairie rattlesnake venoms, bites from those species ordinarily produce more widespread damage, not only to muscles and subcutaneous tissue but also to various body organs. In recent times, the black-tailed rattlesnake has not caused a single human death, at least in Texas. Not since Amaral (1927) made the first serious effort to study the incidence of venomous snakebite in Texas do we find a documented case of human poisoning caused by this locally abundant pit viper. Russell (1960), on the other hand, reported four cases of black-tailed rattlesnake poisoning that occurred outside Texas, none of which resulted in severe tissue destruction. Hardy, Jeter, and Corrigan (1982) mentioned two instances of envenomation by this snake that did produce intense swelling and ecchymosis of the bitten extremities (perhaps because the offending rattlesnakes bit with such tenacity that they had to be forcibly removed), but they observed none of the severe tissue necrosis or hemorrhaging into vital organs that would be expected in serious poisoning by certain other Texas pit vipers. In the first case, the victim was bitten at the base of his left index finger by a 21-inch (53.3 cm) specimen, receiving only a single fang puncture; the other patient was bitten on the right wrist by a captive 33-inch (83.8 cm) black-tailed rattlesnake he was holding. Both victims fully recovered, suffering no local tissue destruction, hemorrhaging of blood into vital organs, or loss of limb or digit function.

MOHAVE RATTLESNAKE. The Mohave's most noteworthy attribute is its venom. Studies conducted over the last 30 years, according to Sherman Minton (pers. com.) show that in many individuals of this species the venom is the most toxic of any North American pit viper, even exceeding that of the eastern coral snake. When introduced into mice, and depending on the route of injection, it can be 10 to more than 50 times as lethal as that of the western diamond-backed rattlesnake. Containing a powerful neurotoxic element called Mohave toxin, it targets the victim's myoneural junctions and creates severe neurological degradation that can result in double vision and interfere with the normal functions of speaking and swallowing. It also affects the cardiovascular system, yet it is described as producing only minimal local effects on the tissues. Death, when it does occur, is the result of respiratory failure. Designated as type A venom by Glenn and Straight (1978), the highly dangerous venom containing Mohave toxin is present in *C. s. scutulatus* populations inhabiting southern California, southwestern Utah, southeastern Nevada, parts of western and southern Arizona, and the Big Bend region of Texas. The average venom yield from an adult specimen is reported by Minton and Minton (1969) as between 50 and 90 mg; the same authors estimated that it takes only 10 to 15 mg of the highly toxic substance to kill an adult human.

But not all Mohave rattlesnakes possess such deadly venom. Most of those occupying a wide geographic zone in south-central Arizona between Phoenix and Tucson contain a much less lethal form of venom, known as type B, which lacks the virulent nerve-damaging Mohave toxin. Unlike the A type, it produces dramatic local symptoms typical of pit viper poisoning, including considerable swelling, bleb formation, ecchymosis, and necrosis.

Because the Mohave rattlesnake, one of Texas' most dangerous serpents, is easily confused with the more common western diamond-backed rattlesnake, it is important for persons residing or traveling in the southwestern part of the state to make a careful distinction between the two. If the source of a snakebite is not accurately identified, the relatively mild local effects produced by the more lethal type A Mohave venom may cause an attending physician to underestimate the gravity of a bite. What may at first be diagnosed as a minor case may later prove to be a life-threatening condition, and when critical systemic manifestations finally appear, it may be too late for the successful administration of antivenin.

Fortunately, this snake is not particularly abundant in Texas, and its distribution is restricted to a relatively small part of the state. If it were even half as common as the western diamond-backed rattler and as widely distributed, the Mohave rattlesnake would represent an extremely serious outdoor hazard for Texans.

PRAIRIE RATTLESNAKE. Overall, the prairie rattlesnake's venom is estimated to be from 2 to 2 $\frac{1}{2}$ times more toxic than that of the western diamond-backed rattler, although the storage capacity of the snake's venom glands is only about one-ninth that of its larger cousin.

According to Russell, Gans, and Minton (1978), the first and most frequently reported symptoms of *C. viridis* poisoning are pain and swelling at the site of the bite, which typically occur immediately following the accident but may be delayed up to half an hour. An early symptom of most North American rattlesnake bites, such pain ordinarily is less severe in this species than in bites by the diamondback. Russell (1960) treated two exceptional cases of poisoning by the northern Pacific rattler (*C. oreganus*), in which the patients described the degree of pain as minor. Envenomation by the prairie rattlesnake and its close relatives frequently results in a tingling sensation involving the tongue, mouth and scalp and occasionally the ends of the fingers and toes as well, symptoms not usually evident following the bites of other Texas pit vipers. Additional signs and symptoms include weakness, giddiness, sweating, faintness, and nausea; in severe cases the victim may experience a weak though rapid pulse, a drop in systemic arterial pressure, respiratory difficulties, and some degree of paralysis. According to Russell, death, when it does occur in humans, results from cardiovascular failure caused by a lethal peptide component in the snake's venom.

DESERT MASSASAUGA. Since neither the snake's venom yield nor lethal toxicity have been studied, and there are no recorded case histories of bites by this subspecies, we know little about the effects of desert massasauga envenomation in humans. Like its close relatives the eastern and western massasaugas, it probably has a highly toxic venom containing a potent neurotoxic component, although this is not certain. If future research reveals that the desert massasauga does indeed possess such a venom, then its bite should be regarded as potentially life-threatening to humans. Even then, the snake's relatively short fangs and modest venom supply make death from a bite unlikely, for this is the smallest of the three massasauga subspecies. Besides, it has a spotty distribution, making an encounter with one of these elusive little rattlesnakes highly improbable. See also the western massasauga account.

WESTERN MASSASAUGA. Endowed with a relatively toxic venom believed to contain some neurotoxic components, the western massasauga can seriously poison a human victim, but its bite rarely causes death in humans. This is partly the result of the snake's relatively short fangs (barely a $1/4$ inch long in the largest specimens) and its conservative venom supply. According to Minton and Minton (1969), the venom averages 25 to 35 mg by dry weight in an adult snake, and they estimate the lethal human dose at 30 to 40 mg. Since rattlesnakes rarely exhaust their venom in one strike, it is unlikely that a massasauga will inject a lethal dose in just a single stab of its fangs.

Symptoms typically associated with massasauga poisoning include immediate, often severe pain at the bite area; some swelling at the site, though usually not extensive; discoloration; a moderate degree of ecchymosis; faintness; and nausea. According to Russell (1980), none of the seven victims of *Sistrurus* poisoning he treated showed any significant changes in their blood picture, and all recovered uneventfully in just a few days. This does not mean that a massasauga bite should be treated as a trivial event. On the contrary, every bite by this species, if it produces signs and symptoms of poisoning, should be seen promptly by a physician experienced in the treatment of such a medical emergency. The lethal toxicity of western massasauga venom has not yet been established, although Glenn and Straight (1982) report that for the closely related eastern race, it is greater than for the majority of other rattlesnakes.

WESTERN PYGMY RATTLESNAKE. Over the last 35 years, in the Houston area alone, five persons have been bitten by western pygmy rattlesnakes that each intentionally handled in the belief that it was a harmless juvenile hog-nosed snake.

Even this short-tempered little rattlesnake usually crawls away from danger if permitted to do so, but if provoked, even slightly, it is apt to launch a strike with the suddenness of a coiled spring. Its striking distance is limited, however, seldom spanning more than 4 or 5 inches (10–13 cm), and its fangs (measuring only $1/8$- to $3/16$ inch long) are not capable of deep penetration. According to Russell (1980), the lethal potency of pygmy rattlesnake venom when administered intravenously in mice is less than that of most other Texas rattlesnake species tested. It is also evident that although the larger eastern races of *S. miliarius* (nearly as big as a full-grown western massasauga) produce venom quantities averaging about 30 mg of dry weight per individual, the glands of the average western pygmy rattler must contain significantly less venom (apparently the amount has not been measured). Snakebite statistics reveal that the western pygmy rattlesnake is responsible for relatively few human snakebites, and a bite from this subspecies, though capable of producing serious medical consequences in humans, rarely if ever causes human death. We can find no record of a human fatality from its bite. According to Vick (1971), envenomation usually produces moderate to somewhat severe local symptoms and, in some of the more aggravated cases, may even result in marked systemic consequences such as hemorrhaging, passing of bloody urine, and breathing difficulty. Although most victims suffer pain, swelling (generally not severe), and some nausea, seldom do they experience significant tissue degeneration, nor is there a dramatic change in their blood picture. Unless the patient is a small child or a debilitated older person (which adds to the gravity of any envenomation), most victims recover completely and uneventfully in just a few days.

SNAKE CLASSIFICATION AND IDENTIFICATION

Taxonomy is the science of classifying and naming animals and plants—the foundation for the development of biological knowledge. The history of classifying animals is perhaps nearly as old as humanity itself. Even natives of various primitive tribes were good naturalists, with specific names for local trees, flowers, mammals, birds, fishes, and other species. Their health—sometimes even their lives—depended on their ability to distinguish between harmless and venomous (or toxic) plants and animals. To survive in nature, they frequently learned the subtle differences between such things as edible mushrooms and deadly toadstools, milk snakes and coral snakes, and a host of other "good-bad" species that they encountered in the wild.

The father of taxonomy is considered to be Carolus Linnaeus, a Swedish naturalist who in the mid-1700s consistently used the binomial system of nomenclature in his pioneer work; that is, he assigned both a generic and specific name to each animal. In those days, taxonomy was a relatively simple science that required only a careful examination of the organism's body parts and a comparison of such features with those of other closely related animals. Since then, however, the science of taxonomy has changed dramatically. Today, instead of relying only on morphological characters to compare species, the taxonomist uses a variety of other, more sophisticated, tools to accomplish the task. Among them are biochemistry, histology, cytology, genetics, and, in the case of venomous snakes, analysis of their venoms by electrophoresis and chromatography.

Beginning at the highest level of animal classification, snakes are grouped with the vertebrates, since they have a backbone consisting of individual segments, or vertebrae. Together with the crocodilians, turtles, lizards, and tuataras (all of which are cold-blooded and share the characteristic of dry, scaly skin), they are included in the class Reptilia. Defining their taxonomic status even more narrowly, snakes are sorted with lizards in the order Squamata, then placed in their own suborder, Serpentes. This suborder is generally considered to be divisible into 13, 14, or 15 living families (depending on which authority one follows), 4 of which occur in Texas. In the main body of this book, the species and subspecies accounts are grouped by family. A brief definition of the relevant families follows the Taxonomic Issues below.

Defining the Snake

Snakes are essentially highly specialized lizards without limbs, movable eyelids, and external ear openings (though some lizards also lack limbs, movable eyelids, and external ear openings). Furthermore, they have neither a sternum nor a urinary bladder, and most species possess only a single functional lung, which is extremely elongated to conform to the snake's long, slender body shape. In snakes, the two lower jaw bones are separated at the front and united there by a flexible ligament, whereas in lizards they are solidly fused at that point. In addition, the quadrate bones of snakes are typically long and loosely connected to the skull, permitting flexibility of movement, but those of lizards are firmly attached to the skull. While lizards have only a few pairs of ribs, those of snakes are numerous and in some species can number more than 300 pairs.

Making an Identification

Before attempting to identify a snake, it is necessary to become familiar with some terms used to define various external features of this animal group. Among the most obvious and useful are those of coloration and markings. A glance at the photographs in this book will quickly show that Texas snakes come in a bewildering array of patterns and colors, ranging from unicolored on top (green and earth snakes) to complex dorsal patterns combining both blotches and spots (long-nosed snake and rock rattlesnake).

Some of the basic pattern types can be defined as follows:

UNICOLORED. A single, solid dorsal color, but with a generally paler hue on the belly.

STRIPE. A narrow, lengthwise line of color, which, if wide, may be called a band.

BLOTCH. A large oval, rectangular, squarish, or diamond-shaped marking, usually arranged with numerous others in a single, lengthwise row along the back. One or more secondary longitudinal rows of blotches often occur on either side of the body below the main series of blotches, although these are sometimes small enough to be considered spots.

SPOT. A marking not as large as a blotch, but one that can be smaller than a single dorsal scale or occupy an area the size of six or eight dorsal scales.

RING. A band of color that completely encircles the body.

CROSSBAND. Similar to a ring, in that it crosses the back and sides of the snake's body, but it fails to cross the belly.

Besides color and pattern, other characteristics that may help to make a positive identification include the size and shape of the snake's head, as well as its markings, if any; unusual features of the snout, such as an upturned or enlarged rostral scale; the presence or absence of a facial pit on either side of the head, in addition to a nostril opening; and whether the eyes have round or elliptical pupils. Another clue is the shape of the snake's body, whether slender, of moderate girth, or heavy-bodied.

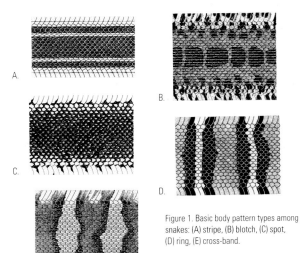

Figure 1. Basic body pattern types among snakes: (A) stripe, (B) blotch, (C) spot, (D) ring, (E) cross-band.

   Although scale characteristics (expressed by kind, number, shape, and arrangement) may prove more reliable for distinguishing certain species and subspecies than either color or markings, such features are not easily recognized by those unfamiliar with them. Furthermore, they are not readily observed, especially in smaller snakes. Yet some scale characteristics, when considered together with other morphological features, often are important aids for identifying snakes, and they are therefore included in the description of each species and subspecies. Among the more important of these are the number of scale rows, called dorsals, that wrap diagonally around the top and sides of the snake's body (usually counted near the middle of the trunk) and the condition of the anal plate (the scale covering the anal opening), which is either single (undivided) or double (divided). An even more fundamental character used to help sort out species is whether a snake has lengthwise-keeled or smooth body scales, though in some snakes the keels are not pronounced and may occur only on the upper few rows of the body.

The simplest and most practical way to begin the task of making an identification is to review the color photographs in the book, keeping in mind the various features that are most important for such purposes. When a match has been found, verify the snake's identification by turning to the text account for that species or subspecies. Compare its key characters with those mentioned in the Description section, and eliminate from consideration any look-alikes by reading the Comparable Snakes section in the same account. The line drawings throughout the book that compare patterns and other features of certain species or subspecies to one another should serve to confirm your choice. If, after completing this procedure, you are still unable to identify the specimen, the next step is to use the taxonomic key, beginning on page 51, which is designed to help trace the snake to the species level. From there, the text descriptions and line drawings should lead you to the correct subspecies. In most instances, the final part of the task will be simplified if you know precisely where the snake was found, since each sub-

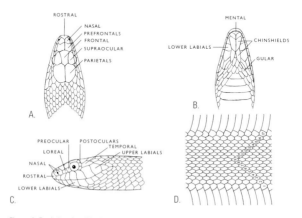

Figure 2. Basic head and body scale arrangement of a typical snake: (A) dorsal head scales, (B) ventral head scales, (C) lateral head scales, (D) method of counting dorsal body scale rows.

species—except for intergrade populations between adjoining subspecies—occupies a separate geographic territory.

Aberrant Snakes

Unfortunately, it is not possible for a novice to identify by such means every snake encountered in the wild, for in nature we can expect each organism to show varying degrees of color and pattern deviation. Moderately atypical specimens, which nevertheless fall within the normal range of variation for their kind, are mentioned in the appropriate species and subspecies text descriptions and should, therefore, present no real obstacle in one's efforts to identify them. Others may be more troublesome. At times, for example, different but usually closely related species may breed with one another and produce offspring, called hybrids, which share certain characteristics of both parents. But since such progeny are themselves generally incapable of producing young, they rarely become established as viable local colonies. Because they do not exactly match the descriptions or illustrations depicted in most field guides, they are normally difficult to identify, even by the experts. Fortunately, such species crosses are rare, and the possibility of encountering one in the wild is extremely remote.

Equally uncommon in nature are snakes with extreme color or pattern abnormalities. Even professional herpetologists, who probably find more snakes in several seasons of field work than most persons see in a lifetime, rarely encounter them in the wild. Among these curiosities, the most frequently reported are partial or complete albinos. Although we usually think of an albino animal as one totally lacking in melanin, Bechtel (1995) defines albinism as either the absence or deficiency of melanin, a condition occurring in approximately one of every 10,000 to 40,000 individuals of a given species.

At the other end of the spectrum are all-black individuals whose normal body patterns have been virtually obliterated by black pigmentation. Two such unusual coral snakes are known from Texas, one of which was found at Lackland Air Force Base near San Antonio. The second, reported by Gloyd (1938), was a melanistic specimen encountered near Victoria by a woman familiar with the local serpent fauna. After concluding from the snake's all-black color that it did not fit the description of any local venomous species known to her, she picked it up, whereupon the reptile bit her on a finger. Although the bite proved serious, the victim recovered.

Just as bewildering as all-black coral snakes are the occasional patternless examples of ordinarily well-marked species, like the completely pale gray mottled rock rattler found near Juno in Val Verde County, the lengthwise-striped western diamondbacked rattlesnakes sometimes reported from Central and West Texas, and the piebald western diamond-backed rattlesnake from Bosque County.

Considering the great odds against finding an aberrantly colored or patterned snake in the wild, it may seem trivial to devote so much space to a discussion of such abnormal specimens. Nonetheless, we feel that the reader should at least be aware of their existence, so that an unexpected encounter with one of these odd serpents, should it be venomous, does not become a medical emergency. Since the striking coloration of an all-white or golden yellow snake is unlike that of any normally colored Texas snake species, it will more than likely be recognized for what it is—an aberrant specimen—and should therefore not be handled unless and until it is determined to be a harmless kind. There is, however, no easy solution for identifying some of the other bizarre color and pattern mutations. By observing many snakes over a period of time, an experienced herpetologist, amateur as well as professional, eventually learns to recognize most native species—even the strange out-of-character individuals—from their general, overall appearance and behavior. Any person seriously interested in the subject can in time achieve the same objective.

If all attempts to classify a particular unfamiliar specimen prove futile, we suggest you call a local zoo, nature center, museum of natural science, or university zoology department, whose staff can assist you in making a determination.

Naming the Snake

Once the snake has been identified, it will be assigned a name, which will probably be a vernacular name (otherwise known as the common name). Because such designations often vary greatly from one part of the continent to another, Collins and Taggart (2002) and Crother et al. (2000, 2003) have attempted to standardize the common names of all North American snakes. We have, with some exceptions, followed their recommendations. A serpent's vernacular name is usually followed by its scientific name. The latter is a Latinized designation that is accepted and understood by scientists and naturalists worldwide, and it also reveals the reptile's relationship with other closely related snakes.

The novice usually finds scientific names intimidating, but they need not be. Early in life, without ever knowing it, we were already using the scientific names of certain familiar zoo animals: alligator, as in *Alligator mississippiensis;* boa constrictor, as in *Boa constrictor;* giraffe, as in *Giraffa camelopardalis;* and hippopotamus, as in *Hippopotamus amphibius.*

Composed of at least two separate words (genus and species), and sometimes three (genus, species, and subspecies), the scientific name may also include the name of the person (the author) who first formally described the snake, in which case his or her name will appear at the end. When the author's name is enclosed in parentheses, it means the snake has been assigned to a different genus from the one in that author's original description. In more formal listings, the year in which the animal was first described will follow the author's name.

The generic name, which always begins with a capital letter, is the first element in a snake's scientific name. It is followed by the species name, which always begins with a lowercase letter. Both are printed in italics, and together they identify a specific kind of organism—the species. Considered the basic unit of classification, a species can be defined as a distinct group of similar organisms capable of interbreeding among themselves but reproductively isolated from other species. An example of a species with no described subspecies is *Crotalus atrox,* the western diamond-backed rattlesnake. In some instances, a species is further divided into two or more geographically different local populations, called subspecies (or races), in which case the scientific name will be composed of three parts—the last part also beginning with a lowercase letter and italicized. For example, the rock rattlesnake consists of several subspecies, two of which, the mottled rock rattlesnake (*Crotalus lepidus lepidus*) and the banded rock rattlesnake (*Crotalus lepidus klauberi*), occur in Texas, each occupying a different segment of the species' range. Subspecies can therefore be defined as geographically distinct populations of a species that are still recognizable at the species level but differ in certain characteristics from other races within the same species. Unlike species hybrids, however, they freely interbreed and produce fertile offspring. The area where two subspecies meet and intermingle reproductively, known as a zone of intergradation, can be as narrow as a few miles or as broad as a couple of hundred miles. Because there are inadequate specimen samples from many such areas, the zones are not always well defined. Within these zones, individual animals can look like either of the two involved subspecies, or they can share certain characteristics of both races.

TAXONOMIC ISSUES

At the beginning of the project, we had to make some decisions about the scientific names of several species of Texas snakes whose taxonomic status is in dispute. Most involve the classification of subspecies within a single species, whose individual geographic ranges apparently do not converge and whose evolutionary pathways seem to be in isolation from those of their closest relatives.

Since evolution is a continuing biological process, the science of classifying snakes is often complex and open to differing taxonomic interpretations. As a result of its dynamic nature, there is frequent disagreement among taxonomists about whether a particular population of snakes represents a subspecies or is, in fact, more correctly classified as a species. For example, when two subspecies (races) of the same species are sufficiently isolated from one another by an impassable geographic barrier (a large body of water, mountains, etc.), preventing any genetic exchange between them, they will probably evolve independently and may over time become separate and distinct species. One issue then is whether there is sufficient evidence to support the contention that the two populations are already completely isolated from one another geographically, and therefore reproductively separated. The question, are they indeed genetically isolated, or have we, as the result of a collecting bias, overlooked areas of contact between them? If they are completely isolated from one another, at what point in time can we conclude that they have evolved into separate species? We should also remember that evolutionarily speaking, such decisions are being made in a tiny slice of time. Who can say whether in the next 500 years, 1,000 years, or longer, the two subspecies will remain separate races, eventually merge again into a single population, or continue on their present evolutionary course to become individual species? Some herpetologists argue that when two adjacent but geographically separated populations of a single species (presently regarded as subspecies) are isolated from one another, they are well on their way to becoming species and should therefore automatically be given species status. We have taken a more conservative approach. It is our belief that before all such subspecies are summarily elevated to species rank, they must be evaluated case by case, using all of the data available. Only then can we adequately decide the outcome of such taxonomic controversies.

Based on that position, we have adopted the proposed change of status for one genus of snake from *Liochlorophis vernalis* to *Opheodrys vernalis;* for seven snakes from subspecies to species rank: *Carphophis amoenus vermis* to *Carphophis vermis, Elaphe guttata emoryi* to *Elaphe emoryi, Leptotyphlops dulcis dissectus* to *Leptotyphlops dissectus, Micrurus fulvius tener* to *Micrurus tener, Pituophis melanoleucus ruthveni* to *Pituophis ruthveni, Tantilla rubra cucullata* to *Tantilla cucullata,* and *Trimorphodon lambda vilkinsoni* to *Trimorphodon vilkinsoni;* and for four snakes from one species to another species, and/or one subspecies to another subspecies: *Drymarchon corais erebennus* to *Drymarchon melanurus erebennus, Elaphe guttata guttata* to *Elaphe guttata slowinskii, Elaphe guttata meahllorum* to *Elaphe emoryi meahllorum,* and *Masticophis taeniatus girardi* to *Masti-*

cophis taeniatus ornatus. We are retaining the subspecies desig-
nation of *Cemophora coccinea copei, Cemophora coccinea lineri,
Coluber constrictor flaviventris, Nerodia harteri harteri,* and
Nerodia harteri paucimaculata.

ORGANIZATION OF FAMILIES, SPECIES, AND SUBSPECIES ACCOUNTS
Arrangement of Families

Taxonomically speaking, families are arranged in a phylogenetic
order—in other words, as groups from the most primitive snakes
to the most advanced snakes. We have arranged the species and
subspecies accounts in order by families—referred to in this field
guide as blind snakes, colubrids, elapids, and vipers. A brief description of each family is summarized below.

Family Leptotyphlopidae
BLIND SNAKES

This family of small, slender, wormlike snakes contains two
genera, one of which is confined to West Africa. The other, Leptotyphlops, embracing more than 80 species, has a worldwide
distribution that takes in Africa, southern Asia, Arabia, Paki-
stan, and the Americas, including the southwestern part of the
United States. Three species are found in Texas, one of which
contains two subspecies. Features that distinguish this nonvenomous family of snakes are the rather solidly constructed skull,
an adaptation for burrowing; the presence of teeth only in the
lower jaw; the degenerate eyes, which can be seen only as small
black dots beneath the translucent ocular scales; the absence of
broad abdominal scales; and the presence of a rudimentary pel-
vic girdle (Fig. 3). Also notable are the small blunt head (which is
no wider than the snake's body), the reduced size of most of the
plates on the crown, and the extremely short spine-tipped tail
that is present in most species.

Family Colubridae
COLUBRIDS

Of all snake families, this is by far the largest and most varied,
containing more than 280 genera and about 1,600 species. It is

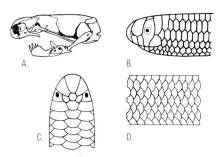

Figure 3. Characteristics of the family Leptotyphlopidae: (A) solid skull with teeth only in the lower jaw, (B) degenerate eyes nearly hidden beneath large ocular scales, (C) small blunt head no wider than neck or body, (D) belly scales same size as dorsal scales.

also the most perplexing, for it includes snakes that do not exactly fit in this family but are included here as a matter of convenience. Indeed, few internal or external characteristics can be used consistently to define all members of the family or those of its subfamilies. Colubrids, which inhabit all of the continents except the polar regions, display their greatest diversity in North America, Eurasia, and tropical Asia but are found only marginally in Australia, whose serpent fauna is dominated by elapid species.

In this large, diverse family, species range from diminutive snakes less than 12 inches (30.5 cm) long to those exceeding 11 feet (3.35 m) in length. All colubrids have large ventral scales (Fig. 4E); some have smooth dorsal scales, and others are covered with strongly keeled dorsal scales; most possess a conventionally rounded snout, while a small number have an oddly modified rostral scale, like those of bull, hog-nosed (Fig. 4F), and patch-nosed snakes; the vast majority have round eye pupils, but in a few the pupil is vertically elliptical (Fig. 4C,D); and though most of them possess upper jaw teeth of nearly equal length, some have enlarged (grooved or ungrooved) (Fig. 4A,B) teeth at the rear part of the upper jaw, including species with modified salivary glands that produce toxic saliva. In Texas, however, such rear-fanged snakes present no danger to humankind.

The family Colubridae is divided into four subfamilies, one of

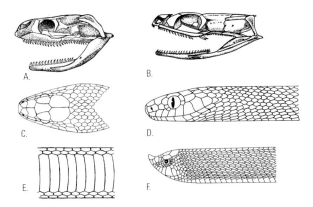

Figure 4. Characteristics of the family Colubridae: (A) Small solid teeth in both upper and lower jaws or (B) last two teeth of upper jaw may be enlarged and sometimes grooved. The majority of colubrids have (C) an unmodified head shape and round eye pupils; some possess (D) elliptical eye pupils. All colubrids possess (E) large ventral scales. A few, like the hog-nosed snakes, have (F) modified rostral scales for digging.

which, the Lycodontinae, is not represented in Texas. The largest subfamily, the Colubrinae, contains the following Texas genera: *Arizona* (glossy snakes), *Bogertophis* (Trans-Pecos rat snake), *Cemophora* (scarlet snakes), *Coluber* (racers), *Drymarchon* (indigo snake), *Drymobius* (speckled racer), *Elaphe* (rat snakes), *Ficimia* (Mexican hook-nosed snake), *Gyalopion* (western hook-nosed snake), *Lampropeltis* (king and milk snakes), *Masticophis* (whip-snakes), *Opheodrys* (smooth and rough green snakes), *Pituophis* (bull and pine snakes), *Rhinocheilus* (long-nosed snake), *Salvadora* (patch-nosed snakes), and *Sonora* (ground snakes). The subfamily Natricinae includes the Texas genera *Nerodia* (water snakes), *Regina* (crayfish snakes), *Storeria* (brown and red-bellied snakes), Thamnophis (garter and ribbon snakes), *Tropidoclonion* (lined snakes), and *Virginia* (rough and smooth earth snakes). In the subfamily Xenodontinae, we find the Texas genera *Farancia* (mud snake), *Carphophis* (worm snake), *Conio-phanes* (black-striped snake), *Diadophis* (ring-necked snakes), *Heterodon* (hog-nosed snakes), *Hypsiglena* (night snake), *Lep-

todeira (cat-eyed snake), *Tantilla* (black-headed and flat-headed snakes), and *Trimorphodon* (lyre snake).

Family Elapidae
CORAL SNAKES AND THEIR ALLIES

Found primarily in tropical and subtropical regions of the world, this family of venomous snakes contains some of the earth's most feared and dangerous serpents, including the cobras and mambas of Africa; the tiger snake, black snake, death adder, and taipan of Australia; and the cobras, kraits, and coral snakes (not closely related to American corals) of Asia. Also included in this family are the venomous sea snakes, whose special adaptations (laterally compressed bodies, paddlelike tails, and nose-valves, among others) allow them to exist in a marine environment. Comprising nearly 60 species in two subfamilies, they are widely distributed across the South China Sea and the Indian and Pacific oceans. The approximately 61 species of American coral snakes, included in the genera *Micrurus, Leptomicrurus,* and *Micruroides,* and distributed from the southern United States to Argentina, are also members of the family Elapidae. Only one, the Texas coral snake, occurs in Texas. These long, slender-bodied serpents typically have smooth dorsal scales and nearly always lack a loreal scale between the nostril and eye. Their fangs, like those of other elapids, are relatively short and incapable of rotational movement, fitting into a groove in the lower jaw when the snake's mouth is closed (Fig. 5).

A.

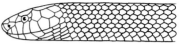

B.

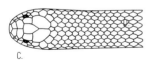

C.

Figure 5. Characteristics of the family Elapidae, the only dangerously venomous native snake species with (A) short, nonmovable fangs near the front of the upper jawbones, (B) smooth dorsal scales and a round pupil, and (C) a nontriangular head that is little if any wider than the neck.

Family Viperidae

VIPERS

This nearly worldwide family of venomous snakes is divided into three subfamilies, only one of which, the Crotalinae, commonly called pit vipers, is represented in Texas. Including about 144 species, the crotalids range throughout the Americas from southern Canada to Argentina, occurring as well in South and Central Asia, Malaysia, and the southeastern edge of Europe, but they are absent from Antarctica and Australia. Like the true vipers of the subfamily Viperinae, they have a wide, somewhat triangular head, vertically elliptical pupils, and a long, hollow fang on either side of the head near the front of the upper jaw. The fang is attached to a short, modified bone (the maxilla) and can be rotated through an arc of about 90 degrees, bringing it from a horizontal at-rest orientation against the roof of the mouth to an extended striking position (Fig. 6). This venom delivery system is the most sophisticated among all venomous snakes.

The single important external feature that immediately distinguishes the pit vipers from the true vipers (and from all other Texas snake species) is the pair of infrared-sensing facial pits, one on either side of the head between the eye and nostril. With

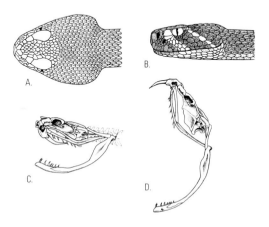

Figure 6. Characteristics of the family Viperidae (pit vipers): (A) a broad, triangular head followed by a relatively narrow neck, (B) elliptical pupils and temperature-sensing facial pits, and (C and D) large movable fangs.

these organs, the serpent can locate warm-blooded prey even in total darkness, gauge its distance, and visualize its size and outline. This unique adaptation allows the snake to hit its mark without the benefit of its eyesight, a decisive advantage when hunting at night or deep inside a mammal burrow.

Texas snakes belonging to the subfamily Crotalinae, in the family Viperidae, include all of the races of copperheads, the cottonmouth, and 10 types of rattlesnakes.

Arrangement of Species and Subspecies

In organizing the species and subspecies accounts in the main text, we have used the standard arrangement found in most general books about snakes. Families are listed first, according to their phylogenetic position, followed by their respective genera, in alphabetical order, then the species, also listed alphabetically. When a Texas species is represented by more than one subspecies, such races are arranged alphabetically as well, unless the nominate race is included (the one in which both species and subspecies names are the same), in which case it comes first regardless of alphabetical order.

Each snake account begins with the serpent's common name, followed immediately by its scientific name. Thereafter, each account is organized into four main headings: Description, Comparable Snakes, Size, and Habitat.

Unless a more recent record length is noted, the maximum measurement mentioned herein for each species and subspecies generally is that listed in Conant and Collins (1991). We have not accepted every new maximum length report, however, particularly if it is unsupported by a voucher specimen.

The amount of natural history information presented for individual species and subspecies is largely a reflection of the documented knowledge available for that snake. An account is long when the published information about it is plentiful and brief when such data are sketchy. Whenever possible, we have based our information about a given species or subspecies on studies conducted in Texas, but when such knowledge was scanty or lacking altogether, we turned to observations made in other parts of the serpent's geographic range.

The Maps

The base map of Texas, drawn and produced by Dr. Ralph W. Axtell, is used here with his permission. It delineates political boundaries (counties); details rivers, major streams, and lakes; and indicates the approximate locations of certain geological features such as faults and ancient beach lines, that affect or limit the distribution of some snake species.

The maps in this book are based solely on actual preserved specimens held in museum, university, and other scientific collections throughout the United States. Although locality dots cannot be illustrated for each map because of their size, we have carefully outlined the edge of the species' range within the state. The presentation of subspecies distributions are less accurate. We have assumed that the contact area between subspecies is best represented by a line that delineates the middle of the intergrade zone (see Werler and Dixon 2000).

A glance at Werler and Dixon's state maps demonstrates that few Texas snakes are shown to be evenly distributed throughout their respective ranges. Such spotty patterns can sometimes be real, reflecting a species' absence from certain local areas of unsuitable habitat, for few serpents are adaptable enough to occupy all of the varied environments within their territories. Inhospitable areas within a snake's range can be smaller than a square mile or involve several hundred square miles. Nevertheless, many of the distributional gaps evident on the maps are not the result of such natural barriers but are traceable to a collecting bias on the part of zoologists and others who capture voucher specimens for university and museum collections. Such voids are particularly evident in West Texas, and to a lesser degree in South Texas, where vast tracts of privately owned land are fenced and therefore not readily accessible to collectors.

Citations

In a book of this kind, frequent citing of references within the text may be an impediment to readability. We believe, however, that such acknowledgment serves two useful purposes: it appropriately recognizes the contributions of those who have added to our body of knowledge, and it provides the reader with additional sources of information, near the material under discussion.

CHECKLIST OF TEXAS SNAKES

FAMILY LEPTOTYPHLOPIDAE

Plains blind snake
Leptotyphlops dulcis dulcis
(Baird and Girard) 1853
South Texas blind snake
*Leptotyphlops dulcis
rubellum* (Garman) 1883
New Mexico blind snake
Leptotyphlops dissectus
(Cope) 1896
Trans-Pecos blind snake
*Leptotyphlops humilis
segregus* Klauber 1939

FAMILY COLUBRIDAE

Kansas glossy snake
Arizona elegans elegans
Kennicott 1859
Texas glossy snake
Arizona elegans arenicola
Dixon 1960
Painted Desert glossy snake
Arizona elegans philipi
Klauber 1946
Trans-Pecos rat snake
*Bogertophis subocularis
subocularis* (Brown) 1901
Western worm snake
Carphophis vermis
(Kennicott) 1859

Northern scarlet snake
Cemophora coccinea copei
Jan 1863

Texas scarlet snake
Cemophora coccinea lineri
Williams, Brown, and Wilson 1966

Buttermilk racer
Coluber constrictor anthicus
Cope 1862

Tan racer
Coluber constrictor etheridgei Wilson 1970

Eastern Yellow-bellied Racer
Coluber constrictor flaviventris Say 1823

Mexican racer
Coluber constrictor oaxaca
Jan 1863

Southern black racer
Coluber constrictor priapus
Dunn and Wood 1939

Black-striped snake
Coniophanes imperialis imperialis (Kennicott) 1859

Prairie ring-necked snake
Diadophis punctatus arnyi
Kennicott 1858

Regal ring-necked snake
Diadophis punctatus regalis
Baird and Girard 1853

Mississippi ring-necked snake
Diadophis punctatus stictogenys Cope 1860

Texas indigo snake
Drymarchon melanurus erebennus (Cope) 1860

Speckled racer
Drymobius margaritiferus margaritiferus (Schlegel)
1837

Baird's rat snake
Elaphe bairdi (Yarrow)
1880

Slowinski's corn snake
Elaphe guttata slowinskii
Burbrink 2000

Great Plains rat snake
Elaphe emoryi emoryi Baird and Girard 1853

Southwestern rat snake
Elaphe emoryi meahllmorum Smith, Chizar, Staley, and Tepedelen 1994

Texas rat snake
Elaphe obsoleta lindheimeri
(Baird and Girard) 1853

Western mud snake
Farancia abacura reinwardti (Schlegel) 1837

Mexican hook-nosed snake
Ficimia streckeri Taylor 1931

Western hook-nosed snake
Gyalopion canum Cope
1860

Plains hog-nosed snake
Heterodon nasicus nasicus
Baird and Girard 1852

Dusty hog-nosed snake
Heterodon nasicus gloydi
Edgren 1952

Mexican hog-nosed snake
Heterodon nasicus kennerlyi Kennicott 1860

Eastern hog-nosed snake
Heterodon platirhinos
Latreille 1802

Texas night snake
Hypsiglena torquata jani
Duges 1866

Gray-banded king snake
Lampropeltis alterna
(Brown) 1902

Prairie king snake
*Lampropeltis calligaster
calligaster* (Harlan) 1827

Speckled king snake
*Lampropeltis getula
holbrooki* Stejneger 1902

Desert king snake
*Lampropeltis getula splen-
dida* (Baird and Girard)
1853

Louisiana milk snake
*Lampropeltis triangulum
amaura* Cope 1860

Mexican milk snake
*Lampropeltis triangulum
annulata* Kennicott 1860

New Mexico milk snake
*Lampropeltis triangulum
celaenops* Stejneger 1903

Central Plains milk snake
*Lampropeltis triangulum
gentilis* (Baird and Girard)
1853

Northern cat-eyed snake
*Leptodeira septentrionalis
septentrionalis* (Kennicott)
1859

Eastern coachwhip
*Masticophis flagellum
flagellum* (Shaw) 1802

Western coachwhip
*Masticophis flagellum
testaceus* Say 1823

Schott's whipsnake
Masticophis schotti schotti
Baird and Girard 1853

Ruthven's whipsnake
Masticophis schotti ruthveni
Ortenburger 1923

Central Texas whipsnake
*Masticophis taeniatus orna-
tus* Baird and Girard 1853

Gulf salt marsh snake
Nerodia clarki clarki (Baird
and Girard) 1853

Mississippi green water snake
Nerodia cyclopion (Dumeril, Bibron, and Dumeril)
1854

Yellow-bellied water snake
*Nerodia erythrogaster
flavigaster* (Conant) 1949

Blotched water snake
*Nerodia erythrogaster
transversa* (Hallowell) 1852

Broad-banded water snake
Nerodia fasciata confluens
(Blanchard) 1923

Florida water snake
Nerodia fasciata pictiventris
(Cope) 1895

Brazos water snake
Nerodia harteri harteri
(Trapido) 1941

Concho water snake
Nerodia harteri paucimaculata (Tinkle and Conant)
1961

Diamond-backed water snake
Nerodia rhombifer rhombifer (Hallowell) 1852

Midland water snake
Nerodia sipedon pleuralis (Cope) 1892

Rough green snake
Opheodrys aestivus (Linnaeus) 1766

Smooth green snake
Opheodrys vernalis blanchardi Grobman 1941

Sonoran gopher snake
Pituophis catenifer affinis Hallowell 1852

Bull snake
Pituophis catenifer sayi (Schlegel) 1837

Louisiana pine snake
Pituophis ruthveni Stull 1929

Graham's crayfish snake
Regina grahami Baird and Girard 1853

Gulf crayfish snake
Regina rigida sinicola (Huheey) 1959

Texas long-nosed snake
Rhinocheilus lecontei tessellatus Garman 1883

Big Bend patch-nosed snake
Salvadora deserticola Schmidt 1940

Mountain patch-nosed snake
Salvadora grahamiae grahamiae Baird and Girard 1853

Texas patch-nosed snake
Salvadora grahamiae lineata Schmidt 1940

Variable ground snake
Sonora semiannulata semiannulata Baird and Girard 1853

Southern Texas ground snake
Sonora semiannulata taylori (Boulenger) 1894

Marsh brown snake
Storeria dekayi limnetes Anderson 1961

Texas brown snake
Storeria dekayi texana Trapido 1944

Florida red-bellied snake
Storeria occipitomaculata obscura Trapido 1944

Mexican black-headed snake
Tantilla atriceps (Gunther) 1895

Trans-Pecos black-headed snake
Tantilla cucullata Minton 1956

Flat-headed snake
Tantilla gracilis Baird and Girard 1853

Southwestern black-headed snake
Tantilla hobartsmithi Taylor 1937

Plains black-headed snake
Tantilla nigriceps Kennicott 1860
Western black-necked garter snake
Thamnophis cyrtopsis cyrtopsis (Kennicott) 1860
Eastern black-necked garter snake
Thamnophis cyrtopsis ocellatus (Cope) 1880
Checkered garter snake
Thamnophis marcianus marcianus (Baird and Girard) 1853
Western ribbon snake
Thamnophis proximus proximus (Say) 1823
Arid land ribbon snake
Thamnophis proximus diabolicus Rossman 1963
Gulf Coast ribbon snake
Thamnophis proximus orarius Rossman 1963
Red-striped ribbon snake
Thamnophis proximus rubrilineatus Rossman 1963
Western plains garter snake
Thamnophis radix haydeni (Kennicott) 1860
Eastern garter snake
Thamnophis sirtalis sirtalis (Linnaeus) 1758
Texas garter snake
Thamnophis sirtalis annectens Brown 1950

Red-sided garter snake
Thamnophis sirtalis parietalis (Say) 1823
Texas lyre snake
Trimorphodon vilkinsoni Cope 1886
Lined snake
Tropidoclonion lineatum (Hallowell) 1856
Rough earth snake
Virginia striatula (Linnaeus) 1766
Western earth snake
Virginia valeriae elegans Kennicott 1859

FAMILY ELAPIDAE

Texas coral snake
Micrurus tener (Baird and Girard) 1853

FAMILY VIPERIDAE

Southern copperhead
Agkistrodon contortrix contortrix (Linnaeus) 1766
Broad-banded copperhead
Agkistrodon contortrix laticinctus Gloyd and Conant 1934
Trans-Pecos copperhead
Agkistrodon contortrix pictigaster Gloyd and Conant 1943
Western cottonmouth
Agkistrodon piscivorus leucostoma (Troost) 1836

49

Western diamond-backed
rattlesnake
  Crotalus atrox Baird and
  Girard 1853
Canebrake rattlesnake
  *Crotalus horridus
  atricaudatus* Latreille 1802
Mottled rock rattlesnake
  Crotalus lepidus lepidus
  (Kennicott) 1861
Banded rock rattlesnake
  Crotalus lepidus klauberi
  Gloyd 1936
Northern black-tailed
rattlesnake
  Crotalus molossus molossus
  Baird and Girard 1853

Mohave rattlesnake
  *Crotalus scutulatus
  scutulatus* (Kennicott) 1861
Green Prairie rattlesnake
  Crotalus viridis viridis
  (Rafinesque) 1818
Desert massasauga
  *Sistrurus catenatus edward-
  si* (Baird and Girard) 1853
Western massasauga
  *Sistrurus catenatus
  tergeminus* (Say) 1823
Western pygmy rattlesnake
  Sistrurus miliarius streckeri
  Gloyd 1935

KEY TO THE SPECIES
OF TEXAS SNAKES

1. Belly scales about same size as dorsal scales (Fig. 7A) 2
   Belly scales much larger than dorsal scales (Fig. 7B)...........................4
2. Supraoculars absent (Fig. 8A); a very small, pinkish snake, with blackish eye spots beneath the scales; body scales all the same size; length about 6 inches, maximum length around 11 inches
   .... Western blind snake
   (Trans-Pecos), *Leptotyphlops humilis*
   Supraoculars present (Fig. 8B); color and scales similar to above; length about 9 inches, maximum length around 13 inches..........................3
3. Two upperlip scales between nose scale and eye scale (Fig. 9A)
   .... New Mexico blind snake,
   Leptotyphlops dissectus
   One upper lip scale between nose scale and eye scale (Fig. 9B)
   .... Texas blind snake
   (plains, South Texas), *Leptotyphlops dulcis*
4. A facial pit between eye and nostril (Fig. 10A) 5
   No facial pit between eye and nostril (Fig. 10B) 14
5. No rattle or button on end of tail 6
   Rattle or button on end of tail 7

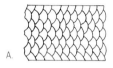 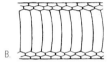

Figure 7. Reduced (A) and normal (B) size of belly scales.

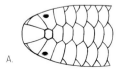 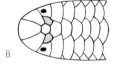

Figure 8. Supraoculars absent (A) or present (B).

Figure 9. Differences in lateral head scales between the subspecies of the Texas blind snake, and the New Mexico blind snake: (A) New Mexico blind snake, *L. dissectus*, (B) plains blind snake, *L. dulcis.*

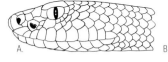 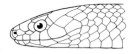

Figure 10. Facial pit present (A) or absent (B).

Figure 11. Loreal scale present (A) or absent (B).

6. Loreal scale present (Fig. 11A), maximum of 23 dorsal scale rows; copper color, dorsal saddles dark to moderate brown, narrow along the middle of the back and frequently not meeting dorsally; dorsal scales weakly keeled, elliptical pupil, and tip of tail frequently yellow, belly pinkish brown; length ranges between 24 and 36 inches, maximum length about 42 inches ....Copperhead

(southern, broad-banded, Trans-Pecos), *Agkistrodon contortrix*

No loreal scale (Fig. 11B), maximum of 25 dorsal scale rows; young occasionally copper colored, but belly dark brown to black; black cheek stripe in young and adults, but frequently faded in adults; black dorsal transverse bands are quickly lost as individual grows; general adult color dark brown to black; frequently swims with most of body visible above water; averages about 36 inches in length, maximum length about 62 inches ....Cottonmouth

(western), *Agkistrodon piscivorus*

7. Head scales generally very small (Fig. 12A) 8

Head scales consist of nine large plates (Fig. 12B) 13

8. Upper preocular divided vertically, anterior division being somewhat higher than posterior part and curved over the snout in front of the supraocular (Fig. 13A); body pattern of widely separated transverse dark bands, occasionally intermixed with dark spots; dark tail bands about one-fourth width of pale bands (Fig. 14C,D); length about 20 inches, maximum length about 32 inches ....Rock rattlesnake

(mottled, banded), *Crotalus lepidus*

Upper preocular not divided vertically (Fig. 13B), or if divided the

A.   B.

Figure 12. Small (A) or large (B) scales on crown of rattlesnake.

A.   B.

Figure 13. Upper preocular vertically divided (A) or not (B).

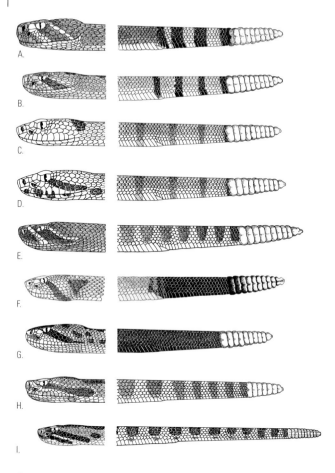

Figure 14. Lateral head and tail markings of Texas rattlesnakes. (A) Western diamond-backed rattlesnake (*Crotalus atrox*). Pale diagonal stripe behind eye intersects mouthline. Dark tail rings are as wide as the intervening pale spaces. (B) Mohave rattlesnake (*Crotalus scutulatus scutulatus*). Pale diagonal stripe behind eye fails to intersect mouthline. Dark tail rings are narrower than pale interspaces. (C) Banded rock rattlesnake (*Crotalus lepidus klauberi*). Usually no dark diagonal stripe behind eye; normally one or two large, dark spots on back of head. Dark tail rings are much narrower than pale interspaces. (D) Mottled rock rattlesnake (*Crotalus lepidus lepidus*). Dark diagonal stripe behind eye usually present; generally no dark spots on back of head. Dark tail rings are much narrower than pale interspaces. (E) Green prairie rattlesnake (*Crotalus viridis viridis*). Pale diagonal stripe behind eye passes above end of mouthline. Dark tail

anterior division not noticeably higher than the posterior part and not curved over the snout in front of the supraocular....................................... 9

9. Anterior body pattern of dark blotches that grade into tan or brown bands on rear part of body and tail(Fig. 14E); length around 40 inches, maximum length about 57 inches .... Prairie rattlesnake

(green prairie), *Crotalus viridis*

Not patterned as above... 10

10. Dorsal pattern of diamond-shaped blotches, tail with black and white bands 11

Dorsal pattern of transverse dark bands or diamonds; tail black 12

11. Dark and pale tail bands of about equal width (Fig. 14A); white cheek stripe extends to mouthline; scales between supraoculars small; length about 48 inches, maximum length about 84 inches

....Western diamond-backed rattlesnake,

Crotalus atrox

Dark tail bands about half the width of pale bands; white cheek stripe passes behind the mouthline (Fig. 14B); scales between supraoculars larger than those on rear of head; length around 30 inches, maximum length 51 inches... Mohave rattlesnake,

Crotalus scutulatus

12. Anterior dorsal pattern with chevron-shaped bands; tail black (Fig. 14F); length about 48 inches, maximum length around 74 inches

....Timber rattlesnake

(canebrake), *Crotalus horridus*

Anterior body pattern with an interconnected chain of dark blotches or diamonds (Fig. 15), tail black; (Fig. 14G) length around 38 inches, maximum length about 49 inches .... Black-tailed rattlesnake (northern), *Crotalus molossus*

13. Upper preocular in contact with postnasal; a series of dark brown to brown body blotches outlined in pale brown, with a lateral alternating se-

bands are irregular in outline, often narrow. (F) Canebrake rattlesnake (*Crotalus horridus atricaudatus*). Dark diagonal stripe behind eye broadly intersects and sometimes crosses the end of mouthline. Tail and posterior end of body are black. (G) Northern black-tailed rattlesnake (*Crotalus molossus molossus*). Dark diagonal stripe behind eye intersects end of mouthline. Tail is black. (H) Massasauga, western (*Sistrurus catenatus tergeminus*) and desert (*Sistrurus catenatus edwardsi*). Dark diagonal stripe behind eye extends backward onto end of jaw. Dark tail blotches may form rings near rattle. (I) Western pygmy rattlesnake (*Sistrurus miliarius streckeri*). Dark diagonal stripe behind eye extends backward onto end of jaw, and usually a narrower dark stripe, paralleling the first, extends onto the lower jaw; upper half of eye is pale, lower part dark. Tail is relatively slender for a rattlesnake, blotched and ending in a series of small rattles.

ries of pale brown spots with ventrolateral darker spots alternating with the pale brown spots; tail bands tan to brown (Fig. 14H); rattles relatively large for a small rattlesnake with a length of 23 inches, maximum length about 34 inches..Massasauga

(desert, western), *Sistrurus catenatus*

Upper preocular not contacting postnasal; usually a pale reddish brown dorsal longitudinal stripe, interrupted by a series of short transverse blackish markings; one or two rows of lateral or ventrolateral blackish spots in addition to the dorsal bands; ground color gray to grayish pink; tail bands similar to body markings in color (Fig. 14I); rattles very small; length around 18 inches, maximum length about 25 inches

....Pygmy rattlesnake

(western), *Sistrurus miliarius*

14. Rings completely encircle the body, red rings alternate with yellow rings that are separated by black rings; snout and anterior head black, followed by a yellow ring, then a black ring; an erect fang at the anterior end of upper jaw; length about 25 inches, maximum length around 47 inches

....Texas coral snake,

Micrurus tener

Body not as above, with transverse bands or blotches, ringlike crossbands never completely encircle the body; no permanently erect fang at anterior end of upper jaw..15

15. Prefrontals more than two (Fig. 16A) 16

Prefrontals two (Fig. 16B); color patterns highly variable; small or large snakes 17

16. A large snake with more than 41 large dark body blotches on a yellowish ground color that contrast more strongly with the ground color at each end of the snake; the dorsal blotches may or may not fuse on the neck; belly marked laterally with large blackish marks on a yellow ground color; tendency to hiss (expel air) loudly; size around 48 inches, maximum length about 100 inches.. Gopher snake

(Sonoran, bull), *Pituophis catenifer*

A large snake with 42 or fewer body blotches; neck blotches normally brown, somewhat obscure, and frequently fusing on the anterior body; blotches just in front of the vent and on the tail brownish red, distinct, and well separated; belly mottled with pale yellow and dark brown spots; length about 51 inches, maximum length around 70 inches

....Louisiana pine snake,

Pituophis ruthveni

17. Scales beneath tail normally in a single row (Fig. 17A); nose appears long; black transverse dorsal bands separated by red ground color; red

Figure 15. Body pattern of northern black-tailed rattlesnake, produced by individual unicolored scales.

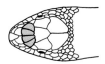 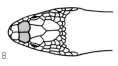

A.   B.

Figure 16. Prefrontals more than two (A) or only two (B) (after Conant and Collins 1991).

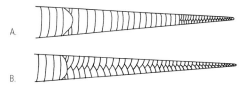

A.

B.

Figure 17. Scales beneath tail in a single row (A) or a double row (B).

scales often obscured with black flecks; belly pale yellow to cream; length about 26 inches, maximum length around 41 inches......Long-nosed snake (Texas), *Rhinocheilus lecontei*

Scales beneath tail normally in two rows (Fig. 17B); color pattern variable 18

18. Loreal scale absent (Fig. 11A) 19

Loreal scale present (Fig. 11B) 27

19. Number of middorsal scale rows normally two more than in front of vent; upturned pointed nose..20

Number of middorsal scale rows the same as those in front of vent; nose neither upturned nor pointed.. 21

20. Prefrontal scales in contact, separating rostral from frontal scale; color pattern of narrow transverse brown bands on a grayish ground color; head also banded; adults usually less than 12 inches in length but may reach 15 inches.. Western hook-nosed snake, *Gyalopion canum*

Prefrontal scales not in contact, rostral contacts frontal; body with small and usually obscure transverse brownish bands or blotches; ground

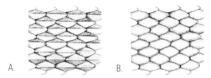

Figure 18. Body scales keeled (A) or smooth (B).

Figure 19. Profile of the Florida red-bellied snake, with white spot on the upper lip scales below and behind the eye.

Figure 20. Lateral head patterns of brown snakes: (A) the dark streak behind the eye of the marsh brown snake and (B) the large dark neck patch and upper lip markings of the Texas brown snake.

color grayish brown to pale brown; head seldom has bands; adults usually less than 12 inches, but may reach 19 inches
.... Mexican hook-nosed snake,
Ficimia streckeri

21. Body scales with keels (Fig. 18A) 22
Body scales smooth (Fig. 18B) 23

22. Body scales in 15 rows; belly yellowish, dorsal color tan or reddish tan, faint yellowish transverse band behind head, head usually dark reddish brown to dark brown; usually a white spot on the edge of the upper lip below and behind the eye (Fig. 19); adults usually 10 inches but may reach 16 inches..Red-bellied snake
(Florida), *Storeria occipitomaculata*

Body scales in 17 rows; belly grayish; dorsal body with tan or pale tan middorsal longitudinal stripe from rear of head to tail, with a series of small black or dark brown dots along each side of stripe; rear of head with a pair of dark spots (Fig. 20); adults usually about 12 inches in length but occasionally 19 inches... Brown snake
(marsh, Texas), *Storeria dekayi*

23. Head brown, tan, or slightly darker than body color (Fig. 21C), upper

lip scales six per side; belly bright pink to almost red; length around 7 inches, maximum length about 9 inches .... Flat-headed snake,
Tantilla gracilis

Head with black cap, contrasting with body color; upper lip scales normally seven per side..24

24. Black head cap with a straight or slightly convex posterior margin (Fig. 21B), extending only about three scales beyond posterior edge of parietals; usually followed by pale border 25

Black head cap with a V-shaped posterior margin (Fig. 21A), extending four to eight scales beyond posterior edge of parietals; the black cap may or may not be interrupted by a white neck band 26

25. Normally one postocular, rear of black head cap straight; mental usually separated from chin shields; length less than 12 inches
.... Mexican black-headed snake,
Tantilla atriceps

Normally two postoculars, rear of black head cap straight; mental usually in contact with chin shields; length less than 12 inches
....Southwestern black-headed snake,
Tantilla hobartsmithi

26. Black cap not extending below end of mouthline, posterior margin V-shaped; body pale brown or tan, midventral area of belly pinkish red; length about 10 inches, maximum length around 15 inches
.... Plains black-headed snake,
Tantilla nigriceps

Black cap extending below end of mouthline and four to eight scales behind parietals, dorsal and ventral surfaces of head completely black, no white cheek patch (Fig. 22C; or black head cap rarely extends beyond posterior tips of parietals, followed by narrow white band which in turn is followed by a broad black band (Fig. 22A,B); snout usually white, a white cheek patch below and behind eye; chin shields white; white band across neck usually one to two scale rows in longitudinal width, occasionally with

A.   B.   C.

Figure 21. Head markings of black-headed and flat-headed snake species: (A) long, pointed cap of the plains black-headed snake, (B) straight-edged cap of Mexican and southwestern black-headed snakes, and (C) faint cap of the flat-headed snake.

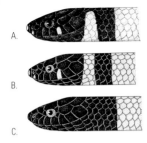

Figure 22. Three head pattern variations of the Trans-Pecos black-headed snake: (A) divided white collar, (B) complete white collar (formerly the Devil's River race), and (C) completely black hood.

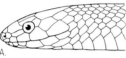

A.   B.

Figure 23. Preocular scale absent (A) or present (B).

a longitudinal black line from parietal to black band, or a black dot, or an interrupted line from parietal to black band; length about 12 inches, maximum length around 25 inches .... Trans-Pecos black-headed snake, *Tantilla cucullata*

27. Two loreals, pupil of eye elliptical; body with about 20 dark brown to brown transverse bands on a gray ground color; the broad dorsal blotches narrow laterally; belly white or cream to dirty yellow; usually three obscure dark spots on back of head; length about 24 inches, maximum length around 41 inches .... Texas lyre snake, *Trimorphodon vilkinsoni*

One loreal, pupil variable, color pattern variable, size variable 28

28. Preocular absent, loreal enters orbit (Fig. 23A) 29
Preocular present, loreal not entering orbit (Fig. 23B) 32

29. Dorsal scale rows smooth, in 19 rows; dorsal body glossy black, belly red and black; body stout; tail short with horny tip; neck not distinguishable from rest of body; usually found around swamps, often burrows in mud; length about 45 inches, maximum length around 81 inches .... Mud snake (western), *Farancia abacura*

Dorsal scale rows keeled or smooth, in fewer than 19 rows 30

30. Dorsal scale rows 13; dorsum black to purplish black, belly pinkish, belly color extends up the sides to the third scale row; 10–12 inches in length, occasionally reaching 15 inches .... Western worm snake, *Carphophis vermis*

Dorsal scale rows 17; dorsal surface gray, brown, or reddish brown; pointed head; length less than 15 inches...31

31. Postocular single, five upper lip scales; pointed snout; scales strongly keeled; a very plain, small brown snake with pale brown to gray belly; length about 8–9 inches, maximum length about 12 inches

.... Rough earth snake, *Virginia striatula*

Postoculars two, six upper lip scales; scales smooth or weakly keeled; gray, brown to reddish snake; length 8–9 inches, maximum length around 15 inches.. Smooth earth snake (western), *Virginia valeriae*

32. Anal plate entire (single scale, Fig. 24A) 33

Anal plate divided (two scales, Fig. 24B)... 45

33. Dorsal scales keeled... 34

Dorsal scales smooth.. 39

34. Belly pattern consisting of two parallel rows of black half-moon spots; three pale longitudinal lines of yellow, orange, white, or gray; length 10–12 inches, occasionally reaching 21 inches ....Lined snake, *Tropidoclonion lineatum*

Belly without two rows of black half-moon spots 35

35..

Pale lateral stripe of anterior body involving fourth scale row (Fig. 25A) 36

Pale lateral stripe on anterior body absent or not touching fourth scale row (Fig. 25B) 37

36. Upper lips, lower lips, and belly with some dark markings, a double row of black spots between pale stripes (Fig. 26A); lateral pale line on scale

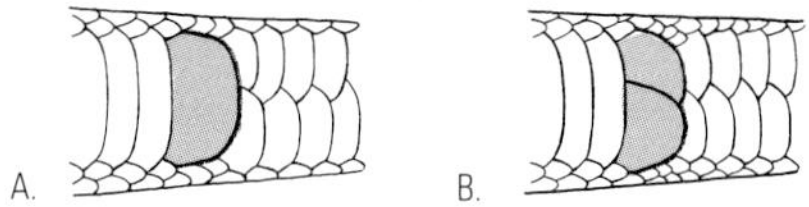

A.   B.

Figure 24. Anal plate single (A) or double (B).

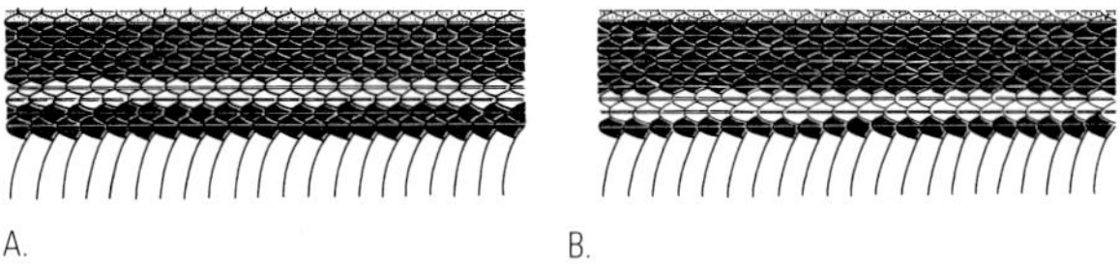

A.   B.

Figure 25. Lateral pale stripe on third and fourth scale rows (A) or on second and third scale rows (B) in garter snakes.

Figure 26. Head markings of (A) garter snake, including vertical black lines along the sutures of the lip scales, and (B) ribbon snake, with no marks on lip scales.

Figure 27. Head markings of the checkered garter snake, including the distinct pale-colored crescent near the end of the mouthline.

Figure 28. Lateral body markings of black-necked garter snake subspecies: (A) double row of black spots on the side of the western black-necked garter snake and (B) a single row on the eastern black-necked garter snake.

rows 3 and 4; outer edge of belly with obscure blackish spots on each side; length around 20–24 inches, maximum length about 41 inches
.... Plains garter snake (western), *Thamnophis radix*

Upper lips (Fig. 26B); lower lips, and belly without dark markings; three pale stripes, the median one highly variable in Texas populations, from pale yellow or grayish white to orange red; two pale spots on the parietal scales; a thin, long-tailed garter snake about 25 inches long, but may reach 48 inches...Western ribbon snake (western, arid land, Gulf Coast, red-striped), *Thamnophis proximus*

37. Lateral pale stripe on third scale row only near head; a checkerboard pattern of squarish black and white spots, black spots frequently invade lateral pale lines; yellowish crescent mark behind the corner of the mouth followed by a large black spot (Fig. 27); scales in 21 rows, anal plate single; about 21 inches in length, maximum length around 41 inches
.... Checkered garter snake, *Thamnophis marcianus*

Lateral pale stripe on second and third scale rows on neck 38
38. Upper lip scales eight to a side; a white to pale yellow mark on the side of the head preceded by a pair of large black neck blotches that may or may not unite across the back of the neck (Fig. 28A,B); head usually gray or bluish gray, contrasting with the black neck blotches; an orange longitudi-

nal stripe from rear of head to tail, but may turn yellowish posteriorly; one or two rows of lateral black blotches between the middorsal and the ventrolateral pale stripes; scale rows usually 19 at midbody, anal plate single; length about 24 inches, maximum length around 41 inches
.... Black-necked garter snake
(western, eastern), *Thamnophis cyrtopsis*

Upper lip scales seven to a side; no pale crescent or paired black blotches behind head; lateral longitudinal pale stripes confined to scale rows 2 and 3; basic colors highly variable, the three longitudinal pale stripes varying from yellow (usual color) to gray, yellowish orange, greenish, or bluish, or occasionally absent; usually two rows of black spots between pale stripes; may have red on scales or skin; belly with a lateral series of small black marks; length about 24 inches, maximum length about 48 inches .... Common garter snake
(eastern, Texas, red-sided), *Thamnophis sirtalis*

39. Dorsal scale rows 17; a large bluish black snake with some indication of black marks below the eye; young with anterior to middle of body brownish yellow to brown, with some indication of an obscure pattern of darker marks; length around 4–5 feet, maximum length about 100 inches .... Central American Indigo snake
(Texas), *Drymarchon melanurus*

Dorsal scale rows 19 or more; always some pattern of blotches, spots, or bands present 40

40. Dorsal scales in 19 rows; snout pointed and red; transverse bands of red bordered with black, and yellow bands between the black-edged red bands (Fig. 29A,B); belly immaculate white to cream; length about 18 inches, reaching a maximum length of about 32 inches .... Scarlet snake
(northern, Texas), *Cemophora coccinea*

Dorsal scale rows 21 or more 40

41. Dorsal scale rows 29 or more; pale brown to tan, moderately large transverse body blotches, with alternating smaller brown body blotches on sides of body; belly white to cream; snout pointed, head with two preoculars; length about 30 inches, with maximum length about 54 inches .... Eastern glossy snake
(Kansas, Texas, Painted Desert), *Arizona elegans*

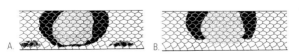

Figure 29. Lateral body markings of (A) northern scarlet snake and (B) Texas scarlet snake.

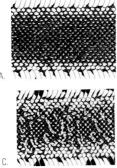

Figure 30. Dorsal patterns of (A) typical phase of the speckled king snake, (B) coastal phase of the speckled king snake, and (C) typical desert king snake (after Blaney 1977).

Dorsal scale rows 27 or less; dorsal body pattern, if consisting of a series of blotches or spots, accompanied by a blotched belly pattern; preoculars single 42

42. Dorsal pattern of narrow blackish gray to gray transverse bands, alternate bands being mixed or split with red color, or a pattern of alternating black-bordered red or orange saddles and white-bordered gray saddles; belly blotched with black or sometimes almost entirely black; length about 25 inches, maximum length about 57 inches
.... Gray-banded king snake,
Lampropeltis alterna

Dorsal pattern not as described above 43

43. Dorsal pattern of small yellow or yellowish white dots on each scale, or obscure black transverse blotches with yellow or pale yellow borders, occasionally forming a chainlike pattern, or a series of transverse black blotches separated by white or yellow bands or spotted scale rows (Fig. 30A,B,C); belly mostly black but may be blotched with yellow and black; scales smooth, anal plate single; length about 40 inches, maximum length about 72 inches .... Common king snake
(speckled, desert), *Lampropeltis getula*

Dorsal pattern of dark brown to brown transverse blotches with alternating small spots on the sides of the body, or pattern of red, black, yellow to white transverse bands that extend onto the belly and may occasionally reach across the belly 44

44. Dorsal pattern of brown to dark brown transverse body blotches; belly with squarish brown blotches alternating with pale tan to cream ground color; length about 36 inches, maximum length around 56 inches
.... Prairie king snake,
Lampropeltis calligaster

Dorsal pattern consisting of various widths of red, black, and yellow (occasionally white) transverse bands that may form rings around the body; belly is typically colored like the dorsum, but bands usually do not meet across the belly (Fig. 31); red bands are always bordered by black bands, which alternate with yellow or white bands; length around 24 inches, maximum length about 42 inches .... Milk snake
(Louisiana, Mexican, New Mexico, Central Plains),
Lampropeltis triangulum

45. Dorsal scales keeled...46
    Dorsal scales smooth...62
46. Dorsal color a uniform green to bright green in life, no other pattern; belly whitish to pale yellow to white or pale green cast; long and slender body and tail; length about 26 inches, maximum length around 45 inches
....Rough green snake,
Opheodrys aestivus

Dorsal surface with some pattern; old individuals may appear unicolored, pattern may be lined, blotched, or spotted 47
47. Nose scale (rostral) turned up...48
Nose scale (rostral) normal, not turned up 49
48. Prefrontal scales separated by small scales; nose scale turned up sharply and keeled; underside of tail not paler than belly; belly and undertail usually black (Fig. 32), marked with yellow areas; dorsum with five rows of brown blotches, a larger middle row and two smaller rows per side; length about 22 inches, maximum about 39 inches
.... Western hog-nosed snake
(plains, dusty, Mexican), *Heterodon nasicus*

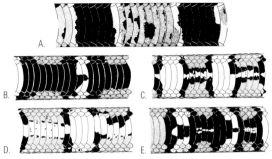

Figure 31. (A) Dorsal rings on belly of the coral snake compared to belly patterns of native milk snakes: (B) Mexican milk snake, (C) New Mexico milk snake, (D) Louisiana milk snake, and (E) Central Plains milk snake.

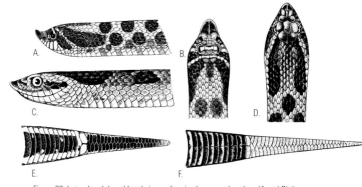

Figure 32. Lateral and dorsal head views of native hog-nosed snakes: (A and B) the more pronounced nose scale of the western species compared to that of (C and D) the eastern species. Undertail views of (E) the black-marked western species and (F) the almost patternless eastern species.

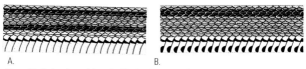

Figure 33. Graham's crayfish snake (A) with dark lateral line and no bold belly spots, and the Gulf crayfish snake (B) with bold belly spots but no dark lateral stripe.

Prefrontal scales contact one another, underside of tail paler than belly; belly often mottled with gray or greenish on yellow-gray or rose (Fig. 32); dorsum normally with transverse brown to black blotches in a single or double row, background color sometimes reddish; occasionally the dorsum appears uniform black or gray; length about 25 inches, maximum length about 45 inches..Eastern hog-nosed snake,
Heterodon platirhinos

49. Dorsal scales in 19 rows..50

Dorsal scales in 21 or more rows..51

50. Dorsum with distinct yellow longitudinal lines on lowest three scale rows; a distinct black line on outer edge of belly adjacent to lowest body scale row (Fig. 33A); occasionally a faint series of dark spots down the center of the belly; scales keeled; belly usually yellow, buff, or grayish yellow; length around 24 inches, maximum length about 45 inches
.... Graham's crayfish snake,
Regina grahami

Dorsum unicolored, occasionally glossy brown, dark brown, or almost black; scales keeled; two rows of distinct black spots down the belly (Fig. 33B); almost meeting at midline, but with a pale space between each pair of dark spots; length about 18 inches, maximum length about 31 inches ....Glossy crayfish snake (Gulf), *Regina rigida*

51. Subocular scales present (row of scales separating upper lip scales from eye (Fig. 34A) 52

Subocular scales absent (Fig. 34B)...53

52. Dorsal pattern rarely blotched, usually consisting of a series of longitudinal H-shaped blotches; a pair of black neck stripes that extend posteriorly to form the outer segments of the H pattern; desert form, nonaquatic; occasionally a blond form with pale yellowish brown blotches in the Lajitas area of West Texas; length about 40 inches, maximum length around 66 inches.. Trans-Pecos rat snake, *Bogertophis subocularis*

Dorsal pattern usually greenish or brownish with dark brown or blackish markings intermixed; belly with distinctive mottling of dark and light, but color variable; strongly keeled scales; aquatic form; length about 36 inches, maximum length around 50 inches .... Mississippi green water snake, *Nerodia cyclopion*

53. Large aquatic form with strongly keeled scales; dorsal pattern of chainlike dark brown to black markings; each dark loop of the chain extends down the sides to the belly, forming a somewhat loose diamond mark; general ground color olive green or dark green to brownish; belly strongly marked with black spots on the outer edge of and scattered smaller black spots down the center; length about 40 inches, maximum length around 63 inches.. Diamond-backed water snake, *Nerodia rhombifer*

Small to large aquatic snake with strongly keeled scales; pattern transverse blotches, bands, or spots 54

54. A double row of somewhat small, reddish brown to pale brown spots on each side of dorsum, on a pale brown to pinkish brown ground color; a row of obscure to distinct dark spots along each side of the belly (known

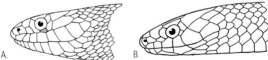

Figure 34. Subocular scales present (A) or absent (B).

only from middle Brazos, Concho, and Colorado river drainages); length about 22 inches, maximum length about 39 inches ..... Harter's water snake (Brazos, Concho), *Nerodia harteri*

Dorsum never with four rows of small spots; belly pale or dark, never with small obscure dark spots along the sides on a pinkish or tannish background 55

55. Belly pale yellow, yellow, or with a slight orange tinge, occasionally with dark markings laterally; dorsum with dark brown to blackish blotches that may fade in larger snakes, usually some indication of pattern remaining even in old snakes; colors often variable in different parts of the state; length around 40 inches, maximum about 59 inches .... Plain-bellied water snake (yellow-bellied, blotched), *Nerodia erythrogaster*

Belly never pale colored; dorsum blotched, banded, or striped 56

56. Ventrals number 160 or fewer... 57
Ventrals number 190 or more 59

57. Dorsum with two yellowish stripes and two brown stripes on each side of the body; belly reddish brown or blackish brown with a longitudinal central row of whitish dots; in addition, there may be a pair of whitish dots along the outer row of belly scales; length about 28 inches, maximum length about 36 inches....................................... Salt marsh snake (Gulf), *Nerodia clarki*

Dorsum with 30 or fewer reddish brown to blackish brown transverse bands 58

58. Dark stripe from eye to angle of mouth; anterior part of body with 17 or fewer broad brown to rich reddish brown bands separated by spaces usually some blend of yellow; belly yellow with squarish red to rust red spots, occasionally scattered and not uniform in size; scales strongly keeled; length about 30 inches, maximum length around 45 inches. .... Southern water snake (broad-banded, Florida), *Nerodia fasciata*

Dark stripe absent from eye to angle of mouth; anterior of body has a few brown bands, remainder of body shows a series of alternating brown to gray blotches; dorsal bands and blotches usually fewer than 30; series of dark markings on belly, often paired; length about 40 inches, maximum length around 59 inches .... Northern water snake (Midland), *Nerodia sipedon*

59. Dark stripe behind eye normally crosses the end of the mouthline and frequently extends onto neck.. 60

Dark stripe behind eye, when present, stops near the end of the mouthline, never crossing or extending onto neck 61

60. Number of brown to grayish brown body blotches variable, 28 to 37; belly with extensive dark squarish blotches, fewer blotches in South Texas and more numerous in North Texas; tail with or without a pair of ventral tail stripes, but stripes more common in East Texas; length about 40 inches, maximum around 72 inches.. Red corn snake (Slowinski's), *Elaphe guttata*

    Grayish brown to dark brown body blotches number 35 to 58, belly with or without extensive black to dark brown markings, undersurface of tail with paired blackish lines or dots along either side; head pattern very similar to corn snake ....Great Plains rat snake (Great Plains, southwestern), *Elaphe emoryi*

61. Young gray with brownish blotches, as they mature the blotches become dark brown to black and frequently disappear; head usually black in adults; length about 45 inches, maximum size around 86 inches ....Texas rat snake, *Elaphe obsoleta*

    Young grayish to greenish brown, with more than 47 narrow brown crossbands; adults with four dark stripes, the two lateral stripes frequently obscure and the two upper ones more distinct but occasionally absent; length about 54 inches, maximum around 62 inches.......Baird's rat snake, *Elaphe bairdi*

62. Same number of dorsal scale rows throughout the body (occasionally 14 or 13 at vent in South Texas).. 63

    Two fewer dorsal scale rows in front of the vent than at midbody ..64

63. Dorsal color tan, brown, reddish brown, with or without small and narrow black transverse bands, or orange or reddish orange longitudinal stripe down the back; length about 10 inches, maximum size around 15 inches.. Ground snake (variable, southern Texas), *Sonora semiannulata*

    Dorsal color uniform green, scales smooth; long, slender body and tail; belly white to pale yellow; length around 15 inches, maximum length about 26 inches.. Smooth green snake, *Opheodrys vernalis*

64. Dorsal scale rows 19 or more... 65

    Dorsal scale rows fewer than 19... 67

65. Dorsal pattern of broad, dark brown to black longitudinal stripes that alternate with tan or pale brown stripes; a white or yellowish line from snout, over eye, to rear of head; belly orange or reddish, without other markings; about 15 inches in length, maximum length around 20 inches .... Black-striped snake, *Coniophanes imperialis*

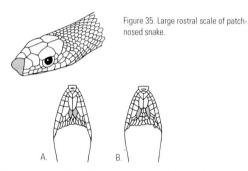

Figure 35. Large rostral scale of patch-nosed snake.

Figure 36. Posterior chin shields touching or separated by a single row of scales (A) or separated by two or more rows (B) (after Conant and Collins 1991).

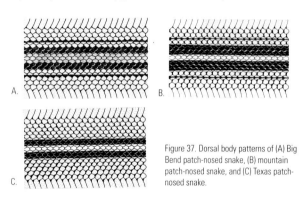

Figure 37. Dorsal body patterns of (A) Big Bend patch-nosed snake, (B) mountain patch-nosed snake, and (C) Texas patch-nosed snake.

Dorsal pattern with blotches or bands, no stripes.............................66

66. Dorsal pattern of large, dark brown to black, roundish blotches or saddles, extending down sides almost to belly, blotches contrast with ground color; pupil elliptical; neck narrow, head broad; belly white or cream to pale yellow; about 22 inches in length, maximum length around 38 inches .... Northern cat-eyed snake, *Leptodeira septentrionalis*

Dorsal pattern of small, brown to dark brown, irregularly shaped blotches that may be in one, three, or more rows; neck and middorsal blotches may be large and fused, while remainder may be paired and much smaller; a black stripe from snout, through eye, to side of neck; neck pattern usually of three longitudinal black marks; lateral dark neck marks may fuse with lateral head stripe; belly cream to white; pupil of eye elliptical; about 15 inches in length, maximum length around 20 inches

....Night snake
(Texas), *Hypsiglena torquata*

67. Nose scale (rostral) much enlarged, shieldlike and with free edges
(Fig. 35) 68

Nose scale not enlarged, not with free edges 69

68. Upper lip scales eight per side; posterior chin shields usually in contact or separated by a single scale (Fig. 36A); dorsum with broad dark brown to blackish longitudinal stripes strongly contrasting with yellowish tan ground color (Fig. 37B,C); paler middorsal stripe may be similar in color to or brighter than the sides of the body; occasionally with a dark longitudinal line on the third row of scales; belly pale yellow to cream; length about 30 inches, maximum length around 47 inches

.... Mountain patch-nosed snake
(mountain, Texas), *Salvadora grahamiae*

Upper lip scales nine per side; posterior chin shields separated by two or three scales (Fig. 36B); two broad blackish lines on the back; a thin dark line usually on scale row 4, but posteriorly on scale row 3; lower edges of the broad blackish stripes often interrupted with ground color, having a zigzag appearance (Fig. 37A); belly peach to rose; length around 27 inches, maximum length about 40 inches .... Big Bend patch-nosed snake,
Salvadora deserticola

69. Preocular single; body and tail long and slender; throat yellowish, ventral surface fading to whitish posteriorly; dorsum with a single yellow dot in the center of a black scale, the base of each scale blue; a black stripe from eye to neck; some blackish marks may be present on the ventral surface of body, most frequently under the tail; length about 35 inches, maximum length around 50 inches..Speckled racer,
Drymobius margaritiferus

Preoculars two 70

70. Anterior temporal scale single; lower preocular almost equal in size to upper preocular, not wedged between adjacent upper lip scales; a small snake with a bright orange or orange-yellow neck band in most populations, neck ring may be interrupted by dorsal ground color; dorsal color gray, blue, bluish green, tan or brown; belly bright orange to yellow, with a series of black spots scattered or densely spaced on the belly, spots may be in a single or paired row; length about 12 inches, maximum length around 19 inches .... Ring-necked snake
(prairie, regal, Mississippi), *Diadophis punctatus*

Anterior temporal scales in two or three rows; lower preocular smaller than upper preocular and wedged between adjacent upper lip scales...... 71

71. Dorsal scale rows just in front of the vent 15; dorsal color highly vari-

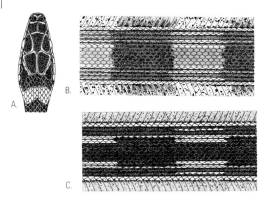

Figure 38. Markings of the Central Texas whipsnake: (A) crown and neck, (B) banded dorsal pattern, and (C) darker, broken-stripe dorsal pattern.

able, black, blue, tan, green, bluish green, with or without brown or reddish brown transverse blotches or bands (especially in young); belly pale yellow, cream, bright yellow, or lemon yellow; normally unicolored dorsally as adults, but some populations may have individual white scales scattered over the dorsal surface; length highly variable by population, usually about 38 inches, maximum length around 73 inches

.... Eastern racer

(buttermilk, tan, eastern yellow-bellied,

Mexican, southern black),*Coluber constrictor*

Dorsal scale rows 11, 12, or 13 just in front of the vent 72

72. Dorsal scale rows at midbody 17; dorsal color pattern highly variable throughout the range of the species; bright red, brown, tan, and black anteriorly to brown, tan, or pale yellow posteriorly; some populations may be completely black; rear of body appears braided to the human eye, resembling a leather whip; belly usually one color, cream, pinkish, or reddish; young have anterior brownish transverse bands or blotches, resembling young racers; length around 48 inches, maximum length about 102 inches.. Coachwhip

(eastern, western), *Masticophis flagellum*

Dorsal scale rows at midbody 15... 73

73. Uniformly black scales predominate on dorsal surface; head black with some scales outlined in white; narrow white transverse band or

paired white nape spots across neck, and normally five (0–10) white bands over the body (Fig. 38); eight longitudinal black lines (four per side) on scale rows 1, 2, 3, and 4 within white areas; anterior two-thirds of belly black, including throat; posteriorly, the ventral black pigment shifts to coral red near the vent and on the ventral surface of the tail; length about 48 inches, maximum length around 72 inches .... Striped whipsnake (Central Texas), *Masticophis taeniatus*

Uniformly bluish gray to greenish gray scales on dorsal surface, each scale with a pair of white, cream, or yellow marks on the anterolateral surface (Fig. 39); usually two white stripes on scale rows 3 and 4 on each side of the body (usually absent in Rio Grande Valley, where it occasionally has a pale stripe at the edge of the belly); throat and neck whitish, sides of neck reddish orange; belly with some speckled bluish marks throughout but turning salmon pink toward the tail; length about 48 inches, maximum length around 66 inches .... Schott's whipsnake (Schott's, Ruthven's), *Masticophis schotti*

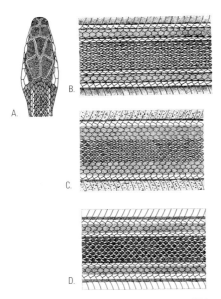

Figure 39. Markings on (A) crown of Schott's whipsnake, (B) dorsal pattern of Schott's whipsnake, and (C and D) dorsal pattern variations in Ruthven's whipsnake.

SPECIES AND SUBSPECIES ACCOUNTS

Family Leptotyphlopidae
BLIND SNAKES

PLAINS BLIND SNAKE
Leptotyphlops dulcis dulcis

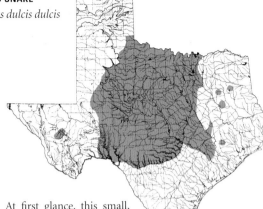

DESCRIPTION At first glance, this small, slender serpent looks more like an earthworm than a reptile. In addition to its diminutive size, several other physical characteristics, some of them unique among Texas snakes, help to emphasize this similarity. The serpent's coloration, like that of a nightcrawler, is earthy and virtually patternless, and the luster of its small, shiny scales resembles the glistening surface of a wet annelid. In addition, its body is cylindrical, being the same diameter throughout, beginning with a blunt head and ending in a very short, stubby tail. Unlike the slender neck of most other serpents, that of the blind snake is just as thick as the reptile's head and trunk, making its appearance even more wormlike. Finally, the snake's tiny, vestigial eyes, barely visible as black dots beneath semitransparent scales, are noticeable only upon close examination. The upper trunk is light brown, reddish brown, or dull pink, while the lower sides and belly are pale gray to pinkish; the entire body of some specimens displays a silvery sheen or delicate iridescence. In this subspecies, three small scales occur on top of the head between the eye plates, and only one upper lip scale is present between the lower part of the eye plate and the lower nasal scale. Moreover, the body scales, which in blind snakes are perfectly smooth and all of equal size (including those on the belly), normally are arranged in 14 rows around the trunk. The number of dorsals from rostral to the tip of the tail vary from 210 to 246, with a mean of 227.

COMPARABLE SNAKES The Trans-Pecos blind snake has only a single small scale on top of the head between the eye plates (see Fig. 8A). The New Mexico blind snake has two upper lip scales instead of one, and the South Texas blind snake has a greater number of dorsal scales, which vary from 222 to 257, with an average of 240.

SIZE Among the smallest of all Texas snakes, the adults of this subspecies usually range in length from 5 to 8 inches (12.7–20.3 cm). The largest known specimen measured 10 3/4 inches (27.3 cm) long.

Adult from Bexar County.

HABITAT Strictly a snake of arid to semiarid regions, it typically occurs in sandy or loamy soils, usually near moisture, for there it can easily dig its way below the surface, where it is safe from numerous predators that search for it above ground. Where those requirements are satisfied, it is found in a variety of habitats, including rocky and sandy desert, rock-strewn hillsides and mountain slopes, thornbrush, live oak and juniper woodlands, and open grassy plains. Milstead, Mecham, and Mc-Clintock (1950) collected two specimens on the Blackstone Ranch in northern Terrell County. One came from the cedar savannah plant community; the other was found in the stomach of a road-runner killed in the cedar-ocotillo plant association. From the southwestern corner of the Panhandle in Dawson County, Fouquette and Lindsay (1955) collected two specimens along a mesquite-lined creek bank.

SOUTH TEXAS BLIND SNAKE
*Leptotyphlops dulcis
rubellum*

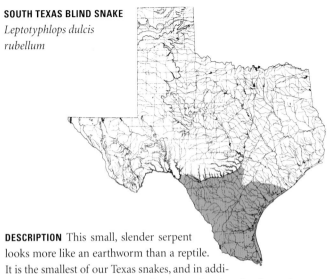

DESCRIPTION This small, slender serpent
looks more like an earthworm than a reptile.
It is the smallest of our Texas snakes, and in addition to its strange appearance, the serpent's coloration is much
like that of an earthworm. There is no pattern, and the luster of
its small, shiny scales resembles the surface of a wet worm. Its
cylindrical body, of the same diameter throughout, begins with a
blunt head and ends in a very short stubby tail. The reptile's neck
is the same thickness as its head and trunk, and the snake's tiny,
vestigial eyes are barely visible as black dots beneath semitransparent scales. The upper trunk is usually reddish brown, hence
the name *rubellum.* Occasionally the color is pale reddish brown,
sliver, or dull pink, depending on its shedding cycle. The lower
sides and belly are pale gray to pinkish. There are three small
scales on top of the head between the eye plates, and only one
upper lip scale is present between the lower part of the eye plate
and the lower nasal scale. The body scales are perfectly smooth
and all of equal size (including those on the belly). The scales
around the trunk are arranged in 14 rows.
COMPARABLE SNAKES The Trans-Pecos blind snake has only a
single small scale on top of the head between the eye plates. The
New Mexico blind snake differs from the closely related plains
blind snake in that two upper lip scales instead of one are pres-

ent between the lower portion of the eye plate and the lower lip scale. Besides the plains blind snake, no other Texas serpent has degenerate, scale-covered eyes and belly scales that are no larger than the dorsals. Unfortunately, such details of scale arrangement in so small a snake are visible only under magnification.

South Texas blind snake.

The major difference between the Plains and the South Texas blind snake is the total number of dorsal scales from the snout to the tip of the tail, averaging 227 in the plains and 240 in the South Texas variety.

SIZE Among the smallest of all Texas snakes, the adults of this subspecies, no thicker than a shoelace, usually range in length from about 5 to 8 inches (12.7–20.3 cm), while the largest known specimen measured 10 1/2 inches (27.1 cm) long.

HABITAT This snake is a burrower. It occurs from arid to semiarid regions of southwestern Texas to the Rio Grande Valley, typically in sandy or loamy soils and only near the surface following rains. It can easily dig its way below the surface, especially near termite and ant colonies where it may follow previously excavated tunnels. It is found in a variety of habitats, including rocky and sandy desert, rock-strewn hills, thornbrush, live oak stands, and open grass plains. In cities it may occur in water meter boxes, under trash in a back yard, or under leaf litter.

NEW MEXICO BLIND SNAKE
Leptotyphlops dissectus

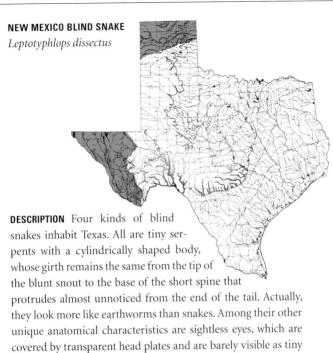

DESCRIPTION Four kinds of blind snakes inhabit Texas. All are tiny serpents with a cylindrically shaped body, whose girth remains the same from the tip of the blunt snout to the base of the short spine that protrudes almost unnoticed from the end of the tail. Actually, they look more like earthworms than snakes. Among their other unique anatomical characteristics are sightless eyes, which are covered by transparent head plates and are barely visible as tiny black spots, and belly scales the same size as the dorsal scales. The smooth body scales encircling the trunk are in 14 rows and glossy, giving the snake a distinctly polished look.

In the New Mexico blind snake, two upper lip scales separate the eye plate from the lower nasal scale, whereas in *L. dulcis*, only one does so. At first glance, the snake appears to be uniformly dark brown, but a closer look often reveals a two-toned creature, one that carries a dark brown band (4 to 6 scale rows wide) down the middle of its back, flanked on either side by a cream or pinkish hue, which continues downward onto the belly. Some individuals even acquire an overall silvery sheen.

COMPARABLE SNAKES The Trans-Pecos blind snake has only one scale between the plates covering the eyes; the New Mexico and plains blind snakes possess three. The New Mexico blind snake has two upper lip scales separating the eye plate from the lower nasal scale, while the plains blind snake has only one; otherwise, they are nearly indistinguishable. It is the only Texas serpent with degenerate eyes and belly plates as small as its upper body scales.

SIZE Although this species reaches a maximum length of about 10 inches (25.4 cm), most adult New Mexico blind snakes are between 5 and 8 inches (12.7–20.3 cm) long. They are the tiniest of all Texas serpents, more apt to be viewed by the novice as earthworms than as reptiles.

HABITAT Usually confined to more arid terrain than that inhabited by the plains blind snake, this serpent nevertheless prefers to establish residence in loose soil where its burrowing tendencies can best be accommodated. Such places, often occurring near permanent or transient sources of water, include arroyos, streams, and canyon bottoms. In the absence of lingering moisture, the snake can frequently be found on sandy soil beneath boulders and large stones, which, shaded from the relentless sun,

Adult from southeastern Arizona. Photo by P. Freed.

often retains a certain degree of dampness, however small, not to mention an equable temperature that tends to attract the snake.

The blind snake is occasionally observed above ground during the early evening hours. Especially after the ground has been soaked by a heavy summer rain and when the air temperature is between 78 and 82 degrees F. At such times it is most likely to be discovered under some large, flat rock, its slender body partially buried in the damp soil. Occasionally several specimens will cluster under a single large rock, as witnessed on one occasion by Rundquist and his coworkers (1978), who discovered 11 individuals of this subspecies beneath one limestone slab. Others have been found in rock crevices and tree stumps, under logs and cactus litter, among the root systems of trees and bushes, and in ant burrows.

TRANS-PECOS BLIND SNAKE
Leptotyphlops humilis
segregus

DESCRIPTION Often mistaken for an earthworm, this small, slender reptile can easily be recognized as a snake both by the scales that cover its body and by the two small dark spots on either side of its head, which are vestigial eyes embedded beneath large, partially transparent scales. Even the snake's dark-hued, cylindrical body has the look of a worm, for it changes little in girth from the blunt snout to the end of the tail. The neck, which in most snakes is narrower than the head and body, is not distinctive in this species. The serpent's other novel features include the short spine at the end of its tail and the small belly scales, which are the same size as the body scales.

The four kinds of blind snakes found in Texas look so much alike superficially that to tell them apart requires an examination of their head scales, a task that in so small a snake is accomplished only under magnification. In the Trans-Pecos blind snake, there is but one scale on top of the head between the plates covering the eyes. The 14 rows of smooth, tightly fitting scales that encircle its body give the blind snake a highly polished look. The upper 5 or 7 dorsal scale rows are usually brown or purplish, often with a silvery tint, while those along the sides and on the belly are subdued pale purple or pinkish.

COMPARABLE SNAKES The plains and New Mexico blind snakes, although similar in coloration to the Trans-Pecos blind snake, generally display a more uniform body pigmentation. In addition, they have three small scales on top of the head between the eye plates instead of one. Blind snakes can be distinguished from all other Texas serpents, by their vestigial, scale-covered eyes and by the size of their abdominal plates, which are no larger than the dorsal scales.

SIZE The greatest length reported for this subspecies is 13¹/₈ inches (36.2 cm). It is the largest of all blind snakes inhabiting Texas. Adults of average size measure between 7 and 10 inches (17.8–25.4 cm) long.

HABITAT Although essentially an aridland serpent of deserts, dry brushland,

Adult from Presidio County.

and regions of desert-grassland transition, the Trans-Pecos blind snake is partial to localities with either permanent or residual moisture, such as those containing springs, streams, arroyos, or canyon bottoms, for it readily succumbs to excessive dehydration. To survive the intolerably hot daytime temperatures of the desert floor, it burrows down into the soil, which in choice habitats is mostly gravelly or sandy and, therefore, easily penetrated. In fact, specimens are regularly plowed up in fields or discovered during routine excavating activities. More specific habitat descriptions for Texas specimens include those of Jameson and Flury (1949), who found a Trans-Pecos blind snake in a plant community of cat-claw acacia and grama grass, and of Milstead, and his colleagues (1950), whose Terrell County specimen was collected in a cedar-ocotillo plant association. In describing the habitat of western forms of this species, Klauber (1940) states that the ideal terrain is generally a bit more arid than that occupied by *L. dulcis* and its subspecies and that, at least in San Diego County, California, stony substrate is favored over sandy terrain. The snakes' preferred territories include rocky canyons and mountain slopes where the vegetation typically consists of mesquite, mountain ash, cotton-wood, or ocotillo, although they generally avoid sandy flats, dry lake basins, and alluvial fans.

Family Colubridae
COLUBRIDS

KANSAS GLOSSY SNAKE
Arizona elegans elegans

DESCRIPTION The dorsal coloration of this moderately slender serpent is tan, yellowish tan, or pastel pink, with a row of 39 to 69 large, distinct, dark-edged, reddish brown to dark brown blotches down the middle of the back. Each blotch is wider than long and narrowly separated from its neighbors. The intervening spaces of pale ground color become darker on the sides, especially in older specimens. Flanking the primary markings on either side is an alternating row of smaller circular spots. The white or yellowish white abdomen is unmarked. The serpent's pattern and coloration are not bold, but its scaly covering is shiny, giving it a distinctive glossy appearance.

The snake's relatively small head, which is not much wider than the neck, begins with a somewhat pointed snout, and the pupil of the eye, unlike that of most nonvenomous serpents, is slightly elliptical. A dark brown bar crosses the crown just forward of the eyes, while on either side of the face a dark stripe extends from the eye to the end of the mouthline. The dorsal scales, all smooth, are in 29 or 31 midbody rows, and the anal plate is single.

The Kansas glossy snake, the Texas glossy snake, and the Painted Desert glossy snake are all subspecies of a single species and differ from one another only in minor details of scalation and color pattern. In the Kansas glossy snake, the primary row of body blotches (not counting those on the tail) usually numbers more than 50 (50 or fewer in *A. e. arenicola*), and the dorsal scales are usually in 29 to 35 midbody rows (only 29 in the Texas glossy). The Painted Desert race, on the other hand, is a paler subspecies whose primary body blotches ordinarily number more than 62 and whose midbody dorsal scales are in no more than 27 rows.

COMPARABLE SNAKES Except for the Texas night snake (which can be identified by its 21 midbody dorsal scale rows), all similar Texas serpents have either keeled body scales *and* a divided anal plate, or the body blotches are squarish *and* the belly is marked with some form of dark pigmentation. Furthermore, the bull snake and Sonoran gopher snake have 4 prefrontal scales (2 in glossy snakes) and an enlarged nose scale, while the crown of the Great Plains rat snake is distinctly marked with a large, dark, forward-directed spearpoint-shaped marking, and the underside of its tail is light-and-dark striped.

SIZE A snake of moderate size, it attains a usual adult length of 20 to 39 inches (66–99.1 cm), though a record-size specimen measured 55³/₄ inches (141.6 cm) long.

Adult.

HABITAT The Kansas glossy snake is encountered in a variety of arid and semiarid regions in the western part of Texas, where the substrate consists of sandy or loamy soils, for this snake, like all species of the genus *Arizona,* is an inveterate burrower. Preferred habitats include sagebrush slopes, sand dunes, pastures, and grass-covered slopes of the Canadian Breaks region in the Panhandle, as well as creosote bush flats of Trans-Pecos Texas. In Big Bend National Park, according to Easterla (1989), it is found from the Rio Grande floodplain to the foothills (Panther Junction and lower Green Gulch). Much farther north, in the Panhandle county of Hutchinson, Fouquette and Lindsay (1955) found it primarily in the deep sand formation above a creekbed floodplain where sage and scattered clusters of cottonwood trees were the principal vegetation on the area's sand dunes and sand flats. According to recent records, it has also been found in the east-central portion of the Edwards Plateau, where sandy soils border some of the region's major stream systems.

TEXAS GLOSSY SNAKE
Arizona elegans arenicola

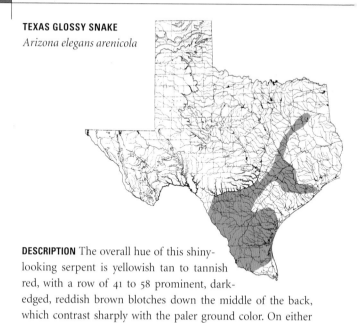

DESCRIPTION The overall hue of this shiny-looking serpent is yellowish tan to tannish red, with a row of 41 to 58 prominent, dark-edged, reddish brown blotches down the middle of the back, which contrast sharply with the paler ground color. On either side of the primary markings is an alternating row of small, dark, circular spots, below which is still another row of even smaller, irregular ones. The white abdomen is unmarked.

The snake's relatively small head, which is not much wider than the neck, begins with a moderately pointed snout, and the pupil of the eye, in contrast to that of most nonvenomous serpents, is slightly elliptical. A dark brown bar crosses the crown just forward of the eyes, while a dark stripe reaches from the eye to the end of the mouthline. The dorsal scales, all smooth, are in 29 to 35 midbody rows, and the anal plate is single. Individuals of this race from South Texas are paler than those from the San Antonio region, while individuals from the northeastern end of the range are the darkest of all.

COMPARABLE SNAKES *See Kansas glossy snake account.*

SIZE Most adult Texas glossy snakes are from 27 inches to 3 feet (68.6–91.4 cm) long, although the largest known specimen measured nearly 55 ¹/₂ inches (141 cm) in length.

Adult.

HABITAT This snake is usually found wherever there is deep, sandy soil, its rather wide range of habitats including open scrubland, prairies, farmlands, beachfronts, sand dunes, and open woodland. While chiefly an inhabitant of the semiarid South Texas thornbrush environment, it also follows the Carrizo Sands geological formation from Central Texas to the northeastern part of the state, where a few specimens have been found in Henderson and Smith counties. The dominant vegetation of this formation, where soils consist of fine to loosely coarse sand from one to several feet deep, is oak-hickory. There are also isolated records for the Texas glossy snake from Waller and Brazoria counties.

PAINTED DESERT GLOSSY SNAKE

Arizona elegans philipi

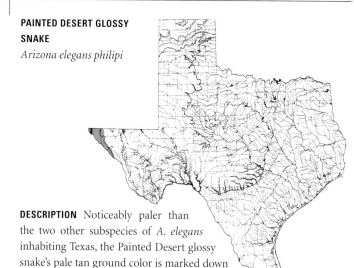

DESCRIPTION Noticeably paler than the two other subspecies of *A. elegans* inhabiting Texas, the Painted Desert glossy snake's pale tan ground color is marked down the center of the back with a row of 53 to 80 (usually 62 or more) fawn to nearly brick red blotches, whose outer margins are only slightly darker than the centers. Flanking them on either side is another longitudinal row of smaller dark spots, somewhat circular in shape, while below these is an additional one or two rows of even smaller dark spots of irregular size and shape. There is a tendency for some of the primary markings to split along the spine so as to form a pair of separated and sometimes offset half-blotches. The belly is white and unmarked.

The snake's rather small head, which begins with a somewhat pointed snout, is little wider than the neck, while the pupils of the eyes are slightly elliptical, a rare condition among local nonvenomous snakes. The dark bar that in other native glossy snakes typically crosses the crown just forward of the eyes is normally faded or absent in this subspecies, as is the dark stripe that runs backward from each eye to the end of the mouthline. The snake's smooth and unusually glossy scales normally occur in 27 rows at midbody, and the anal plate is single.

COMPARABLE SNAKES

See Kansas glossy snake account.

Adult from El Paso County.

SIZE The adults of this, the smallest native glossy snake subspecies, are usually from 15 to 37 inches (38.1–94 cm) long, although the largest known specimen measured 39 inches (99.1 cm) in length.

HABITAT Inhabiting the extreme western end of the state, where it occurs in El Paso County and along the adjacent borderland of Hudspeth County, the Painted Desert glossy snake is found primarily in the sand dunes east and southeast of the city of El Paso and along the creosote- and mesquite-covered benches above the dune areas. Although primarily a snake of moderate to low altitudes, outside of Texas it has been encountered at elevations exceeding 6,000 feet (1,829 m).

TRANS-PECOS RAT SNAKE
Bogertophis subocularis
subocularis

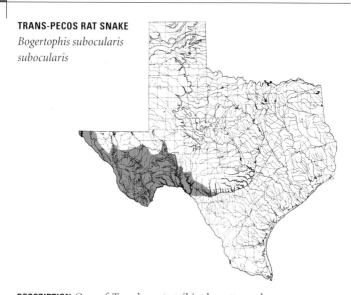

DESCRIPTION One of Texas' most strikingly patterned serpents, this relatively slender snake is easily recognized in its typical form by the conspicuous dark brown or black H-shaped dorsal blotches, which stand out boldly against a contrasting background color of tan, yellow. or pale orange. In a departure from the norm, specimens from the Franklin Mountains near El Paso may also display a steel gray ground color instead. Whatever the snake's overall dorsal hue, the central core of each H marking is paler than its lateral horizontal arms and is flecked with both pale and dark scales, while in the midportions of the arms themselves some scales are edged in white. On the neck and forebody, the outer arms of the blotches are connected, forming two bold, continuous, though sometimes irregular, parallel dark lines that extend down either side of the spine and between which only remnants of the blotches remain. The arms of the other dorsal H markings may be similarly connected, though the intervening horizontal links that unite them are generally obscure. A row of small, indistinct dark spots occurs beneath the larger dorsal series, with every other spot located directly below a primary blotch and each alternate lying between two adjacent blotches.

Not all Trans-Pecos rat snakes fit this description, for specimens from the lower Trans-Pecos River drainage system are quite unlike typical examples. Instead of displaying the characteristic H blotches, the pattern of this blond variety consists of pale, often indistinct, dark-edged oval or vaguely diamond-shaped blotches set against an even paler background hue of yellowish tan.

It is in certain specialized features of the head that the Trans-Pecos rat snake best displays its uniqueness. One is the arrangement of scales around the eye. Whereas in all other native rat snakes, and in most other serpent species for that matter, the lower border of the eye directly meets the upper lip scales, that of *B. subocularis* the is separated from them by an intervening

Yellowish adult from Brewster County. Photo by J. E. Werler.

row of small scales. Of special note also are the serpent's large, somewhat bulging eyes, a useful adaptation for a creature whose aboveground activities are limited mostly to the hours after sundown.

The pale-colored head, rather wide and flat on top, bears no markings. Its upper surfaces are nearly the same pale hue as the background body color, but the chin, throat, and neck are white. The belly, however, is olive-buff, usually with some discrete dark mottling, which may consolidate on the underside of the tail to form a pattern of dusky stripes. At midbody, the dorsal scales are arranged in 31 to 35 rows. Like other native rat snakes, this species has faint keels only on the upper body scales, the others being smooth. The anal plate is divided.

COMPARABLE SNAKES The pattern of an adult Baird's rat snake consists of four dark, lengthwise stripes, whereas the young of this species are marked along the back with a series of narrow, dark crossbars. From other blotched snakes within its range the "blond" variety of *B. subocularis* can be distinguished from other blotched snakes within its range by its pale, rounded dorsal blotches (none of which is linked with either of the adjoining spots) and its unmarked, light-colored head.

SIZE Adults are usually between 3 and 4$^1/_2$ feet (91.4–137.2 cm) long, although the maximum length recorded for this subspecies is 5$^1/_2$ feet (167.4 cm).

HABITAT Dry, rocky terrain between 1,500 and 5,000 feet (457–1,520 m) elevation is the preferred habitat of this aridland dweller. In Texas it occurs chiefly within the confines of the Chihuahuan Desert in a variety of environments, ranging from low basins and valleys where mesquite is the dominant vegetation; through the intermediate regions of chiefly creosote bush in association with tarbush, prickly pear cactus, and ocotillo; to the higher desert slopes where the widely scattered vegetation consists of sotol, lechuguilla, ocotillo, agave, and yucca; and still higher to the more moist oak and juniper woodlands of the mountains. In such environments, where aboveground shelter is often severely limited, the snake finds refuge in the labyrinth of honeycombed or fractured rock formations that lie upon the desert floor, though it seems not to favor any particular type of rock formation. In the Chisos Mountains it occurs among the region's igneous rocks, while along the stretch of the Rio Grande that delineates the southern border of the Big Bend, it occupies pure limestone formations.

WESTERN WORM SNAKE
Carphophis vermis

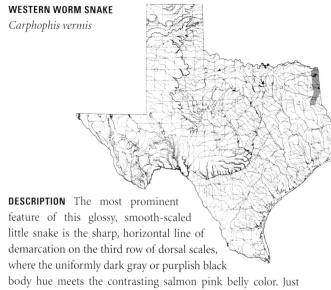

DESCRIPTION The most prominent feature of this glossy, smooth-scaled little snake is the sharp, horizontal line of demarcation on the third row of dorsal scales, where the uniformly dark gray or purplish black body hue meets the contrasting salmon pink belly color. Just days before the snake sheds its skin and until the epidermis is discarded, the dark dorsal tone fades to ashen gray, masking its true color. The serpent's bluntly pointed head is no wider than its neck, its eyes are small, and its short tail ends in a sharp little spine. There are but 13 midbody rows of dorsal scales, and the anal plate is divided.

COMPARABLE SNAKES When first hatched, the mud snake is nearly the same length as an adult worm snake, but with a much thicker body. Although both species are shiny and blackish on the back and sides, the red color of the mud snake's belly extends up along the lower sides of the body as vertical bars instead of terminating in a sharp, horizontal line of demarcation. The ring-necked snake, whose slate gray to blackish dorsum is similar to that of a worm snake, has a narrow, pale-colored ring on the neck and black spotting on its yellowish belly. The Florida red-bellied snake may have a pale orange abdomen, but its color does not extend upward to the third row of body scales. Moreover, it has 15 rows of *keeled* dorsal scales at midbody and a conspicuous pale spot covering all of the fifth upper lip scale.

SIZE Although the known record length for this snake is 14 3/4 inches (37.5 cm), most adults are between 7 1/2 and 11 inches (19–27.9 cm) long.

HABITAT In northeastern Kansas, according to D. R. Clark (1970), the snake's distribution is closely tied to stream valleys adjacent to forested or grassy hillsides where elevations generally rise above 100 feet (30.5 m). Such areas, while damp, contain well-drained, organically rich soils littered with rocks or logs, under which the snake can take cover, and are shaded either by trees or dense ground cover, leafy umbrellas that help to conserve soil moisture. Black, clay-loam soils containing from 10 to 30 percent water, by weight, are preferred, whereas neighboring patches of more cohesive, light-brown clay substrate are avoided. Some open habitats near Lawrence, Kansas, characterized by sparse ground cover as the result of moderate cattle grazing, actually attracted greater numbers of worm snakes than did other, more natural, nearby habitats.

Adult from Titus County.

NORTHERN SCARLET SNAKE
Cemophora coccinea copei

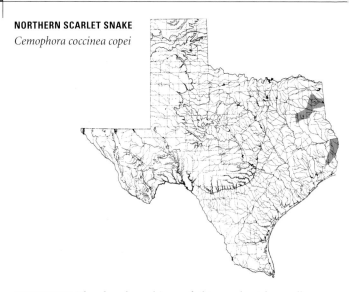

DESCRIPTION The dorsal markings of this moderately small, white or tan snake consist of wide, black-encircled crimson to red-orange saddles that extend down either side of the body to the first or second scale row. Alternating with and located just below them is a series of dark, irregularly shaped spots. The snake's small head is scarcely wider than its neck, and its sharply pointed red or orange snout juts forward prominently beyond the end of the lower jaw. The forward edge of the black rim that encloses the first scarlet body blotch usually reaches the parietal scales and contacts or nearly meets (shy one scale width or less) the transverse black band on the forecrown. This condition is relatively inflexible, despite a wide range of minor variations in the serpent's head markings. Even more constant is the scarlet snake's white or yellow unmarked belly. The smooth dorsal scales are usually arranged in 19 rows, and the anal plate is single.

Not every scarlet snake precisely fits this description, for the species undergoes a remarkable color transformation from the time it first emerges from the egg until it is aged. First of all, the hatchling's red colors are more muted than those of the adult, and there is more white in its coloration. Extending downward on either side of the body to the second or third scale row above the abdomen, the young snake's soft-pink saddles, black-edged front and back, are separated from one another by immaculate white spaces. An intermittent row of black flecks borders the lower edges of the saddles, including a black spot at each white interspace just above the belly line. At this age the scarlet snake appears distinctly blotched.

After it reaches a foot in length (30.5 cm), it experiences a gradual pale yellowing of the white dorsal spaces between the saddles, which hue gradually expands laterally. At the same time, the pinkish saddles become more red and, together with their lateral black margins, gradually extend farther down along the sides of the body nearly to the abdomen. Later the black margins converge under the saddles to encircle them completely, whereas the black flecks between the blotches gradually dimin-

Adult from Newton County.

ish. By the time it is fully adult, the northern scarlet snake, even when seen from the side, looks like it is completely encircled by rings of deep red, bright yellow (paler near the belly), and black. But this is only an illusion, for none of the colors extends across the reptile's pure white belly. Still different looking is the very old scarlet snake, whose colors have gradually darkened over time—eventually becoming somber red-brown instead of scarlet on the saddles and tan or pale gray instead of yellow in the interspaces—and its number of dark-centered, pale-colored scales has increased. The dorsal scales, all smooth, are arranged in 19 rows at midbody, and the anal scale is single.

COMPARABLE SNAKES The coral snake's ringed dorsal pattern continues across its abdomen, the red and yellow markings are side by side, its snout is all black, it has only 15 rows of dorsal scales at midbody (19 in the scarlet snake), and its anal plate is divided. Another species likely to be confused with *C. c. copei* is the Louisiana milk snake, whose black, yellow (or whitish), and red body bands reach well onto its belly and whose midbody dorsal scales are arranged in 21 rows.

SIZE Adults generally range in length from 14 to 20 inches (35.6–50.8 cm). The largest known example of this subspecies measured 32 $^1/_2$ inches (82.5 cm) long.

HABITAT Like most other burrowing serpents, the scarlet snake prefers areas of well-drained, sandy or loamy soil, usually in pine, hardwood, or pine-oak forest, where it can easily dig into the relatively loose substrate. Despite the traditional notion that the species restricts itself to a woodland environment, there is sufficient evidence to show that it frequently inhabits open spaces as well, provided the soils there are penetrable. In the most comprehensive study yet made of the scarlet snake's behavior and occurrence in the wild, Nelson and Gibbons (1972) reported that of 49 specimens collected in pitfall drift fence traps during a survey near the U.S. Department of Energy's Savannah River Plant below Aiken, South Carolina, 28 were taken in woodland and 21 in open areas (abandoned fields, grassy tracts, and roadsides). It is also evident from this and other studies that the scarlet snake often is found in the vicinity of marshes, swamps, or ponds, though we can find no report that this species enters the water. At more northern latitudes it sometimes inhabits rocky, wooded hillsides and even rugged, nearly treeless, slopes.

TEXAS SCARLET SNAKE
Cemophora coccinea lineri

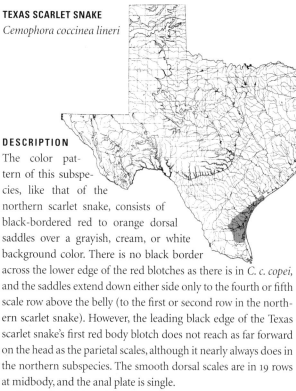

DESCRIPTION

The color pattern of this subspecies, like that of the northern scarlet snake, consists of black-bordered red to orange dorsal saddles over a grayish, cream, or white background color. There is no black border across the lower edge of the red blotches as there is in *C. c. copei,* and the saddles extend down either side only to the fourth or fifth scale row above the belly (to the first or second row in the northern scarlet snake). However, the leading black edge of the Texas scarlet snake's first red body blotch does not reach as far forward on the head as the parietal scales, although it nearly always does in the northern subspecies. The smooth dorsal scales are in 19 rows at midbody, and the anal plate is single.

During its lifetime this subspecies experiences the same gradual color transformation described in the northern scarlet snake account. As a hatchling, its pattern consists of well-defined, soft-pink dorsal saddles separated from each other by white interspaces. With age, these muted markings become redder, and the pale-colored spaces between them turn yellow, first along the middle of the back, then laterally. At the same time, an ever-increasing number of light scales in the snake's pattern develop dark centers. In old specimens the pattern becomes indistinct, the red color having turned dark brown and the yellow hue having changed to a somber tan or light grayish brown. At this age, too, the snake takes on a more speckled appearance.

COMPARABLE SNAKES Unlike the dorsal saddles of the Texas scarlet snake, which fail to reach the belly, the coral snake's brightly ringed dorsal pattern continues across the abdomen and the red and yellow markings are side by side; those of the scarlet snake are separated by black. In addition, the coral's snout is black, its dorsal scales are in only 15 rows at midbody, and its anal plate is divided. Milk snakes living within the range of the Texas scarlet snake can be distinguished by the extension of at least some of the dorsal pattern onto or across the abdomen and by the 21 rows of dorsal scales at midbody. The Texas long-nosed snake's yellow dorsal coloration is confined

Adult from Aransas County.

mostly to narrow lines of demarcation between its much wider black and red crossbands and to dots of similar color in the black markings. Its dorsal scales are arranged in 23 midbody rows; among all of our harmless serpents, only the longnose has most of the scales on the underside of the tail in a single row.

SIZE The known maximum length for this subspecies is 26 inches (66 cm).

HABITAT Although the snake's South Texas coastal habitat is clearly different from the pine-hardwood forest environment of its close relative to the northeast, it is nevertheless restricted largely to areas of loose, sandy soils. Of several specimens collected within the city limits of Rockport, two were found near live oaks scattered across the coastal sand dunes, while two others were dug from the sandy substrate of watermelon patches. Stephen E. Labuda, Jr., (pers. com.) discovered one on the Aransas Wildlife Refuge as it crawled over the sand in a cluster of red bay trees and scattered American beauty berry plants. This subspecies may even occupy dry, sandy flatland where the dominant vegetation is mesquite, black huisache, and prickly pear cactus.

BUTTERMILK RACER
Coluber constrictor anthicus

DESCRIPTION No other adult Texas racer is as curiously marked as this one, its steel blue, blue-green, slate, or dark olive dorsal color randomly speckled with a hodge-podge of white, gray, tan, or pale yellow scales, most of which are of a single, solid hue and arranged both individually and in clusters of diverse sizes. Some display just a few pale-colored scales, while others are densely speckled over nearly their entire bodies. The rear part of the racer's trunk, as well as the tail, is some shade of pale brown. The white or pale gray belly is usually marked with a small number of pale yellow spots, and the racer's snout, throat, and lips are white. The dorsal scales, all smooth, are in 17 rows at midbody, and the anal plate is divided. The juvenile buttermilk's grayish ground color is conspicuously marked with a row of reddish brown saddles down the middle of the back, which are flanked on either side by two or three longitudinal rows of smaller dark spots. During a brief interval in the racer's early life (at a length of approximately 20 inches, when the juvenile loses its baby pattern of bold, dark blotches but before it develops its light dorsal spotting) it is essentially unicolored.

COMPARABLE SNAKES Because its body is heavily flecked with dark spots, the speckled king snake is the serpent most likely to be mistaken for an adult buttermilk racer, although its spots are small (not covering an entire scale), its yellow abdomen boldly checked with black, and its anal plate undivided. The juvenile buttermilk racer can be distinguished from other small, blotched serpents by the following combination of features: it has smooth dorsal scales, no more than 17 dorsal scale rows at midbody, and a divided anal plate.

The buttermilk racer often exhibits features of coloration intermediate between it and its nearest neighbor, making a precise subspecies identification difficult. The most practical course in such cases is to identify the mystery specimen according to geography, assigning it by its collecting locality to the closest ranging subspecies.

Adult from Liberty County.

SIZE This subspecies approaches in maximum size the yellow-bellied racer, whose greatest known length of 71 inches (180.3 cm) is only 1 inch longer than that of its speckled cousin. Most adult buttermilk racers, however, are between 30 and 60 inches (76.2–152.4 cm) long.

HABITAT Restricted to the longleaf pine and mixed pine-hardwood forests of East Texas and adjacent Louisiana, the buttermilk racer is most likely to be encountered in places that have been cleared by humans but not so sanitized as to be without some form of brushy ground cover. Little-used agricultural and urban areas adjacent to woodlands are especially favored. Such forest-edge clearings include pastureland, abandoned farm fields, old oil-field sites, powerline rights-of-way, sawmill sites (especially those no longer in use), and certain open spaces devoted to outdoor recreation, where the buttermilk racer can at times be unexpectedly plentiful. During a single week in mid-May, for example, nine of these elusive reptiles were captured along the brushy perimeter of a golf course in northeastern Harris County by an amateur snake collector employed there as a groundskeeper. Of 40 specimens collected by R. F. Clark (1949) in the Hill parishes of Louisiana, 39 were found in woodlands near brier patches or other brushy ground cover.

TAN RACER
Coluber constrictor etheridgei

DESCRIPTION This long, slender racer has a pale tan to brown body, usually randomly speckled with a few small, pallid spots or, less often, none at all. Its chin, throat, and belly are even paler. The snake's dorsal scales are smooth and arranged in 17 rows at midbody. The anal plate is divided. A very young specimen shows little resemblance to the adult. Like the hatchlings of most other racer subspecies, its pale gray ground color is conspicuously marked with a row of reddish brown saddles down the middle of the back, on either side of which are two or three lengthwise rows of smaller dark spots. All of these markings become gradually more indistinct on the rear of the body, finally fading altogether long before they reach the end of the tail.

COMPARABLE SNAKES Although the speckled king snake is heavily spotted, its overall coloration is dark brown to black instead of light brown. Moreover, virtually every one of its dorsal scales contains a small central light spot, whereas the spots of the tan racer, when present, are randomly distributed over the back and sides; each typically occupies an entire scale. Another similar snake, the adult eastern coachwhip, is generally much darker than a tan racer and unspotted; it also has fewer midbody rows of dorsal scales (13 rather than 17) and a subtle crosshatched pattern on its tail. The juvenile racer can be distinguished from other small, spotted snake species by a combination of characters: it has smooth scales, a divided anal plate, and no more than 17 rows of dorsal scales at midbody.

SIZE Most adults of this uncommon subspecies are 3 to 4 ¹/₂ feet (91.4–137.2 cm) long, although large examples may reach a length of nearly 6 feet (182.9 cm).

HABITAT While most other racer subspecies occurring in Texas inhabit primarily open spaces, this one dwells chiefly among the longleaf pine flatwoods that dominate the eastern part of the state along its south-central border with Louisiana. Land clearing is inexorably reducing its prime habitat. Richard Etheridge (in Fitch 1963) suggested that as ever more prime forest is converted to brushy space by logging, the buttermilk racer, a resident of open habitat, invades the cleared land at the expense of the forest-dwelling tan racer.

Adult from Hardin County.

EASTERN YELLOW-BELLIED RACER
Coluber constrictor
flaviventris

DESCRIPTION The unpatterned
olive-brown to grayish green dorsal hue
of adult Texas specimens contrasts with the
cream to yellow belly color, which is especially
bright under the snake's chin, across its upper lip
scales, and on the sides of its neck. The snake's dorsal scales are
smooth and arranged in 17 rows at midbody, there are usually
seven upper lip scales on either side of the head, and the anal plate
is divided.

The juvenile racer (at least for the first two or three years of
its life) looks strikingly different from the adult. Its back is boldly marked with a longitudinal row of dark, light-edged blotches
and two or more rows of alternating small dark spots along the
sides, all of which become indistinct and finally fade altogether
before reaching the end of the tail. On the abdomen are scattered
dark speckles.

COMPARABLE SNAKES An adult coachwhip snake with no ap-
preciable change of color from head to tail (some are banded
or bicolored) can be distinguished from a grown adult yellow-
bellied racer by its fewer rows of dorsal scales (13 rather than 17),
and by the distinct pale and dark crosshatched pattern on its
tail. The rough green snake is an emerald color in life (dark blue
after death) and has keeled scales. The similarly hued (though
sometimes olive-colored) smooth green snake has no more
than 15 rows of dorsal scales at midbody. Among several small
serpent species whose dorsal markings resemble the blotched
pattern of the juvenile racer, none has the following combina-

tion of characters: smooth scales, a divided anal plate, and no more than 17 dorsal scale rows at midbody.

SIZE This subspecies usually attains an adult length between 23 and 50 inches (63.5–127 cm), although the largest known specimen measured 70 inches (177.8 cm) long.

HABITAT Occupying much of Texas from the Panhandle and the Red River south to the northern edge of the coastal plain and the upper Gulf Coast (but excluding southwestern Texas, most of South Texas, and the pine and pine-hardwood forests of East Texas), this adaptable racer utilizes a wide variety of habitats. In a comprehensive, long-term study of its natural history conducted primarily in northeastern Kansas, Fitch (1963) described in detail the snake's choice habitats, which are scarcely different from those in Texas. We have therefore included some of the Kansas information here. Generally avoiding heavily shaded forest in favor of open, brushy areas, this racer shows a definite preference for tallgrass prairie, pastureland overgrown with high weedy vegetation, brush-covered ravines, brushy woodland edge, streamside thickets, weed-covered fields, and sparse woodland. In southeastern Texas it also favors abandoned farmland and the edges of both active grain fields and old oil-field sites, while along the coast it frequently occupies marshland levees. When choosing a grassland habitation, the snake usually avoids areas that have been closely cropped by humans, for where there is inadequate ground cover, the snake tends to move elsewhere.

Adult from McLennan County.

At more northern latitudes it sometimes changes habitat according to season, migrating each fall from lowland meadows to hilltop rock outcroppings in or near dense woods, where it overwinters in rock crevices below ground.

MEXICAN RACER
Coluber constrictor oaxaca

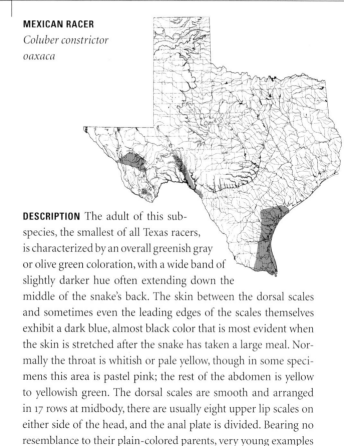

DESCRIPTION The adult of this subspecies, the smallest of all Texas racers, is characterized by an overall greenish gray or olive green coloration, with a wide band of slightly darker hue often extending down the middle of the snake's back. The skin between the dorsal scales and sometimes even the leading edges of the scales themselves exhibit a dark blue, almost black color that is most evident when the skin is stretched after the snake has taken a large meal. Normally the throat is whitish or pale yellow, though in some specimens this area is pastel pink; the rest of the abdomen is yellow to yellowish green. The dorsal scales are smooth and arranged in 17 rows at midbody, there are usually eight upper lip scales on either side of the head, and the anal plate is divided. Bearing no resemblance to their plain-colored parents, very young examples of this subspecies are conspicuously marked with narrow dark crossbars on the forebody, which become gradually less distinct toward the rear of the trunk and disappear altogether before they reach the tail. Below them on either side of the tan body are two or more irregular rows of small dark spots, giving the juvenile snakes a distinctly speckled look.

The infant Mexican racer differs from juveniles of other Texas subspecies of *C. constrictor* in the shape of its dorsal blotches, which are jagged in outline and pointed at their lateral edges; those of other native racers are oval with rounded ends.

COMPARABLE SNAKES A plain-colored adult western coachwhip snake (some are banded) differs from a Mexican racer by its fewer rows of middorsal scales (13 rather than 17) and by the distinct light and dark crosshatched pattern of its tail. The rough green snake has keeled dorsal scales and is vivid green in life (dark blue after death). Among several other small serpent species whose dorsal markings somewhat resemble those of a very young Mexican racer, none has the following combination of characters: smooth scales, a divided anal plate, and no more than 17 dorsal scale rows at midbody.

SIZE This, the smallest of all Texas racers, reaches an adult length between 20 and 40 inches (50.8–101.6 cm).

HABITAT Primarily a Mexican serpent whose geographic range reaches northward into the dry South Texas thornbrush and extends northeast along the Gulf Coast to Corpus Christi, *C. c. oaxaca* generally avoids the more arid sections of the Rio Grande Valley and those that are heavily wooded. Its choice habitats include areas of sparse or scattered brush and open woodland, with a secondary preference for terrain supporting either heavy brush or bare grassland. A couple of hundred miles to the northwest, the snake occurs again in widely scattered populations throughout the Trans-Pecos region of Texas, its highly intermittent distribution there probably representing isolated remnants of a once much wider ranging population that occupied the area in the wetter climate of an earlier geological age. Most of these western locality records, in fact, are associated with some form of natural surface water.

Adult from Cameron County.

SOUTHERN BLACK RACER
Coluber constrictor priapus

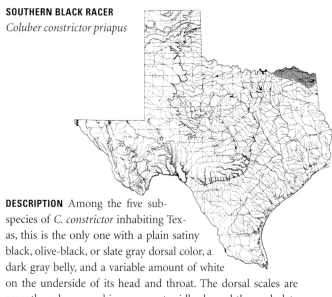

DESCRIPTION Among the five subspecies of *C. constrictor* inhabiting Texas, this is the only one with a plain satiny
black, olive-black, or slate gray dorsal color, a
dark gray belly, and a variable amount of white
on the underside of its head and throat. The dorsal scales are
smooth and arranged in 17 rows at midbody, and the anal plate
is divided. The hatchling of this subspecies looks nothing like the
unpatterned adult. Its dorsal row of reddish brown saddles, which
stand out conspicuously against a light gray background color, is
flanked on either side by two or more rows of smaller dark spots.
Toward the rear of the body the markings become gradually less
distinct and more closely aggregated, until they finally disappear
altogether before reaching the end of the tail. The abdomen is pale
gray and marked along its outer edges with small dark spots.

COMPARABLE SNAKES An adult eastern coachwhip, while sometimes nearly all black, will usually have some reddish brown color
on the rear part of its body, especially on the tail. Furthermore, its
dorsal scales, when counted at a point just ahead of the tail, are
in 13 rows (15 in the racer). The Texas rat snake, whose typically
blotched pattern may occasionally be obscured by an unusual
amount of dark pigmentation, can be distinguished most readily
by the shape of its body, which in cross-section resembles a loaf
of bread instead of a cylinder, and by the keeled scales across the
back of its trunk. No other small, blotched snake species in north-

Adult from Lamar County.

eastern Texas shares the juvenile racer's combination of features: smooth scales, a divided anal plate, and no more than 17 rows of dorsal scales at midbody.

SIZE Adults range from 20 to nearly 65 inches (50.8–165.1 cm) in length. The largest known specimen of this subspecies was collected in Indiana.

HABITAT In Texas the southern black racer is known only from the northeastern corner of the state, where it resides in a rather wide assortment of habitats, including tree-studded pastureland, pine and pine-hardwood forest clearings, grassy hillside rock outcroppings dotted with oak trees, and, according to Jim Yantis (pers. com.), brush-covered terraces along the Red River. In other parts of its geographic range it has commonly been observed in rocky highlands, along brushy stream and lake edges, in the vicinity of limestone bluffs near swamps, and around disturbed areas close to water.

BLACK-STRIPED SNAKE
Coniophanes imperialis
imperialis

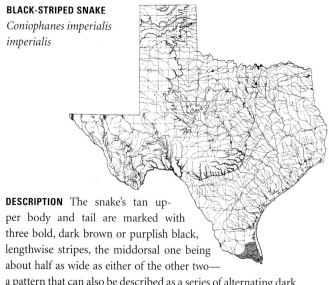

DESCRIPTION The snake's tan upper body and tail are marked with
three bold, dark brown or purplish black,
lengthwise stripes, the middorsal one being
about half as wide as either of the other two—
a pattern that can also be described as a series of alternating dark
and pale brown longitudinal stripes. The serpent's belly, unlike
the rest of its mostly brown body, is pinkish, orange, or scarlet.
A pale, narrow line on either side of the face extends backward
from the snout, crosses the top of the eye, and ends at the back
of the head. Also distinctive are the white, black-dotted upper lip
scales. The dorsal scales are smooth and in 19 rows at midbody;
the anal plate is divided.

COMPARABLE SNAKES The Texas patch-nosed snake's longitudinal pattern consists of four dark lengthwise stripes, not three; its
median stripe is light-colored instead of dark; its belly is white or
cream-colored, never pink, orange, or red; its dorsal scales are
keeled; and its anal plate is single. Ribbon and garter snakes have
a pale spinal stripe, white or pale green bellies, keeled scales, and
a single anal plate.

SIZE The adults of this moderately small snake are usually 12 to
18 inches (30.5–45.7 cm) long, although a specimen of record size
measured 20 inches (50.8 cm) in length.

HABITAT In the lower Rio Grande Valley live several typically
Mexican reptiles, including this one, whose predominantly

Adult from Cameron County. Photo by J. E. Werler.

Latin American ranges continue northward to the southern tip of Texas. Fifty years ago, before intensive agricultural and urban development consumed so much of the Valley's indigenous scrub forest and tropical woodland, the black-striped snake was more widely dispersed throughout the region encompassing Cameron, Hidalgo, and Willacy counties, the only part of the state where it has so far been found. As a result of such widespread disturbance, its habitat has no doubt been considerably reduced. Yet even today, according to Patrick M. Burchfield (pers. com.), it is still relatively common in many Brownsville back yards, being found there in patches of moist humus or leaf litter.

PRAIRIE RING-NECKED SNAKE
Diadophis punctatus arnyi

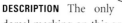

DESCRIPTION The only dorsal marking on this gray, dark olive, or nearly black snake is a prominent yellow or orange-yellow neck ring, which ring is usually separated from the body hue by a narrow black border; the ring's front edge meets the solid black or dark brown dorsal head color. In some specimens the nuchal collar is interrupted along the top of the neck. The snake's pale-colored lips, chin, and throat are speckled with black dots, and the bright yellow belly, grading to pale orange toward the tail, is randomly covered with numerous small black spots. The undertail, by contrast, is scarlet red. The smooth body scales are usually arranged in 17 rows on the forward part of the body (occasionally 15), and the anal plate is divided.

SIMILAR SNAKES The rough earth snake often is born with a pale-colored band across the back of its head, and the juvenile brown snake enters the world with a pale-hued nuchal ring; both species lose such markings long before they reach maturity. Both can be distinguished from the ring-necked snake by their keeled body scales, whitish unmarked abdomens, and brown dorsal color. The Florida red-bellied snake, whose yellowish to reddish orange abdomen sometimes resembles that of a ring-necked snake, differs from *Diadophis* in typically having three small nuchal blotches, keeled body scales, and a virtually immaculate belly. Finally, the three imitator species have a suedelike dorsal surface unlike the glossy appearance of the ring-necked snake.

SIZE Adults of this subspecies usually are 10 to 14 inches (25.4–35.5 cm) long; the largest specimen on record measured 16 ¹/₂ inches (41.9 cm) in length.

HABITAT Much of the information for this account comes from the field studies of Fitch (1975), who has contributed more to our understanding of this snake's natural history than anyone else.

Adult from Dallas County.

The prairie ring-necked snake lives in a variety of habitats, most of which meet the following requirements: moist, but not wet or soggy soil; an adequate surface layer of plant litter, or flat rocks, boards, logs, or other debris under which it can hide; and a canopy of vegetation that while providing some shade allows considerable sunlight to reach the ground. Within those limits it is found most abundantly in old sparsely wooded and brushy hillside pastures, in bottomland pasture dotted with small trees and shrubs, along hilltop limestone outcroppings littered with loose rocks and supporting a modest growth of underbrush, in prairie gullies containing rock outcroppings and brush patches, near streams and ponds, and in old fields carpeted with ground cover. Curiously, in areas impacted by moderate to heavy cattle grazing, Fitch found that prairie ring-necked snakes occurred in higher densities than in similar ungrazed habitat. It so happens that in such places cattle feed on and trample the underbrush, eventually creating open spaces where the sun can filter through to the ground, resulting in more basking opportunities for the snakes.

REGAL RING-NECKED SNAKE
Diadophis punctatus
regalis

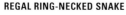

DESCRIPTION Probably the only pure regal ring-necked snakes in Texas are those found in the Guadalupe Mountains, where they live side by side with the prairie ring-necked snake, the two subspecies maintaining their separate identities by shunning one another as mates. The remaining Trans-Pecos populations are considered by Gehlbach (1974) to be intergrades between it and the prairie ring-necked snake, although they more closely resemble *D. p. regalis*. In its unadulterated form, the regal ring-necked snake has an unmarked greenish gray, grayish olive, or slate gray upper body color but lacks the pale-hued nuchal ring that is the hallmark of other native ring-necked subspecies. Yet across the vast area of intergradation between the two involved subspecies, the neck ring may be complete in some specimens, broken along the middle of the back in others, or absent altogether. The belly color, which reaches up along either side of the trunk onto the first row of dorsal scales, is yellow on the forebody but changes gradually to orange-yellow along midbody, then to bright scarlet red near and on the tail. The vividly hued abdomen is randomly decorated with prominent black spots.

The top of the head is usually a bit darker than the upper body, and the lower lips, chin, and throat are sparsely covered with small dark spots. The dorsal scales, all smooth, are arranged in 17 midbody rows, and the anal plate is divided.

SIMILAR SNAKES The Trans-Pecos black-headed snake possesses a brownish instead of grayish dorsal color, and its whitish abdomen has no bold, dark spotting. Although species of black-headed snakes living within the geographic range of the regal ring-necked snake ordinarily display a pinkish belly, this surface area is not spotted, nor is the underside of the tail bright red. The solid color phase of the variable ground snake, which has no prominent black spots on its abdomen, also lacks a bright red undertail, and its dorsal scales occur in only 14 or 15 midbody rows. In the collared variety, the nuchal marking is an abbreviated *dark* bar.

Adult from El Paso County.

SIZE This, the largest subspecies of ring-necked snake in Texas, reaches a record length of 19 1/2 inches (49.5 cm) in the state but attains an even greater size (33 5/8 inches, 85.4 cm) elsewhere within its range. The usual adult length is between 15 and 18 inches (38.1–45.7 cm).

HABITAT Although better adapted to a dry environment than its eastern relatives, the regal ring-necked snake nevertheless prefers moist habitats, steadfastly avoiding the extreme aridity of shrub desert. Suitable habitat, which is discontinuous throughout the snake's geographic range, occurs primarily within the sparse mountain or scarp woodland between about 3,900 and 7,200 feet (1,189–2,195 m) elevation. In a study of the snake's evolutionary history, which involved a survey of its ecological distribution, Gehlbach encountered intergrade specimens in the following Trans-Pecos habitats: evergreen woodland (21 specimens), deciduous woodland or forest (15), succulent desert (3), and desert grassland (1). But in the Guadalupe Mountains, where the two subspecies have essentially retained their respective identities, he found that they mostly inhabited separate and distinctly different sites. The smaller prairie ring-necked snake occupied the damper regions of deciduous woodland, while the larger regal ring-necked snake preferred the drier oak-juniper habitat or occasionally the more arid succulent desert environment.

MISSISSIPPI RING-NECKED SNAKE

Diadophis punctatus stictogenys

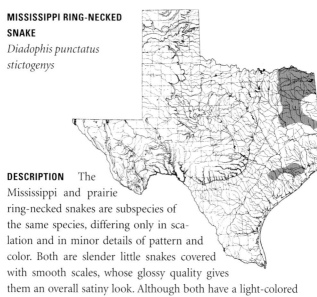

DESCRIPTION The Mississippi and prairie ring-necked snakes are subspecies of the same species, differing only in sca- lation and in minor details of pattern and color. Both are slender little snakes covered with smooth scales, whose glossy quality gives them an overall satiny look. Although both have a light-colored neck ring, the nuchal collar of the Mississippi ring-necked snake is narrower than that of the prairie subspecies. In certain indi- viduals of both races, the collar is incomplete at the top of the neck. In addition, *D. p. stictogenys* has a bright yellow instead of scarlet undertail, and the small, black abdominal spots are not randomly scattered, as in the prairie subspecies, but tend to form an irregular line of pairs down the belly midline. As far back as the yellow neck ring, the top of the head is a bit darker than the slate blue upper body hue, while the lower lips and underside of the chin are unevenly speckled with small black spots. The body scales are usually arranged in 15 rows on the forebody, and the anal plate is divided.

COMPARABLE SNAKES Both the juvenile brown snake's pale- colored nuchal collar and its pale-hued head band, which are sometimes present on very young earth snakes, vanish before the juveniles reach maturity. But even when such markings are present, the two species can be distinguished from the ring- necked snake by their keeled body scales, immaculate whitish bellies, and brown dorsal color. The Florida red-bellied snake, which ordinarily has a yellow to reddish orange abdomen, possesses three small nuchal spots, keeled body scales, and an unmarked abdomen. Also, the three snakes mentioned above all have a suedelike dorsal surface compared to the glossy look of the ring-necked snake.

SIZE A bit smaller than the prairie ring-necked snake, this subspecies reaches a maximum length of about 14 inches (35.6 cm).

HABITAT Essentially a snake of pine forest and pine-oak woodland, this secretive reptile also occurs in adjacent unwooded habitats such as weedy fields and ravine bottoms, provided such places offer both sufficient moisture to prevent the snake's dehydration during times of dry weather and adequate surface debris under which it can hide. It is most often associated with sparse timberland abundantly littered with hollow logs, rotting tree stumps, and other forest-floor debris, all of which it uses as places of shelter. Though it is generally absent from the coastal prairie, Guidry (1953), after nearly half a lifetime of diligent collecting efforts over a large portion of southeastern Texas, discovered only a single specimen of this subspecies in sparse woodland near Port Arthur.

Photo by P. Freed.

TEXAS INDIGO SNAKE
*Drymarchon melanurus
erebennus*

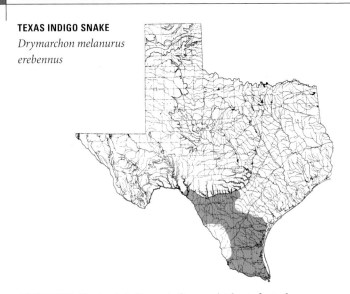

DESCRIPTION Most adult Texas indigos, which at first glance look like large, shiny, all-black serpents, prove on close examination to be blue-black only on the rear half of the body and the tail; on the forward half of the trunk, that color is mottled or discretely banded with gray-brown. Some specimens from the Brownsville area, according to Burchfield (pers. com.), are glossy indigo blue with a reddish blush, resembling somewhat the eastern subspecies of the indigo snake. The chin, throat, and sometimes even the belly as far back as midbody, although generally brown to orange-brown, occasionally display a distinct reddish hue, whereas the rear half of the abdomen is gray, shading to blue-black near the tail. The uniformly dark brown or black color of the crown fades to a paler tone along the sides of the face, where most of the upper lip scales are edged in black. The most prominent of these dark streaks are the two or three that radiate downward from the eye. The large, smooth dorsal scales are in 17 rows at midbody (14 near the tail), and the anal plate is single. A newly hatched Texas indigo snake, however, is dark gray-brown to black, with widely separated, small, white, dashlike spots feebly arranged along the sides of the body as thin, diagonal lines. Evident even at this age are the bold black bars directly below each eye. The young snake's face, as well as its chin and throat, which are whitish or buff-colored, will turn reddish or reddish orange as the snake reaches maturity but will thereafter become dark and nearly colorless.

COMPARABLE SNAKES An especially dark specimen of the Texas rat snake may have its dorsal markings so obscured as to result in a virtually all-black serpent. Unlike the indigo, it will have at least some keeled body scales, a divided anal plate, and no bold vertical dark bars lining its upper lip scales. The adult southern black racer is the only other Texas snake that appears totally black at first glance. However, it lacks the bold black lip marks of the indigo snake.

SIZE One of Texas' largest serpents, both in length and in weight, this snake rivals several other native species as the state's biggest

Adult. Photo by R. A. Odum.

ophidian. Its usual adult length is between 5 and 6 ¹/₂ feet (152.4–198.1 cm), Conant and Collins (1991) give the maximum length for this subspecies as 8 feet, 4 ¹/₄ inches (254.6 cm). An even larger specimen, reported to have measured 9 feet, 5 inches (287 cm) long, was mentioned by Vermersch and Kuntz (1986), although the authors gave no specific reference for such a record. In either case, among our nonvenomous species, only the bull snake grows as long. The western diamond-backed rattler, at an approximate maximum length of 7 feet, 4 inches (223.5 cm), is not as long as a Texas indigo, but with a maximum weight of about 16 pounds, it can be more than three to four times as heavy.

HABITAT Primarily a resident of Mexico, the snake we call the Texas indigo occurs only peripherally in the United States, where its distribution is limited to the thornbrush country of South Texas. This semiarid environment, best characterized as a vast mesquite grassland savannah, will support indigo snake populations only where there is adequate moisture, such as in areas near streams, ponds, resacas, and windmill seeps, for the long-term well being of this drought-sensitive reptile is intimately associated with water.

Much of the thornbrush that constitutes suitable wildlife habitat on the Gulf Coast Plain has disappeared, especially in the lower Rio Grande Valley. As the Valley's remaining brushland succumbs to the unrelenting encroachment of agriculture and urban development, ever more wildlife is displaced. The first to be affected are large species such as this. Despite the ongoing alteration of so much South Texas wilderness, significant parcels of favorable habitat remain, though some of them represent only small isolated pockets. Among the largest of such sanctuaries is the Santa Ana National Wildlife Refuge, a nearly 2,000-acre expanse of brush, trees, and ponds lying along the Rio Grande south of McAllen, where wildlife of all kinds, including the indigo snake, is permanently protected. Below it, near the southernmost end of the state, is the National Audubon Society's Sabal Palm Grove Sanctuary, a unique 172-acre (68.9 ha) tract of remnant subtropical forest whose principal hallmark is the indigenous sabal palm. Within its borders this native palm, together with the indigo and a handful of other distinctly Mexican animal and plant species, enjoys protection from indiscriminate exploitation. From this coastal thornbrush habitat, the snake has traced the major bands of riverine woodland northwestward, extending its range as far inland as Val Verde, Kinney, Uvalde, and Medina counties. Though it occurred along the southern border of Bexar County as recently as the early 1950s, it apparently is no longer found there.

SPECKLED RACER
Drymobius margaritiferus
margaritiferus

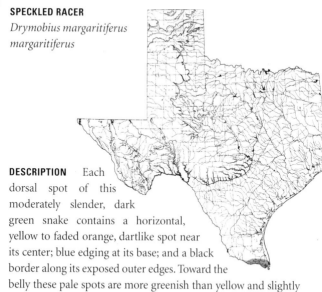

DESCRIPTION Each dorsal spot of this moderately slender, dark green snake contains a horizontal, yellow to faded orange, dartlike spot near its center; blue edging at its base; and a black border along its exposed outer edges. Toward the belly these pale spots are more greenish than yellow and slightly larger than they are on the upper body; those on the neck and tail usually are pale turquoise green. In a newly shed specimen, the overall effect is that of a daintily jeweled piece of oriental ceramic finished in lacquer. A wide, dark, horizontal band extends backward from the eye, and the scales of both the upper lips and the crown are delicately edged in black. Except for the scales under the tail, which are black-edged on their rear margins, the abdomen is usually all white or yellowish. The dorsal scales are only weakly keeled and are aligned in 17 rows at midbody; the anal plate is divided.

COMPARABLE SNAKES The only other serpent in the area with a dark ground color and numerous small, light-colored dorsal spots is the desert king snake, which can be distinguished by the dark chainlike pattern on its back, the 23 or 25 midbody rows of smooth dorsal scales, and the single anal plate.

SIZE The usual adult length for this subspecies is 30 to 40 inches (76.2–101.6 cm), but a specimen of maximum size measured 50 inches (127 cm) long.

HABITAT This is essentially a Latin American serpent whose distribution brings it northward to the very tip of South Texas, the only place in the United States where it occurs. North of the border it is found primarily in the few areas of remnant subtropical forest that remain intact in Cameron County. The most notable remnant is the National Audubon Society's Sabal Palm Grove Sanctuary

Adult from Cameron County.

(6 miles southeast of Brownsville), which probably harbors more speckled racers than any other area in South Texas. Even in such prime habitat the snake remains uncommon to rare. Nevertheless, Pat Burchfield (pers. com.) noted that it is not unusual to see specimens along drainage ditches and low, swampy places in the Southmost area of Brownsville. According to Mrs. L. Irby Davis, naturalist and longtime resident of Harlingen (in Wright and Wright 1957), this snake apparently never was plentiful in the lower Rio Grande Valley. She reported it from only two Valley locations: among the grove of Sabal palms below Southmost and in hackberry woodland along the river near La Feria.

By contrast, the speckled racer is abundant over much of its Latin American range. In Mexico and Central America, living in a variety of moist to wet habitats ranging from sea level to about 4,750 feet (1,453 m) elevation, it favors areas of relatively dense vegetation where leaf litter and other plant debris provide adequate ground cover. It also occurs in open savannahs, especially around marshland pools, and it can even be found in the vegetative debris of village back yards, provided there is some nearby moisture to sustain its amphibian prey.

BAIRD'S RAT SNAKE
Elaphe bairdi

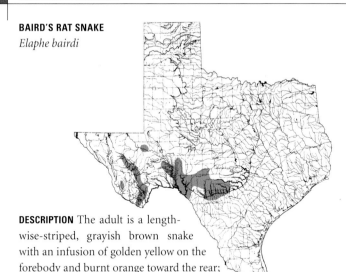

DESCRIPTION The adult is a length-wise-striped, grayish brown snake with an infusion of golden yellow on the forebody and burnt orange toward the rear; the rich highlighting is created by a pale-hued crescent at the base of each dorsal scale. The essential pattern elements are four dark, shadowy stripes running the length of the body and tail. The uppermost pair of stripes is the more prominent; between them sometimes lies a row of indistinct dark crossbars, remnants of the serpent's blotched juvenile pattern. Present also may be a series of smaller but equally vague lateral spots. Aged specimens, however, can be virtually patternless. The head, which is often a subtle bluish gray on the crown, fades to a russet or yellowish hue along the sides but in some specimens is overall pale gray. The snake's underside, often exhibiting small, ill-defined dark blotches, is usually pale yellow on the chin and neck, becoming orange-tan on the rear part of the abdomen. Arranged in 27 midbody rows, the dorsal scales are only slightly keeled. The anal plate is divided.

The juvenile, paler in color than the adult, lacks lengthwise stripes and is strongly blotched; its 48 or more dark brown to black body crossbars (sometimes dumbbell-shaped) stand out clearly against the snake's ground color of pale gray. Similar, though progressively smaller, markings occur on the tail. Alternating with the crossbars is a row of much smaller dark spots low on either side of the body. The head markings consist of a dark transverse band between and just forward of the eyes and a dark line on each side of the face that begins at the orbit and slants back to the mouthline. Also evident may be a pair of longitudinal dark bars, one on either side of the neck directly behind the head. According to Olson (1977), the juvenile pattern of bold, dark crossbars persists until the snake reaches a length between 27 and 31 inches (68.6–78.7 cm), and the adult pattern of lengthwise stripes becomes evident in serpents over 38 or 39 inches (96.5 or 99.1 cm) long. He considered specimens in between (those displaying both stripes and crossbars at the same time) to be young adults. Then there are the occasional very large Baird's rat snakes, whose dark stripes have disappeared altogether, resulting in uniformly gray or yellowish orange individuals.

Adult.

COMPARABLE SNAKES The typical adult Texas rat snake can be distinguished from a mature Baird's rat snake by the median row of large, dark blotches along its back, though some specimens display dark lengthwise body striping as well, and others appear nearly all black, their blotched patterns barely visible through the overall dark pigmentation. Even so, the crown of a Texas rat snake is almost invariably all black or dark gray, whereas that of a Baird's is much paler, particularly along the edges. Although the juveniles of both species are strongly blotched, there are some conspicuous differences between them. The Texas rat snake has only 27 to 37 dorsal body markings (48 or more in Baird's), they are longer than wide (much wider than long in Baird's), and their color is generally a rich brown (gray in Baird's). The dark H-shaped blotches of the Trans-Pecos rat snake, particularly those on the forebody, often merge to give the appearance of lengthwise striping. But in this species the midbody dorsal scales are in 31 to 35 rows, and in a condition unique among our native rat snakes, a row of small scales separates the eye from the upper lip scales. Patch-nosed snakes, also lengthwise striped, have 17 rows of midbody scales, all smooth, and a head not distinctly wider than the neck (clearly so in Baird's). Moreover, the uppermost dark stripes on the body of a patch-nosed snake begin at the snake's eye, while those of *E. bairdi* originate on the neck.

SIZE Most adults are between 28 and 42 inches (71.1–106.7 cm) long. A maximum-size specimen of 63 1/2 inches (161 cm), collected by John Malone in Bandera County, is in the Texas Cooperative Wildlife Collection at Texas A&M University.

HABITAT One of Texas' uncommon serpents, Baird's rat snake has a limited distribution across the west-central part of the state, beginning near the south-central edge of the Edwards Plateau and extending westward through the Stockton Plateau and the Big Bend region to the Davis Mountains. In a recent study, Lawson and Lieb (1990) described the snake's ecology in some detail. Most of the following habitat information is derived from their report.

At the easternmost end of its range, this serpent is confined primarily to the wooded limestone ridges and precipitous canyon walls of the Nueces River, the headwater zones of the Llano and Guadalupe rivers, the high ground separating the Guadalupe and Medina river valleys, and the ridges running along the Medina River valley as far east as Medina Lake. Here, where Baird's rat snake is encircled on three sides by populations of the Texas rat snake, the two species occasionally meet and hybridize. For unknown reasons, *E. bairdi* apparently is absent from similar choice habitat in the eastern and northern parts of the Edwards Plateau. In contrast to the limestone-dominated eastern part of its range, the westernmost portion of the snake's environment in Texas is characterized by the igneous rock formations of the Davis Mountains, especially along the region's wooded canyons and forested uplands. No matter where it occurs, whether at 1,000 or 10,000 feet (305–3,050 m) elevation, this species favors rough, rocky habitats, particularly those containing caves, deep fissures, and steep canyon walls, although it is more catholic in its choice of plant associations, occupying a variety of vegetation types ranging from Chihuahuan desert scrub to Sierra Madrean pine forest (in south-central Tamaulipas, Mexico).

SLOWINSKI'S CORN SNAKE
Elaphe guttata slowinskii

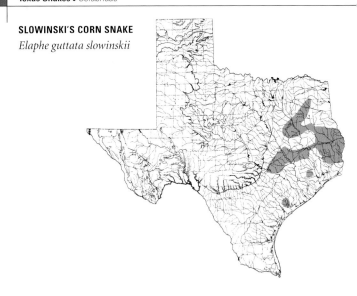

DESCRIPTION In a recent study of *E. guttata* and its subspecies in Texas, Vaughan, Dixon, and Thomas (1996) confirmed the presence of the corn snake in the state. The Texas individuals are not the usual vivid red or bright orange reptile commonly found in the eastern part of the serpent's range. Such brightly hued corn snakes apparently occur no farther west than the Louisiana parishes of Iberia, Point Coupee, and West Baton Rouge. Texas specimens, as well as those in western Louisiana, while they do not display the gaudy red or orange coloration of most individuals found elsewhere, nevertheless fit the description of *E. g. guttata* in other important characteristics. Burbrink (2002) recognized this form as a distinct taxon and described it for a friend and colleague (J. B. Slowinski), who died in Asia.

Texas corn snakes are tan, grayish tan, or orangish tan, with a dorsal row of large brown to reddish brown dark-edged blotches down the middle of the back, below which is another row of smaller alternating blotches, followed by a third series of even smaller spots at the belly line. Their combined dorsal body and tail blotches number 44–59 (average 51), and the combined belly (ventral) and undertail (subcaudal) scales average 282. Furthermore, their numerous squarish, black belly markings, each of which involves at least three ventral scales in sequence, are set against a whitish background, giving the abdomen a conspicuously checkered appearance; the stripes under the tail are bold and black. A characteristic pattern element of all *E. guttata* subspecies is the conspicuous dark, dorsal, spearpoint-shaped marking that begins on the neck as two nearly parallel dark stripes and ends in a point on the crown between the eyes. Just ahead of it, a dark transverse bar connects the eyes, then slants backward along each side of the head past the end of the mouthline, where it sometimes joins the first body blotch. Another short, dark bar may cross the top of the snout. The body scales, of which only the upper several rows are keeled, occur in 27 (rarely 29) middorsal rows, and the anal plate is divided.

Pale adult from Brazos County. Photo by J. E. Werler.

COMPARABLE SNAKES No other East Texas serpent within the corn snake's range has a distinct, dark, forward-directed spear-point marking on the crown and two distinct, lengthwise dark stripes under the tail. The prairie king snake has perfectly smooth scales and a single anal plate. On the adult Texas rat snake, the dorsal blotches often are poorly defined, the top of its head is uniformly dusky, and the underside of its tail lacks two bold, dark lengthwise stripes. The juvenile Texas rat snake also lacks the dark undertail stripes, and the dark stripe behind its eye fails to reach backward past the end of the mouthline. While the color markings of the Great Plains and southwestern rat snake are somewhat similar to the corn snake, the Great Plains rat snake dorsal body and tail blotches number 57–81 (average 67); those of the southwestern rat snake are more similar to the corn snake, varying from 39 to 67 (average 55). However, the latter subspecies has a much paler belly and undertail markings.

SIZE Throughout its range, the usual adult length of this snake is 30 to 48 inches (76.2–121.9 cm); the largest specimen on record measured 72 inches (182.9 cm) long. Five corn snakes collected in Texas from Brazos, Grimes, Milam, and St. Augustine counties were 41 to 55 inches (104.1–139.7 cm) in length and averaged 47.2 inches (119.9 cm) long.

HABITAT The corn snake reaches the westernmost limit of its extensive geographic range in the east-central and southeastern parts of Texas, where it has been found primarily in pine-oak habitat from the eastern edge of the post oak savannah, north to the town of Big Sandy, east to the Louisiana border, and south to Hardin County. It has been found west of Brazos County for more than 40 miles (64.8 km) and south of that county for more than 135 miles (218.7 km), near Port Lavaca. For the most part, collecting records in the state are widely scattered, with most specimens of this subspecies having been obtained in Brazos County. Outside Texas it is encountered in a wide variety of habitats that include sparse woodland, forest edge, rocky hillsides, dry fields, and open grassy areas, but is seldom found in wet bottomlands. Despite its secretive life style, the corn snake is attracted to agricultural and urban areas, especially those in which dilapidated old buildings provide shelter for the snakes themselves and for the small rodents on which they feed.

GREAT PLAINS RAT SNAKE
Elaphe emoryi emoryi

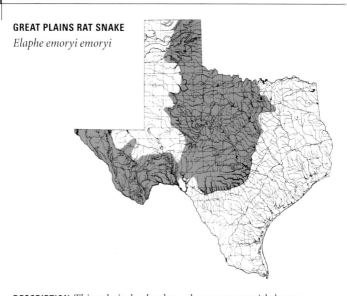

DESCRIPTION This relatively slender pale gray to grayish brown serpent is patterned with a dorsal row of large, rather boldly contrasting dark gray, olive, or grayish brown ovals or roughly four-sided blotches, each narrowly outlined in dark brown or black. Two more lengthwise rows of smaller dark blotches occur on either side of the body. In old specimens, however, the usual bold pattern of dark blotches may be largely replaced by four shadowy lengthwise stripes. When combined, the number of dorsal body and tail blotches in this subspecies (57–81, average 67) is 12 more on average than those of the southwestern rat snake (39–67, average 55). In addition, the combined belly (ventral) and undertail (subcaudal) scales of the Great Plains rat snake vary from 271 to 293 (average 282), but are 12.6 fewer on average than those of the southwestern rat snake (275–312, average 295). The numerous bold and rather large squarish, dark spots randomly distributed across the snake's pale-colored belly give the abdomen a distinctly checkered look. The underside of the serpent's tail features a pair of dark stripes that extend its full length, sometimes discontinuously.

The snake's most easily observed hallmark, present in both *E. guttata* and *E. emoryi,* is the dark spearpoint-shaped marking on top of its head, which, despite its general usefulness as a species characteristic, may be indistinct in very old specimens. It is composed of two bold, nearly parallel dark brown stripes that begin on the neck and extend forward onto the crown, where they normally converge in a point between the eyes. In the middle of this dark outline is an area of light background color. Further forward on the crown, a dark transverse bar connects the eyes, then slants backward along each side of the head past the end of the mouthline, where it sometimes joins the first body blotch. Another, less distinct, dark-colored bar usually crosses the top of the snout.

The body scales, of which only the upper several rows are keeled, occur in 27 (rarely 29) middorsal rows, and the anal plate is divided.

Adult from Terrell County. Photo by J. E. Werler.

COMPARABLE SNAKES Among our native serpent species, only the Great Plains rat and corn snakes have both a bold, dark, forward-pointing spearpoint marked on the head *and* a distinctly dark-striped undertail. The prairie king snake, which is easily confused with *E. emoryi,* has perfectly smooth body scales and a single anal plate, as do the glossy snakes, whose undersides are unmarked. The strongly keeled dorsal scales of the bull snake are arranged in 29 to 37 midbody rows, and the anal plate is single. In the adult Texas rat snake, the dark dorsal blotches do not stand out boldly against the background color, the top of the head is dusky and virtually patternless, there is no downward-slanting dark stripe behind the eye, and the underside of the tail lacks dark striping. Although the juvenile Texas rat snake—with its pale background color, contrasting dark brown blotched pattern, and bold head markings—closely resembles the Great Plains rat snake, it lacks both the dark, forward-pointing spearpoint design on the head and the striped undertail of *E. emoryi.* Furthermore, the dark stripe behind each eye does not extend past the end of the mouthline. The adult Baird's rat snake displays four dark stripes along the full length of its body and has an unpatterned head; the juvenile is marked with numerous narrow, dark crossbars, and the scattered dark markings on its crown do not take the shape of a spearpoint. The blond color phase of the Trans-Pecos rat snake carries no distinct markings on either its head or neck.

SIZE A snake of moderate size, the adult usually attains a length between 24 and 48 inches (61-121.9 cm), although a specimen of record length measured 72 inches (182.9 cm).

HABITAT Generally absent from the western Panhandle and regions east of the limestone extrusions that sporadically surface between Waco and Dallas, this adaptable serpent ranges widely across Central and North Texas, being associated with every major vegetational community in this part of the state. Its distribution stretches from the Edwards Plateau, north through the southern Great Plains of Texas and Oklahoma, and includes the Rolling Plains, Cross Timbers, and grassland prairie, although it generally avoids the Staked Plain. Its preferred microhabitats include rocky bluffs and slopes, partially wooded hillsides, and even caves. In otherwise arid environments, it frequently occurs near springs, streams, and rivers; across the grassy plains, it is often found along dry gullies. Though less disposed than the more precocious Texas rat snake to occupy sites near human habitations, this species sometimes inhabits rural areas where the scattered remains of abandoned farm buildings and similar unoccupied structures harbor an abundance of rodent prey. Burt and Hoyle (1935) found that in the winter, it retires to a deep rock fissure, quarry, cave, or mammal burrow where it can safely pass the season, sometimes in small groups and frequently in association with other serpents, including ring-necked snakes, yellow-bellied racers, and copperheads. One communal den in a rocky ravine in Kansas held a dozen Great Plains rat snakes, numerous yellow-bellied racers, and a few prairie ring-necked snakes.

SOUTHWESTERN RAT SNAKE
Elaphe emoryi
meahllmorum

DESCRIPTION

This somewhat slender snake has a pale gray ground color and a lengthwise row of large, contrasting grayish brown to pale brown oval or nearly four-sided dorsal blotches, each margined with a darker color. The combined number of dorsal body and tail markings of this subspecies vary from 39 to 67 (average 55). Those of the Great Plains rat snake vary from 57 to 81 (average 67), and of the intermountain rat snake from 60 to 84 (average 73). In about half the specimens, a light gray transverse bar crosses through the middle of each dorsal blotch. Usually two more rows of smaller spots lie on either side of the body below the large primary series.

On the forebody the abdomen is white or cream-colored, with normally few if any dark markings except for dark spots along the outer edges of the belly plates, beginning after about the first 50 ventral scales. The degree of ventral spotting, however, can vary from none to moderate. The underside of the tail is irregularly marked with small dark spots, which are seldom arranged in two well-defined lengthwise stripes. Furthermore, of the three subspecies of *E. emoryi,* the southwestern rat snake shows the highest combined average number of belly (ventral) plus undertail (subcaudal) scales, more than 290 in 86 percent of the specimens as opposed to about 282 in both intermountain and Great Plains rat snakes.

The body scales, of which only the upper several rows are weakly keeled (the others being smooth), occur in 27 (rarely 29) middorsal rows, and the anal plate is divided.

COMPARABLE SNAKES In no other Texas snake species do we see the distinct, dark, forward-directed, spearpoint head marking that characterizes the three subspecies of *E. emoryi*. The prairie king snake has perfectly smooth body scales and a single anal plate. Glossy snakes, which display the same scale characters, have an immaculate belly and undertail surface. Bull snakes possess strongly keeled dorsal scales, arranged in 29 to 37 midbody rows, and a single anal plate. On the adult Texas rat snake, the dark dorsal blotches usually are not as well defined as those of the southwestern rat

Adult from South Texas.

snake, the top of its head is uniformly dark, there is no distinct dark stripe behind the eye, and the undertail lacks dark spots. On the other hand, the boldly blotched juvenile Texas rat snake does not appear greatly different from the southwestern rat snake, but it lacks a spearpoint marking on the crown and the dark stripe behind its eye fails to reach beyond the end of the mouthline.

SIZE Adults of this moderately sized subspecies generally range from 24 to 48 inches (61–121.9 cm) long. The maximum known length for the species is 72 inches (182.9 cm).

HABITAT An inhabitant of the South Texas brush country, it occurs as far north as the Balcones Escarpment (along a line extending from Del Rio to San Antonio to Austin), west into the eastern portion of the Chihuahuan Desert, and east to a line between Austin and Corpus Christi. In south-central Texas, according to Vermersch and Kuntz (1986), it is found in juniper, oak, and hackberry woodlands, as well as in the more open adjacent grasslands that support stands of mesquite and scattered yucca.

TEXAS RAT SNAKE
*Elaphe obsoleta
lindheimeri*

DESCRIPTION Except for the occasional adult specimen whose dorsal markings are obscured by the snake's overall black coloration, the typical pattern of this subspecies consists of a median row of large, dark brown to purplish blotches displayed against a background color of yellowish to grayish brown or, on occasion, reddish. Below and alternating with them is a row of smaller dark blotches. Owing to considerable variation in body color among individual specimens, the dorsal and lateral markings either stand out boldly against the background hue or appear almost to blend with it. In some older Texas rat snakes the chief pattern element consists of lengthwise dark stripes, with or without indistinct dorsal blotches.

Whatever the serpent's basic hue, all adult Texas rat snakes have one thing in common: the skin between the body scales and many of the scale edges themselves bear reddish pigmentation. The head, which is uniformly dark gray on top, is white on the lip scales, across the lower jaw, and on the throat. Squarish dark blotches tinted with gray usually mark the pale-colored belly, and the underside of the tail is normally solid gray. At midbody, 27 rows of dorsal scales encircle the snake; only those near the spine bear weak keels, the others being smooth. The anal plate is divided.

A very young rat snake scarcely resembles the adult. Its large, dark brown dorsal saddles stand out boldly against the snake's light gray background color, as do its smaller lateral blotches. On the pale-colored crown, which is only a shade darker than the light gray body, a dark bar crosses the forehead just in front of the eyes. A similar bar extends obliquely backward from each eye, almost reaching the end of the mouthline, while a pair of dark streaks runs back from the rear of the crown to join the first neck blotch.

COMPARABLE SNAKES Nearly all adult Baird's rat snakes have lengthwise dorsal striping, although a few mature Texas rat snakes are also faintly striped. Juvenile *E. bairdi,* with their numerous nar-

row dorsal crossbars (44–61 bars, 2–3 scale rows in length, measured front to back), can easily be distinguished from young Texas rat snakes, which have only 27 to 37 middorsal body blotches that are four to six scales long. In both juvenile and adult Great Plains rat snakes, a dark, forward-pointing,

Adult from Harris County.

spearpoint marking decorates the top of the head, the postocular stripe extends backward onto the neck, and two bold dark stripes occur on the underside of the tail. The body scales of the prairie king snake are all smooth, and its anal plate is also single.

SIZE This is one of Texas' longest serpents. Most adults are between 42 and 72 inches (106.7–182.9 cm) in length; a record individual measured 86 inches (218.4 cm) long.

HABITAT Throughout eastern Texas, this serpent is found most commonly in brushy or wooded areas, particularly those containing large trees, for it shows a strong tendency to climb. It finds not only refuge from ground-dwelling predators but also a convenient source of birds and their eggs, both favored prey items. It utilizes a wide variety of other East Texas habitats, such as rocky hillsides, grasslands, cultivated fields, marshland, and even wooded suburban lots and inner-city parkland. From there it ranges westward through the prairies and Cross Timbers; to the south it penetrates the predominantly grassy and brushy parts of south-central Texas by keeping mostly to the area's countless oak savannahs and mottes and to the woodlands that border the region's numerous watercourses.

WESTERN MUD SNAKE
Farancia abacura
reinwardti

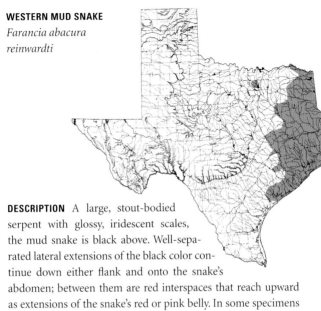

DESCRIPTION A large, stout-bodied serpent with glossy, iridescent scales, the mud snake is black above. Well-separated lateral extensions of the black color continue down either flank and onto the snake's abdomen; between them are red interspaces that reach upward as extensions of the snake's red or pink belly. In some specimens the black bars cross the abdomen in regular sequence, and in others they break up to form a red and black checkered pattern. Among the mud snake's other distinctive features are a somewhat flattened head that is no wider than its neck, tiny eyes, and a sharp spine on the end of its short, stout tail. The head is mostly black on top, whereas the center of each light-colored upper and lower lip scale contains a distinct central dark spot. Similar dark markings occur on the yellow or orange chin and throat. The smooth dorsal scales are arranged in 19 rows at midbody, and the anal plate is nearly always divided.

COMPARABLE SNAKES Within the mud snake's range, the only other serpent having a similar color pattern is the western worm snake, but it has a nearly straight line of demarcation between its contrasting dorsal and ventral coloration, and its dorsal scales are in 13 midbody rows. Although the undertail color of ring-necked snakes is red or orange-red, the belly is never pink or scarlet, the neck is nearly always circled by a partial or complete light-colored ring, and there is a double row of small dark spots along the length of the abdomen.

SIZE The usual adult length for this subspecies is 3 to 4 feet (91.4–121.9 cm); however, Guidry (1953) reported a record specimen from southeastern Texas that measured 6 feet, 2 inches (188 cm) long.

Adult from Liberty County.

HABITAT This semiaquatic snake is most likely to be found in or near still or slow-moving bodies of water with muddy bottoms and an abundance of aquatic and shoreline vegetation, usually in the vicinity of open woodland. Its favorite haunts are wooded swamplands littered with rotting logs, but it also frequents mud- or sand-bottomed lakes, ponds, marshes, sloughs, ditches, and sluggish streams, particularly those surrounded by muddy lowlands. It is also known to inhabit brackish marshes and tidal streams.

MEXICAN HOOK-NOSED SNAKE
Ficimia streckeri

DESCRIPTION

The most distinctive feature of this relatively stout-bodied little snake is its enlarged, upturned snout; it is flat or slightly concave near its base, but the front part is fashioned into a hooked point. Marking the brown, light olive, or grayish dorsal color is a row of narrow, dark brown crossbars, each of which reaches down along the sides of the body to about the second row of scales above the belly, where the dorsal color fades to a paler hue. In some specimens these markings are reduced to large spots, and in others they are obscured by a darkening of the snake's ground color. In addition, most specimens display one or more lengthwise rows of small, irregular dark spots low on each side of the body along the edge of the pale lateral hue. Some of the spots are aligned directly under the ends of the crossbars; others occur between them.

The snake's head and neck are the same width. The crown, usually unpatterned, is generally a bit darker than the dorsal body coloration, and on the upper lip scales beneath and behind each eye there is often an indistinct dark brown spot. Like the belly, the lower lip scales and throat are immaculate white or pale yellow. In the absence of internasal scales, the rostral plate makes direct contact with the frontal scale. There are 17 rows of smooth dorsal scales at midbody, and the anal plate is divided.

COMPARABLE SNAKES The strongly keeled dorsal scales of hog-nosed snakes occur in 23 or 25 midbody rows, and the upturned rostral plate bears a lengthwise keel down its center.

SIZE Although most adult hook-nosed snakes are between 7 and

11 inches (17.8–27.9 cm) long, the greatest length reported for this species is 19 inches (48.3 cm).

HABITAT Chiefly an inhabitant of the South Texas thornbrush woodland, this burrowing serpent also occurs in the floodplain of the lower Rio Grande Valley. Low in elevation, covered mostly with tight gravelly soil, and generally dominated by endless thickets of mesquite and prickly pear cactus, the region contains rela-

Adult from Duval County.

tively few natural bodies of standing water, though human-made tanks, ponds, and resacas are common. It is near such sources of moisture that the Mexican hook-nosed snake is most likely to be encountered. During the spring and summer of 1935, Mulaik and Mulaik (1943) found this ordinarily secretive species in greatest numbers in the vicinity of Edinburg, stranded in concrete irrigation canals from which the snakes apparently had been unable to escape. Axtell (1969) states that this species prefers tight alluvial and even stony soils, avoiding the sizable areas of dune sands and sandy loam that occur in Kenedy, Brooks, east Jim Hogg, and north Willacy and Hidalgo counties. Similar kinds of sandy barriers in La Salle and Dimmit counties, he believes, may effectively limit the snake's spread any farther northwest.

WESTERN HOOK-NOSED SNAKE
Gyalopion canum

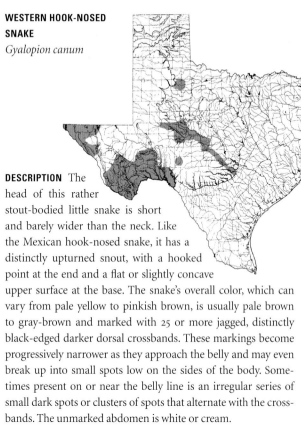

DESCRIPTION The head of this rather stout-bodied little snake is short and barely wider than the neck. Like the Mexican hook-nosed snake, it has a distinctly upturned snout, with a hooked point at the end and a flat or slightly concave upper surface at the base. The snake's overall color, which can vary from pale yellow to pinkish brown, is usually pale brown to gray-brown and marked with 25 or more jagged, distinctly black-edged darker dorsal crossbands. These markings become progressively narrower as they approach the belly and may even break up into small spots low on the sides of the body. Sometimes present on or near the belly line is an irregular series of small dark spots or clusters of spots that alternate with the crossbands. The unmarked abdomen is white or cream.

The most prominent markings are on top of the head, where a dark brown bar crosses the snout between the eyes, followed by another dark bar, sometimes interrupted medially, that crosses the crown behind the first one. Following the last marking is a large, lengthwise nape blotch colored like the body crossbands; on either side of the head, a large dark brown spot occupies the upper lip scales just below the eye. There are two internasals, and the rostral plate makes contact with the prefrontal scales. The dorsal scales are smooth and in 17 midbody rows. The anal plate is divided.

COMPARABLE SNAKES Hog-nosed snakes have strongly keeled

dorsal scales in 23 or 25 midbody rows; they are patterned with large, dark body blotches; and their oversized, upturned rostral plates have a lengthwise keel down the center.

SIZE Although the record length for this species stands at 15 $\frac{1}{6}$ inches (38.5 cm). adults are generally between 7 and 11 inches (17.8–27.9 cm) long.

HABITAT Essentially an inhabitant of the Chihuahuan Desert, the western hook-nosed snake ranges northward from Mexico into Trans-Pecos Texas and the central and western parts of the Edwards Plateau, with a few isolated records from as far north as the southern Panhandle counties of Dickens, King, and Scurry. A single Wise County record from the western Cross Timbers is questionable and requires further confirmation. In Texas it has typically been found in plant associations of mesquite, mesquite-creosote, creosote-agave, persimmon–shin oak, oak-juniper, and the pinyon-juniper woodland of Big Bend National Park. In the prairie grasslands of the southern Panhandle, where this species reaches the northernmost limit of its distribution in the state, Ferguson (1965) described the topography as normally flat to rolling, with some gypsum and limestone outcroppings. In addition to various grasses, the vegetation consisted of mesquite, often interspersed with lotebush, and juniper.

Adult from Jackson County, Oklahoma. Photo by R. W. Van Devender.

PLAINS HOG-NOSED SNAKE
Heterodon nasicus
nasicus

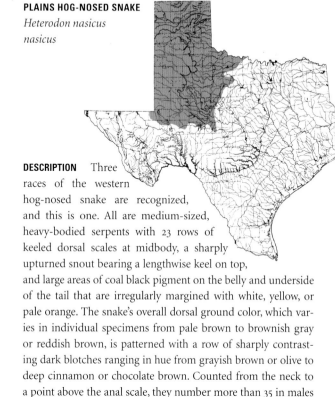

DESCRIPTION   Three races of the western hog-nosed snake are recognized, and this is one. All are medium-sized, heavy-bodied serpents with 23 rows of keeled dorsal scales at midbody, a sharply upturned snout bearing a lengthwise keel on top, and large areas of coal black pigment on the belly and underside of the tail that are irregularly margined with white, yellow, or pale orange. The snake's overall dorsal ground color, which varies in individual specimens from pale brown to brownish gray or reddish brown, is patterned with a row of sharply contrasting dark blotches ranging in hue from grayish brown or olive to deep cinnamon or chocolate brown. Counted from the neck to a point above the anal scale, they number more than 35 in males and more than 40 in females. One to three rows of smaller dark spots occur below the primary series, each spot alternating with the one just above it.

The snake's pale-colored head is conspicuously marked with a white-edged, transverse, dark brown bar on the crown between the eyes; a wide, dark brown cheek mask that reaches obliquely downward from each eye to the end of the mouthline; and a large, V-shaped mark of the same color, whose apex lies on top of the head between the eyes and whose arms slant downward and backward to either side of the neck. In this subspecies, as in the dusty hog-nosed snake, the small scales on top of the head just behind the large nose scale number nine or more. The anal plate is divided.

COMPARABLE SNAKES The larger eastern hog-nosed snake resembles the western species in its heavy build and general head configuration but differs in its less sharply upturned snout and uniformly pale-colored tail undersurface. The western hook-nosed snake, which looks like a miniature hognose, possesses a shallow depression on top of the head behind the snout instead of a lengthwise keel, and its body scales are smooth and in 17 rows at midbody. The massasauga also resembles the western hog-nosed snake, but it lacks the

Photo by R. A. Odum.

upturned snout, has a pale-colored undertail, and a rattle.

SIZE The usual adult length for this subspecies is 16 inches to 2 feet (40.6–61 cm). A record specimen from Hale County measured 35 $1/2$ inches (90.2 cm) long.

HABITAT The snake's preferred habitat in Texas is the shortgrass or mixed-grass prairie of the arid High Plains, where the ground cover is sparse and gravelly or sandy soils provide good surface drainage and a loose substrate into which the snake can easily burrow. In such an environment it is encountered chiefly in the vicinity of sandy hills, sand dunes, sandy prairies, and river floodplains. In Hutchinson County, Fouquette and Lindsay (1955) frequently found it on the High Plains escarpment where the principal vegetation of the deep-sand habitat consisted of sage, sumac, and some grass cover.

Because the snake occurs in a number of isolated populations outside its known continuous range, the boundaries of its geographic distribution have not been clearly defined. To the east its range apparently is limited by the increasing plant density of the tallgrass prairie and deciduous woodland, or by the more compact soil associated with such habitats.

153

DUSTY HOG-NOSED SNAKE
Heterodon nasicus gloydi

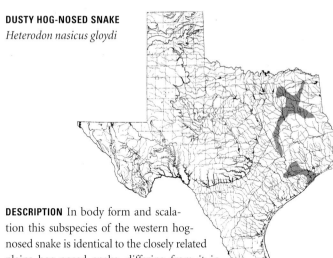

DESCRIPTION In body form and scalation this subspecies of the western hog-
nosed snake is identical to the closely related
plains hog-nosed snake, differing from it in
having fewer dorsal body blotches. It possesses fewer than 32 dark
blotches down the middle of the back in males (not counting
those on the tail) and fewer than 37 in females. In common with
the plains and Mexican subspecies, it displays a sharply upturned
snout bearing a longitudinal keel on its upper surface, prominent
black blotching on the underside of the body and tail, keeled dorsal scales in 23 rows at midbody, and a divided anal plate.

COMPARABLE SNAKES The eastern hog-nosed snake is similar to
the dusty hognose in body shape and general head configuration, but it has a less upturned snout and lacks bold, dark markings on the underside of its tail. The slightly upturned snout
of the little western hook-nosed snake, though resembling the
prominently raised rostral of a hognose, bears no longitudinal
keel on its upper surface, nor is the underside of its tail pigmented with well-defined black blotches. Moreover, the hook-nosed
snake has only 17 rows of midbody dorsal scales, none of which is
keeled. The venomous massasauga, also relatively stout-bodied,
has a narrow neck, pits between the eyes and nostrils, elliptical
eye pupils, and rattles on the end of its tail.

SIZE Mature adults generally measure 15 to 25 inches (38.1–

63.5 cm) long; maximum-size specimens reach a length of nearly 3 feet (91.4 cm).

HABITAT Like all subspecies of the western hog-nosed, this one occupies relatively dry, sandy grassland, although where streams, irrigation ditches, and other bodies of water are present, it will often be encountered near their banks. Broadly distributed in Texas, often in isolated local populations, it is nevertheless rare or absent in the Blackland and Fayette prairies, the Cross Timbers, the Edwards Plateau, and the oak-hickory-pine forests of extreme eastern Texas. In cordgrass prairies and marshlands near the Gulf, where it is also scarce, the dusty hognose is recorded along the coast as far north as Chambers County.

Adult.

MEXICAN HOG-NOSED SNAKE
Heterodon nasicus kennerlyi

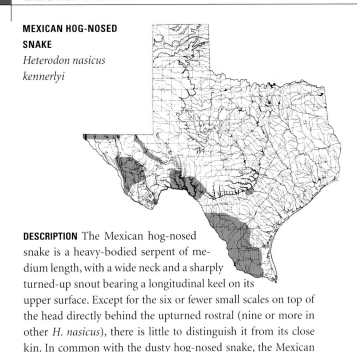

DESCRIPTION The Mexican hog-nosed snake is a heavy-bodied serpent of medium length, with a wide neck and a sharply turned-up snout bearing a longitudinal keel on its upper surface. Except for the six or fewer small scales on top of the head directly behind the upturned rostral (nine or more in other *H. nasicus*), there is little to distinguish it from its close kin. In common with the dusty hog-nosed snake, the Mexican subspecies possesses fewer than 32 dorsal blotches in males and fewer than 37 in females, counting from just behind the head to a point above the anal plate. These sometimes indistinct, cinnamon brown to dark brown markings, rounded or narrowly elongate, rest on a tan to yellowish background color.

Two alternating rows of smaller dark spots occur along each side of the body, the upper row usually more pronounced. As with all western hog-nosed snakes, the serpent's most distinctive color feature is the squarish black blotching on its bottom, especially under the tail, where the dark pigmentation is particularly bold. The dorsal scales are keeled and arranged in 23 rows at midbody. The anal plate is divided.

COMPARABLE SNAKES The eastern hog-nosed snake is the species most likely to be confused with *H. n. kennerlyi,* but it has a less sharply turned-up nose than its smaller counterpart, and the undersurface of its tail is uniformly pale, not boldly splotched with black. In both western and Mexican hook-nosed snakes, the snout, which is turned up only slightly, lacks a longitudinal keel on its upper surface. In addition, neither of these serpents displays conspicuous dark pigmentation under its tail, and each has but 17 rows of scales at midbody, none of which is keeled. The venomous massasauga, which bears some re-semblance to the Mexi-can hog-nosed snake in build and coloration, is easily distinguished from its distantly related look-alike by its slender neck, heat-sensing pits between the eyes and nostrils, elliptical eye pupils, and the rattle at the end of its tail.

Adult from Cameron County.

SIZE The average adult length of this subspecies is between 15 and 25 inches (38.1–63.5 cm).

HABITAT Although most abundant in the mesquite grassland and thorn scrub environment of the lower Rio Grande Valley, this snake also occupies the sandy and gravelly prairies of Trans-Pecos Texas. In such habitats it can be found most frequently in the vicinity of floodplains, streams, and arroyos, where the loose, well-drained soil provides a substrate suitable for burrowing.

In Cochise County, Arizona, according to Fowlie (1965), the Mexican hog-nosed snake appears for a brief time along the edges of temporary bodies of water created when summer rains drench the parched ground; it may also appear under similar circumstances in the more arid parts of its West Texas range. It exists as well in desert scrub, dry mountain canyon basins, and open woodland associated with watercourses, not to mention areas disturbed by humans. Even farmland in extremely arid country may offer the serpent an attractive habitat. This is indi-cated by Tanner (1985), who stated that a local farmer in western Chihuahua, Mexico, collected five of these snakes from a single cultivated field.

EASTERN HOG-NOSED SNAKE
Heterodon platirhinos

DESCRIPTION
Since this moderately large species comes in a range of colors, it is most easily recognized by its head and body shape. Like other hog-nosed snakes, it has a stocky build, a broad head scarcely wider than its neck, an enlarged and pointed upturned snout with a longitudinal keel on its upper surface, and keeled body scales.

The snake's overall color is commonly yellowish brown, individual specimens can be various shades of yellow, orange, red, brown, olive, gray, or black. All-red specimens, for example, are sometimes found southeast of San Antonio and in southeastern Texas, and solid brown examples occur only rarely throughout the snake's range. The usual dorsal pattern consists of rather large, dark brown or black blotches or saddles typically separated from one another by interspaces of a lighter hue. On the tail's upper surface these markings become alternating light and dark half-rings; the tail's underside is nearly always lighter in color than the belly. A transverse dark bar crosses the snake's head between the eyes before slanting downward on either side of the face to the back of the mouthline. In the absence of such a bar, the conspicuous black or dark brown nuchal blotches stand alone. Either 23 or 25 rows of · dorsal scales occur at midbody, and the anal plate is divided.

COMPARABLE SNAKES All subspecies of the western hog-nosed snake are predominantly black on the belly and underside of the tail, and they have a more sharply upturned snout. Copperheads and juvenile cottonmouths, two other serpents likely to be confused with the eastern hog-nosed snake, possess clearly defined crossbands on the body and also have facial pits and elliptical eye pupils. The western pygmy rattlesnake, whose close resemblance to an eastern hog-nosed snake has been the reason for at least two human snakebite accidents in Harris County alone, has a distinctly narrow neck, facial pits, 21 mid-dorsal scale rows, an undivided anal plate, and a tiny rattle on the end of its tail.

Typical adult color phase from Harris County.

SIZE The usual adult length is between 20 and 33 inches (50.8–83.2 cm), but the largest known specimen measured 45 1/2 inches (115.6 cm) long.

HABITAT This snake is most abundant in regions of well-drained, loose, or sandy soil for easy burrowing, where plant cover is sufficiently sparse to allow sunlight to bathe the ground. It favors relatively open deciduous forest, sparsely wooded pine forest, and woodland edge, usually near streams, ponds, and lakes. Around Beaumont and Port Arthur, according to Guidry (1953), it also inhabits moist bottomland. By following the major stream systems westward in Texas, it has managed to invade the arid grassland prairies of the state's High Plains. As would be expected, the snake is not abundant in such areas of limited marginal habitat. Nor is it common on the Edwards Plateau, where scattered populations of this species occur only in locally suitable places within this essentially dry region. The species reaches the southern limit of its distribution in the mesquite-acacia savannah of the South Texas Coastal Plain, where increasing aridity confronts the snake with an unfavorable habitat. Similar environmental conditions restrict its westward movement as well. It is one of the most common snakes found in towns with large suburban locations containing large lawns that require frequent watering. This action seems to invite toads to visit and, in turn, the eastern hog-nosed snake as a predator.

159

TEXAS NIGHT SNAKE
Hypsiglena torquata jani

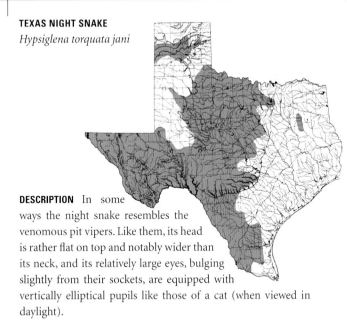

DESCRIPTION In some ways the night snake resembles the venomous pit vipers. Like them, its head is rather flat on top and notably wider than its neck, and its relatively large eyes, bulging slightly from their sockets, are equipped with vertically elliptical pupils like those of a cat (when viewed in daylight).

The most distinctive markings of this relatively small, slender serpent consist of three (sometimes only two) conspicuous, large dark blotches that extend from the back of the snake's head onto its neck. These elongated spots are sometimes irregularly shaped and occasionally joined at their common borders, in which case the snake appears to have but a single large nuchal collar. Another significant pattern element on the snake's head is the lateral dark brown or nearly black bar that runs backward and slightly downward from each eye, standing out in sharp contrast against the adjacent whitish upper lip scales. The tip of the chin and sometimes the leading edge of the throat are dark.

The body, normally gray, gray-brown, or tan in hue, carries a row of dark brown blotches down the middle of the back; a second row of alternating smaller spots lies below the first. Another series of even smaller dark spots occurs low on the sides near the belly, which is white or dull yellow and unmarked. Every Texas night snake possesses a divided anal plate and smooth body scales that are arranged in 21 rows at midbody.

COMPARABLE SNAKES A young glossy snake, though colored and blotched somewhat like a night snake, has a head scarcely wider than its neck. Moreover, the pupils of its eyes are round. Racers, which are also blotched when very young, have round pupils and 17 rows of dorsal scales at midbody. In young Baird's and Great Plains rat snakes, a distinct dark bar crosses the top of the head between the eyes, the pupils are round, and the upper rows of body scales are faintly keeled.

Dark adult from Pecos County.

SIZE Adults of this moderately small snake usually measure between 10 and 14 inches (25.4–35.6 cm) in length, although a 24-inch (61.5 cm) specimen from Brewster County is on record (Yancey 1997).

HABITAT Except for several isolated, out-of-range records for Anderson, Brazoria, Calhoun, Henderson, and Smith counties, where the surroundings are not typical for the species, this wide-ranging serpent occupies a variety of arid to semiarid environments across the western two-thirds of the state, ranging from sea level to an elevation of about 5,000 feet. Most commonly associated with rocky, dissected terrain covered with sandy or gravelly soil, it also occasionally occurs in the pine-hardwood forests of northeastern Texas. Typical natural regions in the state where it is found include the grassy, sometimes broken plains of the Panhandle and north-central Texas; the scrubby oak-juniper savannahs and hills of the Edwards Plateau; the nearly flat thornbrush country of South Texas; and the highly variable topography of the Trans-Pecos, whose rugged hillsides and fractured mountain slopes, sparsely covered with desert plants, contain areas generously littered with loose flat rocks and talus slopes—favorite habitats for this retiring reptile.

GRAY-BANDED KING SNAKE
Lampropeltis alterna

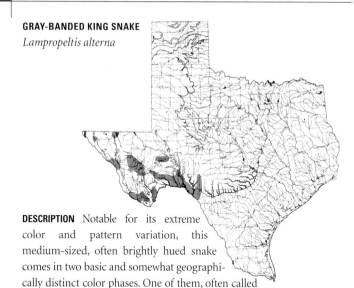

DESCRIPTION Notable for its extreme color and pattern variation, this medium-sized, often brightly hued snake comes in two basic and somewhat geographically distinct color phases. One of them, often called the *blairi* phase, occurs at the eastern end of the species' range in Terrell and Val Verde counties. Ordinarily the more colorful of the two, it is typically marked with fewer than 16 wide, reddish or orange saddles enclosed by narrow black bands, which are separated from one another by broad, dark gray saddles thinly edged in white. Individual snakes can vary greatly. In some specimens, dark pigmentation so completely overwhelms the pattern that it obscures all of the orange and gray colors, leaving only the narrow white edges of the gray bands clearly visible. Between these two extremes, a number of other pattern variations occur as well. The second basic color type, known as the *alterna* phase, is found primarily west of Terrell County. In its typical form, which generally consists of 16 moderately narrow, white-bordered, black bands on a slate gray background, it is the only color variety found at higher elevations in the Chisos, Davis, and Guadalupe mountains. In such snakes, the spaces between the primary dark markings are occasionally occupied by narrower, sometimes broken, secondary black bands. In some, the primary bands may be unusually wide and split across the back by varying amounts of red.

In summarizing the morphology of the gray-banded king snake, Miller (1979) reported that the greatest degree of color and pattern variation in this species was in a series of specimens collected in southern Brewster County along a 1 1/4-mile stretch of Texas Highway 118 that runs north to south through the Christmas Mountains. In this tightly diverse group of snakes, he found specimens fitting the descriptions of both basic color phases, others with an overall brown-orange appearance, and some with deep-red saddles but without white edging along the gray bands. Even more unusual was a single specimen whose background color was an overall gunmetal blue.

Two other areas of southern Brewster County have also been identified as harboring colonies of curiously patterned gray-banded king snakes. According to Michael Forstner (pers. com.), the most bizarre and dramatic color pattern deviations to be found within the snake's range occur at Black Gap, where he found patternless, striped, speckled, and diamond-blotched individuals in addition to specimens exhibiting near-normal features of pattern and coloration.

The snake's moderately wide head, narrow neck, and fairly large and slightly protruding eyes bear little resemblance to the

Adult *alterna* color phase from Terrell County. Photo by J. E. Werler.

cephalic features of other native species of king snakes. Its pale-colored belly is marked with irregularly shaped dark blotches that sometimes merge with one another. The dorsal scales are smooth and in 25 rows at midbody, and the anal plate is single.

COMPARABLE SNAKES The Texas coral snake has no gray in its pattern (only red, yellow, and black rings), nor does the gray-banded king snake exhibit bright yellow in its pattern. Furthermore, the coral snake's body markings completely encircle its body, whereas those of the gray-banded king snake fail to cross the snake's abdomen. In addition, the more slender coral snake has a small head, with black covering the front part and yellow crossing the back, tiny dark eyes, and a divided anal plate. Milk snakes also possess small heads and eyes, and their dorsal scales are in 21 rows at midbody. The pattern of the Texas long-nosed snake is heavily speckled with yellow, the dorsal scales are in 23 rows at midbody, and most of the scales under its tail are in a single row. Although rock rattlesnakes may resemble some specimens of the gray-banded king snake's *alterna* phase, their body scales are keeled and in 23 midbody rows, they have mostly small scales on top of the head (compared to large plates on the king snake's crown), and rattles.

SIZE Adults are usually 24 to 36 inches (61–91.4 cm) long but reach a maximum known length of 57 3/4 inches (116.7 cm).

HABITAT Long considered the rarest of Texas' serpents, the gray-banded king snake is now regarded as a relatively common, though highly elusive, dweller of the Trans-Pecos highlands. In Texas, the species' known range extends from the Hueco Mountains of El Paso and Hudspeth counties in the west, eastward to Dunbar Cave in Edwards County (about 23 miles southwest of Rocksprings), north to the slopes of Guadalupe Peak (although it is apparently absent from the Franklin Mountains of El Paso County), then south to the Chisos Mountains and the Del Rio area. Outside Texas, it is known in the United States so far only from a single documented New Mexico specimen collected recently at the southern end of Eddy County, a Guadalupe Mountains locality near the Texas border, where the elevation is about 3,800 feet (1,156 m) (Painter, Hyder, and Swinford 1992).

Most of this region lies within the northern portion of the Chihuahuan Desert, that part of southwestern Texas character-ized largely by great expanses of barren limestone hills and can-yons interspersed with flat basins, where sotol and lechuguilla grow on rock-strewn hills, and the lower elevations support the growth of desert scrub plants, primarily mesquite trees and creo-sote bush. At the eastern end of its geographic range, the reptile's habitat consists of acacia-lechuguilla plant associations.

In Val Verde County, according to Miller, the snake is most frequently encountered near the Rio Grande, Pecos, and Dev-il's rivers and their tributaries. Few specimens have been found more than 5 miles from these waterways.

A more detailed account of the species' typical habitat (except for *alterna* phase mountain populations) is provided by Michael Forstner (pers. com.), who described the snake's environment as open, fissured limestone hills with a surface accumulation of small or broken stones but without the sizable expanses of large, monolithic outcroppings and boulders usually inhabited by rock rattlesnakes. Throughout its range, it occurs at elevations of 1,200 to 7,500 feet (670–2,286 cm).

PRAIRIE KING SNAKE
*Lampropeltis calligaster
calligaster*

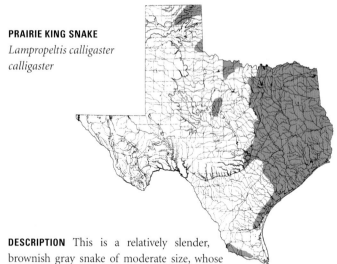

DESCRIPTION This is a relatively slender, brownish gray snake of moderate size, whose dark brown, reddish brown, or greenish dorsal blotches are usually wider than long and narrowly edged in black. As a rule, these markings are slightly concave at front and back and sometimes divided down the midline of the back to form two smaller blotches, one on either side of the spine. Flanking the primary markings on each side of the body is another row of smaller dark spots. In juveniles, the blotches not only are more reddish, but they also show greater contrast with the ground color. The ground color of older specimens may be so dark that the snake's dorsal markings are scarcely visible. In addition, such individuals may develop an indefinite pattern of four wide, dark stripes, one on either side of the spine and another low along each side of the body. Squarish dark spots mark the yellowish belly. The head pattern, when clearly defined, consists of a dark, backward-pointing V-shaped mark on the crown and a dark stripe from the eye to the end of the mouthline. The dorsal scales, in 25 to 27 rows at midbody, are smooth, and the anal plate is single.

COMPARABLE SNAKES The Great Plains rat, southwestern rat, and corn snakes, all of which closely resemble the prairie king snake, have weakly keeled scales on the back, a divided anal plate, and a prominent dark V that points forward instead of backward on top of the head. Furthermore, the underside of their tails bear two dark, lengthwise stripes or bold squarish spots. Glossy snakes have white, unmarked undertails and 29 or more rows of midbody dorsal scales.

SIZE While it is known to reach a maximum length of 54 inches (137.2 cm), the adult prairie king snake is generally 28 to 42 inches (71.1–106.7 cm) long.

HABITAT Primarily an inhabitant of open grassland, this snake prefers prairies, pastures, cultivated farmland, and coastal salt-grass savannah, although it is also found in open woodland and among rock ledges, especially those associated with clearings. Fitch (1978) found it in a variety of grassland habitats as well as in areas of open woodland and along woodland edges. He also frequently encountered it in areas that once were shortgrass prairie but, having lain fallow over time, had become overgrown with tall grass and heavy brush. Although Fitch found that certain other reptile species ultimately abandoned such densely weed-covered places, the prairie king snake continued to thrive there. He also found it in virgin tallgrass prairie and on rolling sand prairies covered chiefly with big bluestem grass.

Adult from Harris County.

SPECKLED KING SNAKE
Lampropeltis getula holbrooki

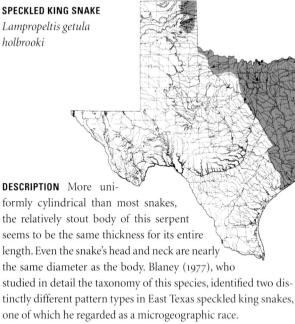

DESCRIPTION More uniformly cylindrical than most snakes, the relatively stout body of this serpent seems to be the same thickness for its entire length. Even the snake's head and neck are nearly the same diameter as the body. Blaney (1977), who studied in detail the taxonomy of this species, identified two distinctly different pattern types in East Texas speckled king snakes, one of which he regarded as a microgeographic race.

The predominant type, which ranges over most of the region from the Red River nearly to the upper Texas coast, is glossy black or dark brown with a single small, yellowish spot at the center of nearly every dorsal scale. The snake's head, like its body, is also black and covered with scattered yellow spots, and its yellow underside is checkered with large, squarish black blotches, or else each light-colored belly scale has a black margin along its posterior edge. The second type, confined to the state's coastal marshes from near Corpus Christi to the Louisiana border, is characterized by a pattern of irregular, pale-colored dorsal bands and by the expansion and intermingling of many of the remaining spots, resulting in the formation of small splotches of diverse shapes and sizes. In both types, the dark ventral markings become progressively more prevalent toward the rear of the snake's body. The dorsal spots of very young speckled king snakes coalesce at regular intervals along the back to form numerous narrow, pale dorsal crossbars with little evidence of pale spotting between them, while the sides of the body are heavily speckled. The dorsal scales are smooth and shiny and arranged in 21 rows at midbody. The anal plate is single.

Intergradation between this subspecies and the desert king snake occurs in Texas along a broad band extending from the Panhandle and the western two-thirds of the Red River southward to the mid-Texas coast. In this region, where the two subspecies meet and intermingle, speci-mens are apt to be in-termediate in pattern. **COMPARABLE SNAKES** The buttermilk racer of East Texas also has an abundance of pale-colored spots cover-ing its generally dark-hued body and tail, but its markings are scattered indiscrimi-nately over the dor-

Adult. Photo by J. E. Werler.

sum. Furthermore, instead of each pale spot being confined just to the center of a scale, as it is in the speckled king snake, each of the racer's spots covers an entire scale. In addition, the racer's ab-domen is not boldly checkered or otherwise decorated with black pigmentation, its neck is distinctly narrower than its head, and its anal plate is divided.

SIZE The usual adult length of the speckled king snake is 3 to 4 feet (91.4–121.9 cm), but this subspecies is reported to attain a maximum length of 6 feet (183 cm).

HABITAT Although it shows a strong preference for moist environments such as those near swamps, marshes, and grassy waterways, the speckled king snake occupies a wide variety of other habitats that include dry woodlands, rocky hillsides, mixed prairies, and overgrown pastures. Along the Texas Gulf Coast and on the state's offshore barrier islands it occurs commonly along the edges of saltwater marshes, where local populations frequently exceed in numbers those found in drier inland environments.

DESERT KING SNAKE
*Lampropeltis getula
splendida*

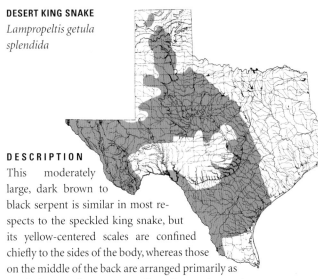

DESCRIPTION
This moderately
large, dark brown to
black serpent is similar in most respects to the speckled king snake, but
its yellow-centered scales are confined
chiefly to the sides of the body, whereas those
on the middle of the back are arranged primarily as
regularly spaced, narrow crosslines. In certain specimens, some
of the scales between the crosslines are also light centered; in
others the crosslines are absent. The abdomen of this subspecies
is mostly black, except for the pale-hued, undivided anal scale
and the yellow pigmentation irregularly distributed on the outer
edges of the belly plates. The snake's dorsal scales are glossy and
unkeeled, those at midbody arranged in 23 or 25 rows.

In Texas, this subspecies intergrades with the speckled king
snake over a wide band stretching from the Panhandle and the
western two-thirds of the Red River southward to the mid-Texas
coast. Specimens from near the middle of this zone may appear
intermediate in pattern between the two races, whereas those
from either side of the intergrade region will tend to look more
like the nearest subspecies.

COMPARABLE SNAKES Each of the speckled racer's small dorsal
spots consists of three colors—yellow, blue, and black—whereas
those of the desert king snake are solid yellow or whitish. Unlike the light-colored dots of *L. g. splendida,* which on the snake's
back are usually restricted to thin, yellow crosslines, those of the
speckled racer occupy almost every scale on the snake's body. In
addition, the racer has a conspicuous dark mask behind each eye,

only 17 rows of midbody scales (the upper row weakly keeled), a pale-colored belly, and a divided anal plate.

SIZE Most adults are between 36 and 45 inches (91.4–114.3 cm) long, although a specimen of record size measured 60 inches (152.4 cm) in length.

Adult.

HABITAT Although the desert king snake occupies a wide range of habitats throughout the semiarid and desert regions of South and West Texas, it seldom wanders far from moisture. Vermersch and Kuntz (1986) stated that in south-central Texas it favors scattered woodlands near streams, especially those in which small mammal and tortoise burrows abound, providing the snakes adequate refuge from the hot summer sun. Other habitats mentioned included savannah-woodland interface and the Blackland Prairie, where vertical, underground, drought-caused fissures also offer cool daytime retreats. In the arid Sierra Vieja Mountains of southwestern Texas, Jameson and Flury (1949) collected two specimens in the yucca-tobosa plant association of the Valentine Plain. In southeastern Arizona, Fowlie (1965) found it near streamside homes and along the margins of temporary bodies of water formed by torrential midsummer rains.

171

LOUISIANA MILK SNAKE
Lampropeltis triangulum amaura

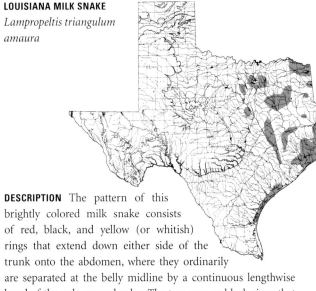

DESCRIPTION The pattern of this brightly colored milk snake consists of red, black, and yellow (or whitish) rings that extend down either side of the trunk onto the abdomen, where they ordinarily are separated at the belly midline by a continuous lengthwise band of the pale ground color. The two narrow black rings that border each wide red one usually do not continue horizontally across the bottom of the red ring to enclose it, but typically the red band extends across the belly, where a lengthwise row of irregular black spots replaces the lowest portion of dark edging. Each yellow ring continues uninterrupted across the belly. The snout is normally speckled with black and white or may even be mostly black, and the rest of the head is black except for a yellow or whitish band just forward of the neckline. The dorsal scales, all smooth, are usually arranged in 21 rows at midbody, and the anal plate is single.

COMPARABLE SNAKES The red and yellow rings of the Texas coral snake are always in contact with one another, whereas in the milk snakes the two colors are invariably separated by a black ring. Furthermore, the coral snake's black rings, which are as wide as its red ones, are much broader than those of the milk snake, and all of the coral's rings cross the belly uninterrupted. Except for small, discreet spots on the very outside edges of some belly plates, the abdomen of the northern scarlet and the Texas scarlet snake is white and unmarked. The belly of the Texas long-nosed snake also is unmarked white; the sides of its black dorsal blotches are prominently speckled with yellow, and the red interspaces are spotted with black. Moreover, it has 23 midbody rows of dorsal scales, and most of the scales under its tail are in a single row (double in milk snakes).

Assigning a particular specimen of *L. triangulum* to the correct subspecies may at times be difficult. Not only are the four Texas races generally similar to each other in color and pattern, but also wherever two subspecies converge geographically individual specimens normally carry the genes of both races, compounding the difficulty of assigning the specimen to either one. The simplest recourse in such cases is to assign the doubtful specimen to the nearest race, based on its collecting locality.

SIZE Adults usually range in length from 16 to 22 inches (40.6–55.9 cm), but a record specimen measured 31 inches (78.7 cm) long.

HABITAT Generally distributed over the eastern third of the state, this snake is most frequently encountered in the low-lying oak-cypress-tupelo forests of southeastern Texas and the pine-hardwood forests that occur in the east-central part of the state. In such regions it is most prevalent in moist, sandy situations where trees and shrubs provide adequate shade, although under less typical circumstances it has been found at a few isolated localities on the treeless, grass-covered sand dunes of the Gulf Coast barrier islands.

Adult from San Jacinto County. Photo by T. J. Hibbitts.

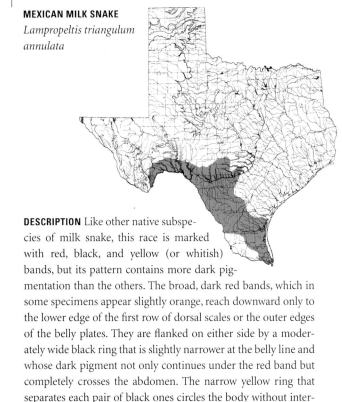

MEXICAN MILK SNAKE
Lampropeltis triangulum annulata

DESCRIPTION Like other native subspecies of milk snake, this race is marked with red, black, and yellow (or whitish) bands, but its pattern contains more dark pigmentation than the others. The broad, dark red bands, which in some specimens appear slightly orange, reach downward only to the lower edge of the first row of dorsal scales or the outer edges of the belly plates. They are flanked on either side by a moderately wide black ring that is slightly narrower at the belly line and whose dark pigment not only continues under the red band but completely crosses the abdomen. The narrow yellow ring that separates each pair of black ones circles the body without interruption. The snout is entirely black or nearly so; the top of the head as far back as the parietals (the largest paired scales on the crown) is also black, as are the sides of the head down to and including the lower lip scales. A yellow collar crosses the back of the head. The dorsal scales, all smooth, are in 21 rows at midbody, and the anal plate is single.

COMPARABLE SNAKES In the Texas coral snake, which is also patterned with red, yellow, and black, the red and yellow rings touch one another; in the milk snakes these two colors are always separated by a black ring. Moreover, all of the coral snake's bands cross the belly almost uninterrupted, and its black rings are as long as its red ones and much broader than those of the Mexican milk snake. Except for a few insignificant dark spots along the outside edges of some belly plates, the abdomen of the Texas scarlet snake is white and unmarked. The Texas long-nosed snake, in addition to its similarly immaculate white belly, has distinct yellow spots

in the lower portions of its black dorsal markings and black ones in the intervening red spaces. Furthermore, its midbody scales are in 23 rows, and the scales beneath its tail are mostly in a single row (double in milk snakes).

SIZE This is the largest subspecies of milk snake in Texas; adult specimens usually range from

Adult from Duval County. Photo by J. E. Werler.

24 to 30 inches (61–76.2 cm) long. The largest known Mexican milk snake measured 41 1/2 inches (105.4 cm) in length.

HABITAT Primarily an inhabitant of the South Texas thornbrush savannah, where caliche and sandy soils support such aridland vegetation as mesquite, catclaw, prickly pear cactus, lotebush, white thorn, blackbrush, and granjeno, this milk snake subspecies ranges north to the southern portion of the Edwards Plateau, where it occurs chiefly in the vicinity of the region's limestone creekbeds and arroyos to an elevation of about 2,350 feet. Snakes from Del Rio to the Davis Mountains all appear to be intergrades between this subspecies and the New Mexico milk snake. On the barrier islands just off the Texas Gulf Coast it can be found at sea level.

NEW MEXICO MILK SNAKE
Lampropeltis triangulum celaenops

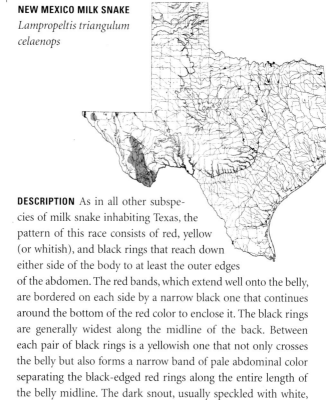

DESCRIPTION As in all other subspecies of milk snake inhabiting Texas, the
pattern of this race consists of red, yellow
(or whitish), and black rings that reach down
either side of the body to at least the outer edges
of the abdomen. The red bands, which extend well onto the belly,
are bordered on each side by a narrow black one that continues
around the bottom of the red color to enclose it. The black rings
are generally widest along the midline of the back. Between
each pair of black rings is a yellowish one that not only crosses
the belly but also forms a narrow band of pale abdominal color
separating the black-edged red rings along the entire length of
the belly midline. The dark snout, usually speckled with white,
may be nearly or entirely black in some specimens; the rest of the
head is black, except for a yellowish collar near the neckline. The
dorsal scales, all smooth, are in 21 rows at midbody, and the anal
plate is single.

COMPARABLE SNAKES The red and yellow bands of the Texas coral snake are side by side. Those of a milk snake are separated by
a black ring. Not only are the coral's red rings much longer than
those of the New Mexico milk snake, but all its colors completely
encircle the body. The black, red, and yellow colors of the Texas
long-nosed snake are not arranged in well-defined rings that encircle its body but consist of black dorsal blotches whose sides

contain numerous bold yellow spots and whose red interspaces are similarly spotted with black. Furthermore, the long-nosed snake's belly is white and unmarked, its midbody dorsal scales are in 23 rows, and the scales under its tail are mostly in a single row (double in milk snakes).

SIZE Adults are generally between 18 and 22 inches (45.7–55.9 cm) long, but the subspecies is reported to reach a maximum length of 25 inches (63.5 cm).

HABITAT This milk snake occurs in a variety of habitats ranging from 2,500 to 7,000 feet (762–2,134 m) elevation, including open woodland as well as rocky grassland. Generally avoiding the intolerably arid desert floor of West Texas, it does inhabit both the dry grasslands and the pinyon-oak zones of the desert mountains, as well as the grass–shin oak prairie of the Llano Estacado region in the western Panhandle.

Adult from West Texas.

**CENTRAL PLAINS MILK
SNAKE**
*Lampropeltis triangulum
gentilis*

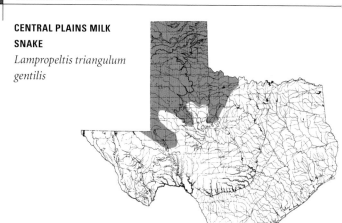

DESCRIPTION Although banded in red,
black, and yellow, like all Texas milk snake
subspecies, this race often appears more faded
than the others. Its red markings sometimes assume
an orange hue, and the yellow bands frequently take on a subdued
greenish yellow or even whitish tone. The red bands (the longest
of all measured from front to back) seldom cross the belly, for
they are normally separated there by the lengthwise expansion of
the black rings, which flank them on either side. In addition, the
black rings frequently become wider along the spine, particularly
on the rear part of the body and also along midbelly, encroaching
on the red bands in both places. The yellowish or white band that
separates each pair of black-margined red ones frequently is pep-
pered with dark pigment along its sides and may be mottled with
large black blotches at the midline of the belly. The snout ordinarily is mottled with light and dark pigment (often as far back on the
crown as the eyes), though occasionally it is mostly black. It may
also be completely white, except for a few scattered black spots.
From the eyes to the back of the parietals (the largest paired scales
on the crown) the top of the head is black, as are the sides of the
face down to and including the upper edges of the lower lip scales.
Thereafter, a pale yellow or whitish collar crosses the back of the
head. The dorsal scales are smooth and usually in 21 rows, and the
anal plate is single.

COMPARABLE SNAKES Not only do the red and yellow rings of a coral snake touch one another (these colors are separated by black in milk snakes), but all of the rings completely encircle the snake's body. Moreover, the coral's black rings are much broader than those of milk snakes. The Texas long-nosed snake can be distinguished from the milk snake by its plain white belly, prominent yellow speckling in the black blotches, and black spotting in the red interspaces. Furthermore, a close examination of the scales under the long-nosed snake's tail will reveal that most of them are arranged in a single row (double in milk snakes).

SIZE Adults attain a modest length of 16 to 24 inches (40.6–61 cm), but the largest documented specimen measured 36 inches (91.4 cm) long.

HABITAT Stone-covered grassland prairie, particularly in the vicinity of rocky ledges, is the preferred habitat of this uncommon milk snake, though it also occurs in wooded streambed valleys and along sparsely forested mountain slopes. In a long-term study of the red milk snake, a subspecies closely related to *L. t. gentilis,* Fitch and Fleet (1970) found that it preferred low, sparse ground cover to taller, more dense vegetation, a condition seemingly favored as well by the Great Plains milk snake.

Adult from Colorado. Photo by R. W. Van Devender.

NORTHERN CAT-EYED SNAKE

Leptodeira septentrionalis septentrionalis

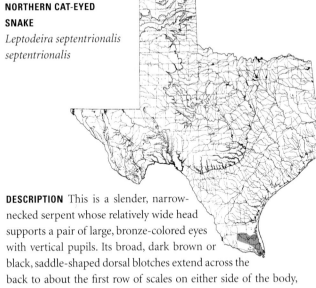

DESCRIPTION This is a slender, narrow-necked serpent whose relatively wide head supports a pair of large, bronze-colored eyes with vertical pupils. Its broad, dark brown or black, saddle-shaped dorsal blotches extend across the back to about the first row of scales on either side of the body, contrasting boldly with the snake's much lighter cream to apricot-buff ground color. These markings gradually narrow as they approach the belly, and occasionally two of them merge to form a single, large H-shaped blotch. The snake's pale orange abdomen is especially vivid on the underside of the tail, and the rear edge of each belly scale is margined with dark pigment. The head markings are variable but usually consist of a nearly horizontal dark streak on each cheek and two or more randomly shaped dark spots on the crown that often terminate in a rearward-pointing, arrowlike mark close to the neck. The smooth dorsal scales are in 21 or 23 rows at midbody, and the anal plate is divided.

COMPARABLE SNAKES The ground snake may occur in a cross-banded phase with dark brown or black markings set against a pale ground color, but its head is only a little if any wider than its neck, and its dorsal scales are in 13 or 15 midbody rows. In the southwestern rat snake the dorsal blotches reach only halfway down the sides of the body, and a lateral row of dark blotches occupies the spaces below them. The belly is patterned with some dark pigmentation. The snake's head markings consist of a bold and well-defined dark, transverse band across the forecrown and a large, forward-pointing, spearpoint mark that dominates the rest of the head. In addition, its midbody dorsal scales are in 27 or 29 rows. Like the cat-eyed snake, the Texas night snake has relatively large eyes with vertical pupils, but its dorsal blotches are small and bordered by a lateral row of smaller spots.

Adult from Cameron County.

SIZE Adults of this subspecies generally are 18 to 24 inches (45.7–61 cm) long, but the largest known specimen measured 38 $^3/_4$ inches (98.4 cm) in length.

HABITAT Essentially an inhabitant of semiarid scrub forest and tropical deciduous woodland, this subspecies of cat-eyed snake ranges northward from east-central Mexico to the southern tip of Texas, generally occupying areas of low to moderate elevation. In some parts of Mexico, where it occasionally occurs as high as 6,500 feet (1,981 m), the northern cat-eyed snake has been taken in cloud-forest clearings. In the South Texas chaparral, however, it usually keeps to thick brush near ponds, streams, and resacas where there is apt to be anuran prey. Such prime habitat is scarce in the lower Rio Grande Valley, largely because of the region's expanding urban and agricultural development. Thus, to insure the survival of this alien rarity in extreme southern Texas, it is important to preserve the region's wildlife refuges, both governmental and private. Such protected parcels of remnant subtropical forest, although scattered and few, may well be the only hope to conserve the northern cat-eyed snake and the host of other rare animal species found there with it.

EASTERN COACHWHIP
*Masticophis flagellum
flagellum*

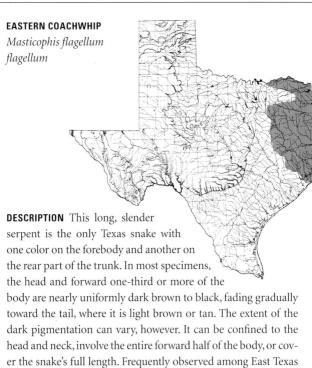

DESCRIPTION This long, slender
serpent is the only Texas snake with
one color on the forebody and another on
the rear part of the trunk. In most specimens,
the head and forward one-third or more of the
body are nearly uniformly dark brown to black, fading gradually
toward the tail, where it is light brown or tan. The extent of the
dark pigmentation can vary, however. It can be confined to the
head and neck, involve the entire forward half of the body, or cover the snake's full length. Frequently observed among East Texas
coachwhips are nearly all-black specimens with a reddish tail, as
well as those with small, widely spaced, light-colored blotches or
banding across the back. Whatever the dorsal body coloration, all
eastern coachwhips exhibit dusky scale margins on the tail, giving this part of the snake the appearance of a braided whip, which
is probably the reason for the serpent's common name. The dorsal scales, arranged in 17 rows at midbody and in 13 rows just in
front of the anal plate, are all smooth. The anal plate is divided. In
contrast to the adult, the hatchling coachwhip is an overall tan or
brown, with indistinct and somewhat jagged, narrow, dark crossbars on the back, which disappear altogether before they reach
the tail, and a double row of dark spots on the forward part of
the abdomen. In addition, the pronounced cream-colored spots
and white-margined scales on the young snake's head are scarce
or absent in the adult.

COMPARABLE SNAKES Except for the buttermilk and tan racers, which usually have some dorsal spotting, adult racers have a uniformly colored dorsum from head to tail tip, and the number of dorsal scale rows is 15 just ahead of the anal plate (13 in the coachwhip). Furthermore, the tail of racers lacks the braided look of the eastern coachwhip.

Black adult from Angelina County.

SIZE Although the largest known eastern coachwhip measured nearly 8 $1/2$ feet (259.1 cm) in length, most adults of this subspecies are between 3 $1/2$ and 5 feet (106.7–152.4 cm) long.

HABITAT It inhabits a wide variety of dry, open places, including pine flatwoods, rocky hillsides, open or broken prairie, fields, pastures, and coastal plain grasslands in the southeastern corner of the state (Jefferson, Orange, Newton, and Hardin counties); Guidry (1953) also encountered it in woodland habitats.

WESTERN COACHWHIP
Masticophis flagellum
testaceus

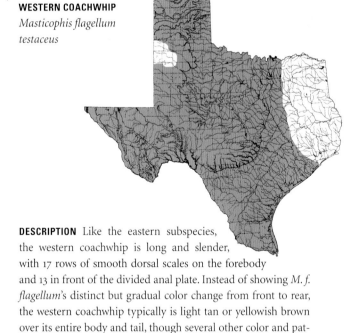

DESCRIPTION Like the eastern subspecies, the western coachwhip is long and slender, with 17 rows of smooth dorsal scales on the forebody and 13 in front of the divided anal plate. Instead of showing *M. f. flagellum*'s distinct but gradual color change from front to rear, the western coachwhip typically is light tan or yellowish brown over its entire body and tail, though several other color and pattern variations occur within the state, none of which is restricted to any particular part of the snake's range. They were defined in a study by L. D. Wilson (1970), from which we have drawn freely to prepare the following descriptions.

The most common is the narrow-banded variety, whose slender, dark dorsal crossbands, each only 1 ¹/₂ to 2 scales wide (measured front to back), occupy much of the body. About 94 percent of the specimens from throughout the serpent's range are so marked, but little more than half the individuals from Trans-Pecos Texas are of this type. About one-third of the coachwhips from this region are essentially unpatterned, particularly those with a light tan coloration. Less common are the boldly broad-banded individuals, whose distinctive markings consist of wide, dark crossbands 10 to 15 scales wide (measured front to back) that are separated from one another by a light tan space of equal width. This particular pattern type is not found in the Texas Panhandle and, in fact, is so uncommon that it never represents more than 20 percent of any regional population. Another color phase consists of the pinkish, sometimes brick red, individuals found in Presidio and Brewster counties, particularly in the deserts that circle the Chisos Mountains, as well as in Big Bend National Park and the Black Gap Wildlife Management Area. Such specimens are among the most strikingly colored of all West Texas serpents. The often black-tipped head and body scales stand out sharply against the serpent's wine red body, making it one of the most elegant serpents found in the desert. Whatever the snake's color or pattern, the tan or yellowish throat and underside of the serpent's forebody ordinarily are marked with two longitudinal rows of dark spots. The hatchling coachwhip, which displays little of the variation seen among the adults, is consistently tan to yellowish brown and marked by dark crossbars that are most prominent on the forward part of the body.

Uniformly tan adult from Bexar County.

In El Paso County, where it is extremely uncommon, the western coachwhip apparently intergrades with the lined coach-whip, a more westerly tan or gray subspecies of *M. flagellum* whose tail is salmon pink underneath. Each of its forebody dorsal scales bears a horizontal dark streak through its center.

COMPARABLE SNAKES The several subspecies of racer occurring within the Texas range of the western coachwhip have 15 dorsal scale rows just in front of the anal plate (the coachwhip has only 13), and the juveniles are boldly blotched, not finely cross-band-ed. Ruthven's whipsnake, which has 15 midbody rows of dorsal scales (17 in the coachwhip), also shows some lengthwise striping on the neck. Ruthven's whipsnake also have a pale of marks on the anterior lateral edge of each dorsal scale, which are absent in the western coachwhip.

SIZE Among the longest of Texas snakes, the adults are generally 4 to 5 1/2 feet (121.9–167.6 cm) in length, with a reported record size of 6 feet, 8 inches (203.2 cm).

HABITAT The western coachwhip is widely distributed in a variety of open, arid, or semiarid habitats throughout the western three-quarters of the state, usually where there is sandy or rocky terrain. They include the Chihuahuan Desert scrub, the gently rolling High Plains, the grass-covered North Central Plains, the rock-strewn Edwards Plateau, the western edge of the Post Oak Savannah, and the scrubby Rio Grande Plain together with its grass-covered coastal prairie.

A good example of the snake's habitat diversity is reported by Milstead, Mecham, and McClintock (1950), who captured 3 western coachwhips in cedar savannah, 15 in mesquite-creo-sote, 3 in mesquite-sumac-condalia, and 2 in live oak, all within the boundaries of Terrell County. Jameson and Flury (1949) likewise found this serpent in a range of plant associations. Of 10 specimens they collected in the Sierra Vieja Mountains of southwestern Texas, 4 came from catclaw-tobosa, 1 from creo-sote-catclaw-blackbrush, 1 from mesquite-huisache-blackbrush, and 1 from yucca-tobosa, all in the plains belt. In addition, 2 were taken in the roughland belt, one from a streambed at the bottom of a canyon and the other in the lechuguilla-beargrass plant association on top of a mesa. Axtell (1959) encountered 7 western coachwhips in the Black Gap Wildlife Management Area of Brewster County, where he found 5 specimens in the floodplain, 1 in a dry streambed, and another in low limestone gravel hills, all in terrain with little vertical relief. When all of these records are considered, it is clear that the coachwhip favors relatively flat, semiopen situations rather than steep, uneven terrain.

SCHOTT'S WHIPSNAKE
Masticophis schotti
schotti

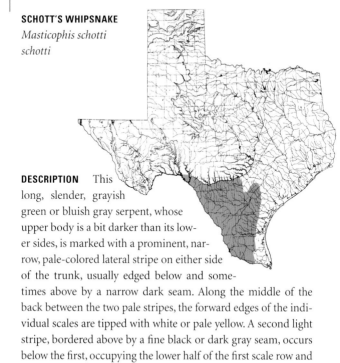

DESCRIPTION This long, slender, grayish green or bluish gray serpent, whose upper body is a bit darker than its lower sides, is marked with a prominent, narrow, pale-colored lateral stripe on either side of the trunk, usually edged below and sometimes above by a narrow dark seam. Along the middle of the back between the two pale stripes, the forward edges of the individual scales are tipped with white or pale yellow. A second light stripe, bordered above by a fine black or dark gray seam, occurs below the first, occupying the lower half of the first scale row and the outer edges of the belly plates. The abdomen, which is whitish or cream-colored behind the chin, becomes pastel blue, then pale salmon toward the rear, with bluish gray stippling at midbody. The most vivid coloring is usually under the tail, where it is most often salmon or coral pink but occasionally yellow.

The top of the head is uniformly olive or dark gray, with no white edging on the head plates. Beginning at the end of the mouthline, several rows of reddish orange scales extend backward several inches onto the neck and the edge of the abdomen. The dorsal scales, all smooth, are arranged in 15 rows at midbody, and the anal plate is divided.

The body pattern of a hatchling is different from that of the adult, primarily in lacking both the paired white or cream-colored dashes on the forward edges of the individual dorsal scales and the bright pink or coral hue under the tail. The body is also darker, being dark olive green or blackish brown instead of gray-green, and bears two white or cream-colored lateral stripes on either side of the body.

COMPARABLE SNAKES The Central Texas whipsnake is an overall darker serpent with paired, narrow, longitudinal white bars along the upper back, at least on the forebody, and a light-hued collar or two pale neck blotches at the back of its head. There are no white or cream-colored dashed margins on the forward edges of its upper body scales, and no white borders on the large plates of its crown.

Other lengthwise-striped snakes occurring within the range of Schott's whipsnake include patch-nosed as well as garter and ribbon snakes, all of which have a pale-colored spinal stripe. The patch-nosed snakes have 17 rows of dorsal scales at midbody and an enlarged nose shield, and the garter snakes' body scales are keeled, with 19 or more rows of dorsal scales at the middle of the trunk and a single anal plate.

SIZE The adults ordinarily are between 40 and 56 inches (101.6–142.2 cm) long, but a record specimen of this subspecies measured 66 inches (167.6 cm) in length.

HABITAT The geographic range of Schott's whipsnake is restricted to the Rio Grande Plain of South Texas, a region embracing the dry, rocky, and often sandy mesquite savannah and thornbrush woodland between the southern edge of the Edwards Plateau (the Balcones Escarpment) and the southernmost tip of the state. Vermersch and Kuntz (1986) noted that in south-central Texas, where it occupies a variety of aridland habitats, the snake favors those associated with streambeds and ponds.

Adult from Atascosa County.

RUTHVEN'S WHIPSNAKE
Masticophis schotti
ruthveni

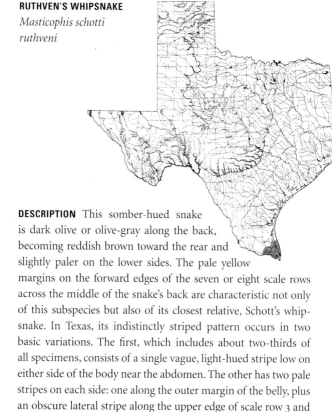

DESCRIPTION This somber-hued snake
is dark olive or olive-gray along the back,
becoming reddish brown toward the rear and
slightly paler on the lower sides. The pale yellow
margins on the forward edges of the seven or eight scale rows
across the middle of the snake's back are characteristic not only
of this subspecies but also of its closest relative, Schott's whipsnake. In Texas, its indistinctly striped pattern occurs in two
basic variations. The first, which includes about two-thirds of
all specimens, consists of a single vague, light-hued stripe low on
either side of the body near the abdomen. The other has two pale
stripes on each side: one along the outer margin of the belly, plus
an obscure lateral stripe along the upper edge of scale row 3 and
the lower edge of scale row 4. The belly is either heavily speckled
on its outer edges or only lightly so along its midline. The bright
yellow on the forebody gradually changes to pale blue-gray or
olive at midbody, then to pink toward the rear, and finally to red
under the tail.

   The crown is uniformly dark olive without white margins on
the head plates. From near the end of the mouthline on either
side of the head, a few rows of reddish orange scales extend several inches backward onto the neck and abdomen. The dorsal
scales, all smooth, are arranged in 15 rows at midbody, and the
anal plate is divided.

In color and pattern, the hatchling is probably similar to a baby Schott's whipsnake, which has two conspicuous light-hued stripes on each side of the body but lacks both the paired white or cream-colored dashes on the front edges of individual dorsal scales and the reddish undertail that characterize the adult.

COMPARABLE SNAKES The Mexican racer has dorsal scales in 17 midbody rows, none of which has pale margins on its forward edges. Neither does it have any pink or red coloration on its belly or under its tail. The rough green snake, which is completely green above and yellow on the belly, shows no sign of body striping.

SIZE The usual length of an adult is 40 to 56 inches (101.6–142.2 cm), although the record for this subspecies is 66 1/8 inches (168 cm).

HABITAT This is chiefly a Mexican subspecies that ranges northward from central Veracruz to the southern tip of Texas, where it is known to occur in Cameron, Hidalgo, Starr, Willacy, and south-central Kenedy counties. In this region of semiarid brushland, where continuing urban and agricultural development is assimilating ever more natural landscape, its specific microhabitats have not been documented.

Adult from Cameron County.

**CENTRAL TEXAS
WHIPSNAKE**
*Masticophis taeniatus
ornatus*

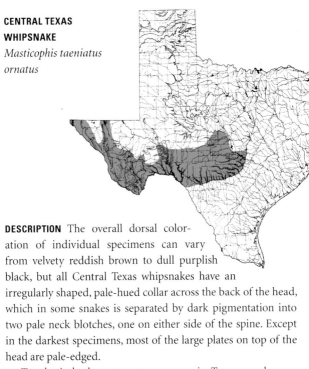

DESCRIPTION The overall dorsal coloration of individual specimens can vary
from velvety reddish brown to dull purplish
black, but all Central Texas whipsnakes have an
irregularly shaped, pale-hued collar across the back of the head,
which in some snakes is separated by dark pigmentation into
two pale neck blotches, one on either side of the spine. Except
in the darkest specimens, most of the large plates on top of the
head are pale-edged.

Two basic body pattern types occur in Texas: a paler one
encountered most frequently in the Trans-Pecos region and a
darker one that is more common on the Edwards Plateau. Both
types consist of light and dark lengthwise stripes. In the light variety, a wide alternating light and dark band runs down the middle of the back, flanked by four narrow, dark stripes that stand
out against a pale background color. In the other type, a narrow
light stripe occupies the outer edges of the belly plates and part
of the first row of dorsal scales, and each of the upper light stripes
is reduced to a series of intermittent, long, whitish bars. Actually composed of two closely adjacent light stripes separated by a
fine black seam, they ordinarily occur only on the forward one-
quarter to one-half of the snake's trunk, becoming progressively
less distinct toward the rear. Conant and Collins (1991) aptly

compared them to the successively weaker imprints made on the pavement by an automobile tire after it has crossed a freshly painted center stripe. Moderate to heavy dark splotching covers the gray belly. On the undertail, where the hue is a striking bright pink or coral red, such dark pigment is confined to the lateral edges of the scales. The dorsal scales are smooth and arranged in 15 rows at midbody, and the anal plate is divided.

Adult from Burnet County.

Except for the pale crossband on the back of the head, which is also present in the adult, the color pattern of a hatchling differs markedly from that of a full-grown specimen. The young snake's most prominent features are its bold lengthwise stripes; unlike those of a mature individual, are never interrupted along their length. Each side of its olive green body is marked by a pair of distinct white or cream-colored stripes. The first one occupies the lowest row of dorsal scales and the outer edges of the belly plates, where a diffuse dark line defines its lower margin.

The yellow to pale orange abdomen is otherwise unmarked. The other stripe, which occurs on the upper half of scale row 3 and the lower half of scale row 4, is more pronounced.

COMPARABLE SNAKES The closely related Schott's and Ruthven's whipsnakes both have paired, pale, dashed spots on the front corners of their individual dorsal scales and reddish orange scales on each side of the neck just behind the end of the mouthline. Absent, however, are the light margins on the scales of the crown, a distinguishing feature of the adult Central Texas whipsnake.

SIZE The adult length of this slender serpent is 40 to 60 inches (101.6–152.4 cm). A record specimen measured 72 inches (182.9 cm) long.

HABITAT In Texas, this snake lives in the desert-dominated Trans-Pecos region of the state, then ranges eastward across the Edwards Plateau, where the southernmost limit of its distribution is defined almost precisely by the Balcones Escarpment. Although habituated to dry environments, it ordinarily does not stray far from moisture; most specimens are found near some form of surface water such as rivers, streams, or springs. It likewise shows a clear predilection for rock-encumbered canyons, especially those containing streambeds, either dry or water-filled.

Typical Central Texas environments include cedar brakes and the oak-juniper woodlands that unevenly cover the rocky limestone hills and canyons, as well as arid, brush-covered valleys. In the Hill Country just north of San Antonio, for example, Quillan (in Wright and Wright 1957) frequently found it along rock-covered limestone ridges. It also occurs on the Llano Uplift, where some floodplains, with their jumble of large and small granite boulders, provide ideal shelter for this rather common indigenous serpent. Along the rock-strewn shores of Lake Marble Falls, for example, we encountered three specimens in one day. Farther west, in northern Terrell County, Milstead, Mecham, and McClintock (1950) observed it in a variety of habitats: the cedar savannah of mesa tops, in the cedar-ocotillo plant community characteristic of sparsely vegetated mesa slopes, dense mesquite-sumac-condalia thickets, the streamside environment of walnut and desert willow, and the persimmon–shin oak plant association of the steep rimrock, as well as the narrow strip of ground along the base of each limestone outcropping.

Throughout the Trans-Pecos region of Texas the snake occupies habitats that range from Chihuahuan Desert scrub vegetation—such as occurs in the limestone Hill Country around Amistad Reservoir at about 1,200 feet (366 m) elevation—to the higher and slightly wetter montane evergreen woodland below about 6,000 feet (1,829 m), which covers the upper reaches of the taller desert mountains. Murray (1939) described it as one of the most common snakes he encountered in the Chisos Mountains above 4,000 feet. In Brewster County, Minton (1959) found it mostly in rocky desert foothills. In the Sierra Vieja Mountains of Presidio County, Jameson and Flury (1949) encountered six of seven specimens in rocky canyon streambed microhabitats, another in a plant association of catclaw and grama grass, and one in an ocotillo–creosote bush association.

GULF SALT MARSH SNAKE
Nerodia clarki clarki

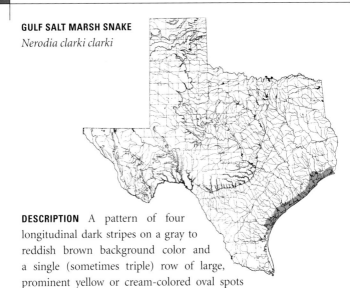

DESCRIPTION A pattern of four longitudinal dark stripes on a gray to reddish brown background color and a single (sometimes triple) row of large, prominent yellow or cream-colored oval spots down the center of the dark brown to maroon belly separate this species from all other Texas snakes. The stripes are located one on either side of the spine and one low on each side of the body near the belly, their edges often irregularly shaped. In some snakes the lateral stripes are interrupted in several places along their lengths by the lighter ground color. A dark stripe on the side of the head passes from the eye to the back of the mouthline. The body scales are keeled and in 21 or 23 middorsal rows; the anal plate is divided.

COMPARABLE SNAKES Gulf Coast and Graham's crayfish snakes have striped patterns but are less boldly marked and possess only 19 midbody scale rows. Garter and ribbon snakes, whose bodies are also longitudinally striped, lack the conspicuous pale belly spots of *N. c. clarki,* and their anal plates are single.

SIZE The largest known specimen of this species measured just 3 feet (91.4 cm) in length. Most adults are between 2 and 2 1/2 feet (61–76.2 cm) long.

HABITAT In Texas, this species is restricted almost entirely to the brackish coastal marshes stretching from the Sabine River southwestward to the vicinity of Corpus Christi Bay on the lower

Texas coast. At least along the upper Texas coast, much of this salt marsh habitat is dominated by seashore saltgrass; marshy, smooth, and Gulf cordgrass; and annual seepweed. As Pettus (1963) pointed out, the snake's striped pattern and grayish background color closely match the ground cover of these slender-bladed grasses. A bit farther inland, the snake also occurs in shallow, freshwater marshes, though they are the snake's second choice for a home. Here we find a different set of aquatic plants; the most common are arrowhead, sedge, and naiad. On nearby dry land grow yaupon bushes and such trees as sweet gum, white ash, and loblolly pine.

Adult from Brazoria County.

Before the postwar building boom of the 1950s visibly accelerated development of the coastal marshlands, *N. c. clarki* was still an abundant snake along the Texas coast. Then collectors could capture a dozen or more specimens in a single day. During one afternoon in July 1946, for example, we captured 23 Gulf salt marsh snakes on Bolivar Peninsula near Gilchrist, where they had aggregated along a series of levees constructed into the salt marshes of East Bay. Since then, alteration of the habitat by dredging, construction, and chemical pollution has seriously reduced the snake's numbers in many parts of its historical range. Nevertheless, Gulf salt marsh snakes can still be found in the vicinity of Freeport and along certain coastal areas to the southwest, though in fewer numbers than before. It is probable that in relatively undisturbed marshlands, such as those just west of the Louisiana-Texas border, the snake still exists in moderate numbers.

MISSISSIPPI GREEN WATER SNAKE
Nerodia cyclopion

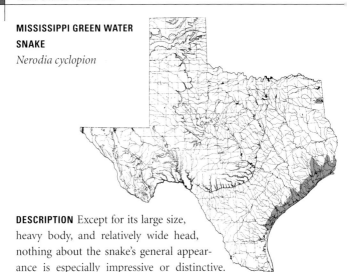

DESCRIPTION Except for its large size, heavy body, and relatively wide head, nothing about the snake's general appearance is especially impressive or distinctive. Its drab olive green to olive-brown dorsal color is marked with numerous obscure, narrow black crossbars along the back that are closely spaced and often slightly wavy in outline. Along each side of the body, a series of similar black bars alternates with the row above. The snake's most conspicuous markings are on the abdomen. Consisting of numerous yellowish, half-moons, they cover most of the belly, which is typically yellowish white on the forward third and grayish or brownish at midbody and the rear. In addition to the distinctive belly pattern, the species' most diagnostic feature is the arrangement of scales under the eyes, for no other native water snake has a row of small scales separating the orbit from the upper lip scales.

COMPARABLE SNAKES No other Texas water snake has scales between the eyes and the upper lip plates, and none exhibits a belly pattern of randomly distributed, pale half-moons. The western cottonmouth, Texas' only semiaquatic venomous serpent, has a pit on each side of its head between the eye and nostril, a vertically elliptical eye pupil; the scales under its tail are arranged mostly in a double row (single in water snakes).

SIZE The adult Mississippi green water snake is generally 30 to 40 inches (76.2–101.6 cm) long. The largest specimen for which there is a confirmed record measured 50 inches (127 cm) in length.

HABITAT Despite being one of Louisiana's most abundant water snakes, this serpent occurs only sparingly in Texas. Most Texas records represent scattered localities along the state's coastal marshes from the Sabine River south to Nueces County, yet Guidry (1953) described it as extremely plentiful in both Jefferson and Orange counties, where he found it as often in brackish water as in fresh water, and moderately abundant just to the north in Hardin and Newton counties. Dundee and Rossman (1989) stated

Adult from Brazoria County.

that in areas of prime southern Louisiana habitat it can be exceedingly common.

Occupying a variety of habitats ranging from woodland swamp to grassy coastal prairie, it prefers environments characterized by quiet waters with some shoreline vegetation. Such habitats include lakes and ponds, rivers and bayous, swamps and marshes, flooded woodland, sloughs and oxbows, as well as canals, ditches, and rice fields. In Alabama, Mount (1975) described it as a common reptile in the tupelo gum and cypress swamps of the Tensaw and Mobile river systems, the same kind of habitat it occupies in the wooded swamplands of south-central Louisiana.

Its occurrence in some brackish marshes has been reported by several zoologists. Indeed, over the years we have observed more than 20 Mississippi green water snakes in the brackish marshes along the west side of Bolivar Peninsula, some swimming with Gulf salt marsh snakes through aquatic vegetation near shore and others crawling across State Highway 87, which runs northeast to the mainland.

YELLOW-BELLIED WATER SNAKE
Nerodia erythrogaster flavigaster

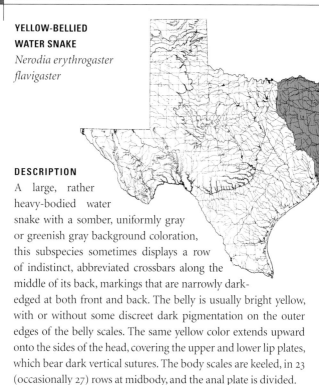

DESCRIPTION
A large, rather heavy-bodied water snake with a somber, uniformly gray or greenish gray background coloration, this subspecies sometimes displays a row of indistinct, abbreviated crossbars along the middle of its back, markings that are narrowly dark-edged at both front and back. The belly is usually bright yellow, with or without some discreet dark pigmentation on the outer edges of the belly scales. The same yellow color extends upward onto the sides of the head, covering the upper and lower lip plates, which bear dark vertical sutures. The body scales are keeled, in 23 (occasionally 27) rows at midbody, and the anal plate is divided.

The infant bears little resemblance to the adult. It is patterned with large, dark, clearly defined middorsal blotches and a lateral row of similar but smaller markings that alternate with the larger ones. Spaces between the markings typically are pinkish or reddish.

COMPARABLE SNAKES Some other adult water snakes are dark-colored with little trace of dorsal markings and may be mistaken for this one, but their prominently patterned bellies make them easily recognizable. The sometimes patternless cottonmouth, which closely resembles this harmless water snake, can be recognized by the heat-sensing facial pits, elliptical eye pupils, and the mostly single row of scales under its tail (double in water snakes).

SIZE Although a specimen 53 ¹/₈ inches (134.9 cm) long represents the record for this subspecies, the usual adult length is between 2 and 3 feet (61–91.4 cm).

HABITAT In the Atchafalaya River basin of south-central Louisiana a (a vast ecosystem involving one of the country's largest expanses of freshwater swampland), Kofron (1978) studied the habits and feeding behavior of the region's aquatic snakes. Much of the following informa-

tion is from that survey and from three similar studies: one conducted in southern Louisiana by Mushinsky and Hebrard (1977), a second by Mushinsky, Hebrard, and Walley (1980) in Ascension Parish, and the other by Diener (1957) in parts of four central and south-central states, including Texas, where the

Adult from Jasper County.

yellow-bellied water snake is abundant.

Those studies reveal that the yellowbelly prefers aquatic environments with still or slow-moving water, including the sluggish portions of streams and rivers, small isolated ponds, lakes, swamps, bayous, wet bottomland forest, and even rice fields and muddy ditches. So habituated is it to quiet waters that streams flowing faster than 50 feet per minute are normally avoided, as are clear streams with rocky bottoms. It is also partial to waterways with brush and trees growing near or at the water's edge and supporting emergent aquatic vegetation, the kind of plant growth characteristic of shorelines adjacent to still or slow-moving currents.

In the south-central Louisiana study, 16 yellow-bellied water snakes were encountered in the following places: bottomland forest (6), river (4), grasses (3), swamp bottomland forest (1), flooded bottomland forest (1), and miscellaneous habitat (1). Those collected in swamp-bayou systems of southern Louisiana were taken in an area broadly described as partly cypress swamp and partly bottomland hardwood forest, although in this study habitat niches were not specifically identified.

BLOTCHED WATER SNAKE
*Nerodia erythrogaster
transversa*

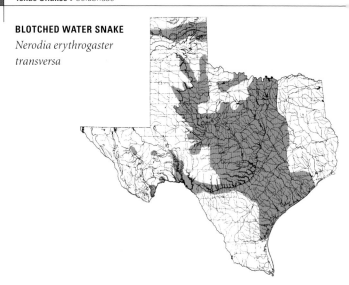

DESCRIPTION Like the yellow-bellied water snake, its nearest relative to the east, this large, heavy-bodied water snake has a dark
dorsal coloration and an unmarked belly, though it shows more
variation in its upper body color than that subspecies, ranging
from light brown to dark gray. The main difference between the
two is the loss in the full-grown yellow-bellied water snake of the
strongly blotched juvenile pattern and the continued presence of
such a pattern in mature *N. e. transversa*. The black-edged, dark
brown dorsal markings of this subspecies alternate with smaller
lateral spots of the same color, although in some older individuals
(those with an overall dark brown or olive coloration) the pattern
has all but disappeared. If there are any markings at all in such
specimens, they consist of abbreviated light-colored crossbars
along the spine, each one edged in black, both front and back.
Narrow dark spots are usually present on the outer edges of the
snake's yellow or sometimes orange belly, but no markings occur
on the underside of its pale orange or reddish tail. Although most
specimens fit the overall description portrayed above, those from
the arid western end of the snake's range ordinarily are much

lighter in hue. The body scales, 23 to 27 in a row at midbody, are keeled, and the anal plate is divided.

The juvenile is prominently blotched on the back and sides, the belly is whitish, and a pair of tiny, pale spots normally marks the top of its head.

COMPARABLE SNAKES Other adult water snakes living within the range of this subspecies, though also dark-colored and dorsally marked, possess boldly patterned bellies. The cottonmouth has elliptical pupils and heat-sensing facial cavities, and the scales under its tail are arranged mostly in a single row, features not seen in our harmless water snakes.

SIZE The usual adult length is 30 inches to nearly 4 feet (76.2–120.7 cm) although this subspecies is reported to reach an extreme length of 58 inches (147.3 cm).

HABITAT In the eastern end of its range, the snake's typical habitat is little different from that of the yellow-bellied water snake. It includes most bodies of water with slow-moving currents sup-

Adult from Bexar County.

porting a growth of emergent vegetation. There it intergrades with the yellow-bellied water snake, producing some serpents intermediate in pattern and coloration. By moving upstream along the major river systems that penetrate into far West Texas, it has managed to invade the drier, more hostile, environment of the Edwards Plateau and the Trans-Pecos region. Reliable evidence shows that it once ascended the Rio Grande drainage system at least to Calamity Creek in Brewster County, to Balmorhea in Reeves County, and to the Black River system in southeastern New Mexico, but today it is no longer found farther up the Rio Grande than the town of Boquillas in Big Bend National Park. Besides serving as convenient aquatic highways, such watercourses contain the prey the snakes must have to survive. In this inhospitable land, where stream levels can fluctuate dramatically according to seasonal periods of severe flooding and extreme drying, the blotched water snake manages to persevere, though its continued existence within some parts of its Chihuahuan Desert range is in doubt.

Even more harmful to the snake's welfare than natural calamities are the effects of human agricultural practices, specifically deep well drilling and excessive long-term pumping of underground water. The implications are obvious. We know that water from aquifers has been so grievously depleted in parts of southwestern Texas that in many places the snake's spring-fed microhabitats have been severely diminished or have disappeared altogether. Despite such losses, *N. e. transversa* continues to hang on in many areas where major sources of surface water have been eliminated. Obviously it does not need large watercourses to endure, since even under ordinary circumstances it often survives in irrigation ditches, small ponds and cattle tanks; during extended dry periods it likewise can be found in rain-filled pools and roadside ditches at a considerable distance from permanent water. It is inclined to wander farther from its aquatic haunts than any of the other races of its species—out of bare necessity, for in this parched land the watercourses on which it depends for its survival are sometimes transitory.

Curiously, the blotched water snake has not been discovered in the Rio Grande Valley south of Kingsville. The reason is not clear, although Conant (1955) speculated that the presence of eolian sand deposits and sand dunes in Kenedy County and in much of the area to the west may thwart its southward movement into the Valley.

BROAD-BANDED WATER SNAKE
Nerodia fasciata confluens

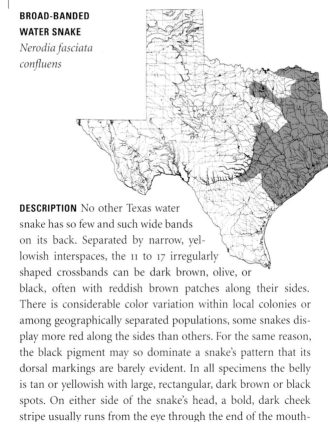

DESCRIPTION No other Texas water snake has so few and such wide bands on its back. Separated by narrow, yellowish interspaces, the 11 to 17 irregularly shaped crossbands can be dark brown, olive, or black, often with reddish brown patches along their sides. There is considerable color variation within local colonies or among geographically separated populations, some snakes display more red along the sides than others. For the same reason, the black pigment may so dominate a snake's pattern that its dorsal markings are barely evident. In all specimens the belly is tan or yellowish with large, rectangular, dark brown or black spots. On either side of the snake's head, a bold, dark cheek stripe usually runs from the eye through the end of the mouthline. The dorsal scales are keeled and arranged in 21 to 25 rows at midbody. The anal plate is divided.

The young broad-banded water snake is more vividly colored than the adult, its bright yellow interspaces standing out conspicuously between the dark crossbands, and each side of its head is covered with a pale orange hue.

COMPARABLE SNAKES Other adult unstriped water snakes inhabiting the broad-banded's range lack its prominent facial mask and its large, dark, rectangular belly spots. The cottonmouth's elliptical pupils, facial pits, more angular head profile, and single row of scales under its tail distinguish it from the broad-banded water snake.

SIZE Most adults of this subspecies measure 20 to 30 inches (60.8–76.2 cm) long; the record length is 45 inches (114.3 cm).

HABITAT This moderately large water snake prefers the quiet, shallow waters of swamps, marshes, bayous, sloughs, ponds, and lakes, whose shorelines are bordered by woodland or vegetation of some sort. It also occupies rice fields, canals, and slow-moving streams. Although it inhabits coastal prairie marshland near brackish water, it cannot live permanently in a saltwater environment, for to survive it must have access to fresh drinking water.

Young adult from Liberty County.

This was convincingly demonstrated by Pettus (1958), whose laboratory experiments showed that when the broad-banded water snake was deprived of fresh water and was forced by circumstances to drink salt water instead, it invariably died.

No comprehensive study has examined the serpent's habitat preferences in Texas, but Kofron (1978) initiated such a survey to determine the snake's preferred haunts in the floodplains of south-central Louisiana. In the vast wetlands and waterways of the Atchafalaya River delta, a region covering 2,100 square miles of mixed hardwood forest and swampland, he collected 48 specimens in the following habitats: grassy areas (16), bottomland forest (8), flooded bottomland forest (7), disturbed swamp–bottomland forest (6), river (2), freshwater marsh (2), bayou canal (2), tidal ditch (2), miscellaneous habitat (2), and flooded field (1).

FLORIDA WATER SNAKE
Nerodia fasciata
pictiventris

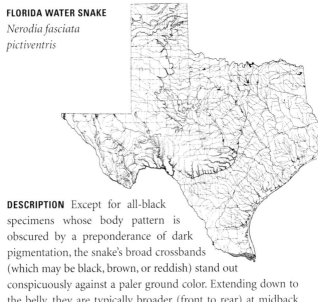

DESCRIPTION Except for all-black specimens whose body pattern is obscured by a preponderance of dark pigmentation, the snake's broad crossbands (which may be black, brown, or reddish) stand out conspicuously against a paler ground color. Extending down to the belly, they are typically broader (front to rear) at midback than along the sides and often edged with widely scattered, single, pale scales. Usually a large, dark spot occupies the pale interspace between each pair of adjacent bands. The snake's head, which is distinctly wider than its neck, generally is dark on top and lighter on the sides, where a dark stripe extends from the eye to the end of the mouthline. The vertical margins of both upper and lower lip scales are edged in black. The belly markings are distinctive, consisting of black, red, or dark brown wormlike markings that cross the yellowish abdomen along the edges of the abdominal plates. The dorsal scales are keeled and in 25 rows at midbody. The anal plate is divided.

COMPARABLE SNAKES The moderately stout-bodied Florida water snake can be mistaken for the venomous cottonmouth, but the cottonmouth does not range as far south in the state as Cameron County. The large, heavy-bodied diamond-backed water snake, a semiaquatic serpent living side by side with *N. f. pictiventris* in the Brownsville area, can be distinguished by the dark brown chainlike markings on its back, the dark half-moons on its belly, and the absence of a dark bar running backward from each eye.

SIZE Adults are generally 24 to 42 inches (61–106.7 cm) long, although the maximum size recorded for this subspecies is 62 ¹/₂ inches (158.7 cm) in length.

HABITAT The snake's natural range includes the extreme southeastern edge of Georgia and nearly all of peninsular Florida, where it inhabits a wide variety of freshwater environments, particularly those characterized by small or shallow bodies of water.

Dark adult from Florida.

Not a native Texas subspecies, it was introduced here accidentally by the South Texas animal dealer known as Snake King, whose wild-animal compound in Brownsville held a constant succession of reptiles, both local and extralimital. Among them were various species of water snakes commonly sold to circuses, sideshows, and zoos. When a severe hurricane devastated the animal compound on September 5, 1933, an untold number of Florida water snakes escaped from their flimsy cages and eventually established a breeding colony in the area. It is also believed that over the years others were intentionally released into local resacas, to be recaptured later as needed. Since then this alien subspecies has become an established part of the South Texas snake fauna.

Three factors in particular may have favored the Florida water snake's successful colonization in Texas. One, of course, is the semitropical South Texas climate; its high average annual temperature and high relative humidity are not markedly different from those in peninsular Florida. Another is the abundance of resacas in the Brownsville region, which replicate the snake's choice Florida habitats of small, shallow waterways. Finally, the snake's large number of offspring—up to 57 per litter—no doubt gave it an edge when it was first liberated into its new habitation.

BRAZOS WATER SNAKE
Nerodia harteri harteri

DESCRIPTION
This relatively small, light brown to grayish brown water snake is marked by four lengthwise rows of large, olive-brown spots, the two upper rows usually separated from each other but sometimes connected along the spine by a continuous dark median stripe. The spots of each lateral row alternate with the adjacent dorsal series, as the two upper rows frequently do with each other. The snake's greenish or yellowish abdomen, whose rear half is pink or rose-colored down the middle, is conspicuously marked with a row of dark spots near the outer edges of the belly plates. Normally the rear pair of chin shields is separated by two rows of small scales. The dorsal scales, all keeled, are arranged in 21 or 23 rows at midbody, and the anal plate is divided.

COMPARABLE SNAKES Other native water snakes have fewer than four distinct rows of large, dark spots on the back, numbering fewer than 52 in a single longitudinal row. Furthermore, the primary markings of the juvenile blotched water snake (adults are essentially one color above) are four or five times the size of the lateral spots, whereas those of the Brazos water snake in both juveniles and adults are nearly the same size as the lateral spots. The diamond-backed water snake is less likely to be mistaken for the Brazos water snake, for its dorsal pattern consists not of spots but of a chainlike network of dark markings with lateral bars reaching down the sides to the edge of the belly.

SIZE More slender than most other Texas water snakes of the genus *Nerodia,* the adults of this subspecies are usually 20 to 30 inches (50.8–76.2 cm) long. The largest known specimen measured 35 $^1/_2$ inches (90.2 cm) in length.

HABITAT Found only in a limited section of Central Texas, the Brazos water snake has evolved to fill a distinct niche, one not ordinarily exploited by the two other water snakes living in the region. That niche is typified by certain shallow, fast-flowing portions of the upper Brazos River and two of its tributaries.

Inhabiting swift, rocky streams riffles along approximately 182 miles of the upper Brazos River drainage, in addition to

Adult from Palo Pinto County.

the shorelines of Lake Granbury and the upper portion of Possum Kingdom Lake, the Brazos water snake occurs as far upstream as Paint Creek in Throckmorton County and Deadman's Creek, another tributary of the Clear Fork of the Brazos, approximately 15 $^1/_2$ miles by stream above the town of Lueders in Jones County. Downstream it ranges as far south on the Brazos as the bridge crossing at FM 1118, east of Brazos Point in Bosque County. The snake's preferred microhabitat is a shallow riffle where the water is usually no more than a foot deep. Among the underwater stone fragments, infant snakes can find a good supply of easily accessible small fish. It is further characterized by a rocky shoreline of unshaded, loose, flat stones under which the young snakes can find shelter from predators and, in cool weather, a reliable source of solar-generated heat. Finally, it must have gently sloping stream banks and be free of dense vegetation close to the water's edge. This subspecies and the Concho water snake are races of a single species, *N. harteri,* which, together with the Trans-Pecos blackheaded snake, are the only snake species endemic to the state. Few other serpent species in the United States occupy such a restricted geographic range.

CONCHO WATER SNAKE
Nerodia harteri
paucimaculata

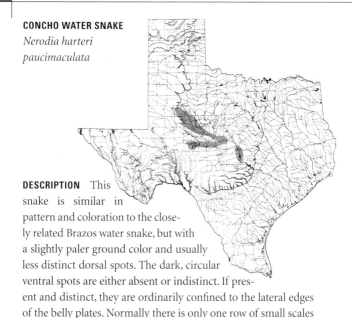

DESCRIPTION This snake is similar in pattern and coloration to the close-ly related Brazos water snake, but with a slightly paler ground color and usually less distinct dorsal spots. The dark, circular ventral spots are either absent or indistinct. If pres-ent and distinct, they are ordinarily confined to the lateral edges of the belly plates. Normally there is only one row of small scales between the rear pair of chin shields instead of two.

The snake's pale brown to grayish brown back is marked with a longitudinal row of somewhat circular dark brown spots on either side of the spine, flanked below by an alternating row of similar but slightly smaller dark spots or vertical bars. Extend-ing down the center of the abdomen is a band of pale orange or rose-colored pigment, which is most distinct on the rear portion of the body. The dorsal scales, all keeled, are arranged in 21 or 23 rows at midbody.

COMPARABLE SNAKES Two other species of *Nerodia* frequently share the Concho water snake's aquatic habitat. One is the diamond-backed water snake, whose pale brown or yellowish back is marked by a dark brown chainlike dorsal pattern; the other, the blotched water snake, has but a single row of large dark blotches down the middle of its back.

SIZE One of Texas' smallest water snakes, the adults of this rela-tively slender species usually 16 to 26 inches (40.6–66 cm) long but reach a known maximum length of nearly 42 inches (106.7 cm).

HABITAT Until recently, this snake was among the least understood of all Texas serpents. Several comprehensive field studies made over the last few years have yielded a surprising wealth of information about its distribution, habitat, and behavior, making it one of the best chronicled of all snakes. These reports, from which we have drawn freely in this account, include those by Dixon, Greene, and Mueller (1988, 1989); Dixon, Greene, and Whiting (1990); B. D. Greene (1993); Greene et al. (1994); Mueller (1990); Scott et al. (1989); Whiting (1993); and N. R.

Adult from Coleman County.

Williams (1969). The natural habitat of the Concho water snake, according to Scott and his colleagues, is confined chiefly to the numerous riffle areas scattered along approximately 238 miles of the upper Colorado and Concho river drainage systems in Central Texas. Even when the limited distribution of this subspecies is added to the equally small range of the Brazos water snake (both races of a single species, *N. harteri*), their combined geographic ranges are relatively meager. Few other snake species in the United States have such a restricted distribution. The Concho water snake is strictly confined to water and to a narrow ribbon of shoreline on either or both sides of such waterways. Its principal habitat is the riffle, a rock-filled section of streambed or riverbed 30 feet to over a mile long, where a drop in elevation, usually over a short distance, causes the water to rush over and through the layers of rocks before collecting in a shallow pool at the downstream end of the riffle.

The principal vegetation in the general area of the rivers consists of mesquite, pecan, cedar elm, western soapberry, hackberry, buttonbush, salt cedar, willow, agarita, prickly pear and slender stem cactus, spiny aster, greenbrier, poison ivy, Johnson grass, and switchgrass, but the streams themselves are relatively free of aquatic plants.

DIAMOND-BACKED WATER SNAKE
Nerodia rhombifer rhombifer

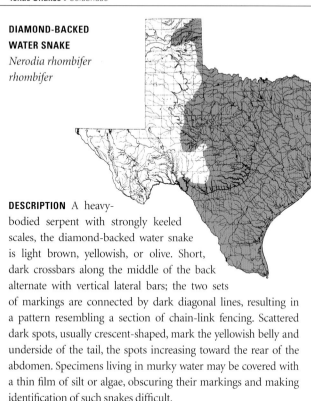

DESCRIPTION A heavy-bodied serpent with strongly keeled scales, the diamond-backed water snake is light brown, yellowish, or olive. Short, dark crossbars along the middle of the back alternate with vertical lateral bars; the two sets of markings are connected by dark diagonal lines, resulting in a pattern resembling a section of chain-link fencing. Scattered dark spots, usually crescent-shaped, mark the yellowish belly and underside of the tail, the spots increasing toward the rear of the abdomen. Specimens living in murky water may be covered with a thin film of silt or algae, obscuring their markings and making identification of such snakes difficult.

The head of an adult diamond-backed water snake is large, somewhat flattened, and distinctly wider than the neck. Its yellowish lip scales usually margined with vertical black bars. Under the chin of older males are many small, prominent tubercles, a feature that distinguishes such diamond-backed water snakes from all other Texas serpents. Although the purpose of these papillae is still unknown, they are probably related to courtship. The strongly keeled dorsal scales are in 25 to 31 rows at midbody, and the anal plate is divided. The dorsal ground color of infants is paler than that of adults and the pattern darker and more pronounced; the abdomen is generally bright yellow, often with an orange tinge.

COMPARABLE SNAKES The cottonmouth has a pit on each side of the face between the eye and nostril, elliptical pupils, and a more angular facial profile. The scales under its tail are mostly in a single row, whereas those of the diamond-backed water snake are arranged in a double row. Other Texas water snakes that may be confused with the diamond-backed water snake have little or no distinct dorsal pattern or are marked with spots, solid blotches, or crossbands; none has the distinctive chainlike markings of *N. rhombifer.*

Photo by R. A. Odum.

SIZE Although the yellow-bellied water snake may approach this species in length, large diamond-backed water snakes, because of their greater girth, are Texas' largest *Nerodia.* Mature individuals are usually 30 to 48 inches (76.2–121.9 cm) long, with a maximum known length of 68 $1/2$ inches (173.5 cm), according to Betz (1963).

HABITAT Occasionally found along fast-flowing streams and rivers, this snake prefers the calmer waters associated with swamps, marshes, bayous, lakes, ponds, stock tanks, drainage ditches, and water holes. Studying this species in Louisiana's Atchafalaya River basin, one of North America's largest swamps, Kofron (1978) encountered the snake in a wide variety of wetland niches. The 308 specimens captured during his two-year survey came from the following habitats: bayous and canals (68), tidal ditches (48), grassy locations (28), swamp–bottomland forest (26), freshwater bays (26), freshwater marshes (25), flooded fields (23), rivers (21), flooded bottomland forest (18), bay inlets (12), unflooded bottomland forest (4), and various other locations (9). In western Texas, where suitable water-snake habitat is scarce, it has made its way into the otherwise inhospitable arid terrain by following the Rio Grande upstream to the Devil's River, the westernmost outpost of its geographic range.

MIDLAND WATER SNAKE
Nerodia sipedon pleuralis

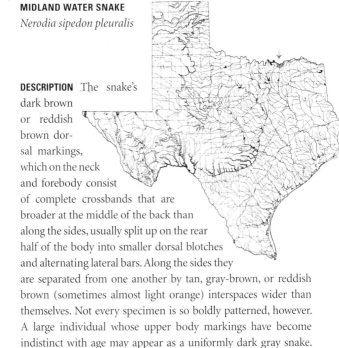

DESCRIPTION The snake's dark brown or reddish brown dorsal markings, which on the neck and forebody consist of complete crossbands that are broader at the middle of the back than along the sides, usually split up on the rear half of the body into smaller dorsal blotches and alternating lateral bars. Along the sides they are separated from one another by tan, gray-brown, or reddish brown (sometimes almost light orange) interspaces wider than themselves. Not every specimen is so boldly patterned, however. A large individual whose upper body markings have become indistinct with age may appear as a uniformly dark gray snake. Especially distinctive is the pattern of red or reddish brown half-moons that extend longitudinally along the serpent's abdomen in two somewhat uneven, parallel rows. Irregular dark spotting is usually also present on the outer edges of the belly plates.

The snake's head, which is relatively large and distinct from the neck, is brown on top and essentially unmarked except for dark sutures along the lateral edges of the upper and lower lip scales, which are paler than the crown. Ordinarily there is no dark line from the eye to the back of the mouthline. The dorsal scales are keeled and usually in 23 rows at midbody. The anal plate is divided.

COMPARABLE SNAKES The dorsal crossbands of the blotched water snake are neither clearly defined nor do the bands on the forebody extend down either side of the trunk to the edge of the abdomen. Its obscure abdominal spots are not half-moons and they are confined to the outer edges of the belly plates. Unlike the midland water snake's wide, crossbands, the dark brown dorsal pattern of the diamond-backed water snake resembles the interwoven strands of chain-link fencing, and the small, blackish half-moons on its abdomen are not arranged in a double, longitudinal row but are randomly scattered down the belly, mostly along the sides. The western cottonmouth also shows some resemblance to the midland water snake, but it is stouter, its head is chunkier and more angular, its pupils are vertical, and it has a pit on either side of the head between the eye and nostril. Furthermore, the bold black-and-white (or yellowish) mottling on its abdomen is unlike the half-moon belly pattern of the midland water snake.

Adult from Missouri. Photo by Suzanne L. Collins, The Center for North American Herpetology.

SIZE Adults are generally 22 to 40 inches (55.9–101.6 cm) long. The largest known specimen measured 59 inches (149.9 cm) in length.

HABITAT We include this snake in our list of Texas serpents based on two specimens in the Carnegie Museum collected in Grayson County 5 miles north of Sherman. They may, however, actually represent an intergrade population between northern and midland water snakes (Conant and Collins 1991). Over most of its geographic range, the snake seems to prefer clear, slow-moving streams with sand, gravel, or rock bottoms, but it also lives in a wide variety of other aquatic environments including rivers, lakes, ponds, swamps, and marshes. It is less attracted to mud-bottomed watercourses with poorly defined shorelines (where broad-banded, yellow-bellied, and diamond-backed water snakes are more at home), and it usually avoids swift-flowing rivers and streams. Yet even ditches, if they are wet for most of the year, can support small numbers of midland water snakes.

ROUGH GREEN SNAKE
Opheodrys aestivus

DESCRIPTION Like a number of other arboreal serpents, the rough green snake has
a long, emerald-hued, pencil-thin body and
an elongated, gradually tapering tail of the same col-
or. This unpatterned dorsal tone extends down either side of the
body nearly to the abdomen, where it fades to yellow or yellowish green, the same pale color that marks the snake's immaculate
belly, throat, and lips. Correctly identifying a dead specimen is
another matter, for soon after it dies, the reptile's normal coloration turns to deep blue. Its dorsal scales are keeled and arranged
in 17 rows at midbody. The anal plate is divided.

COMPARABLE SNAKES The only native serpent species likely to
be confused with the rough green snake is the smaller and extremely rare (in Texas) smooth green snake, whose dorsal scales,
arranged in only 15 rows at midbody, lack keels.

SIZE Although adults are generally 22 to 32 inches (55.9–81.3 cm)
long, a specimen of record size measured 45 5/8 inches (115.9 cm)
in length.

HABITAT The rough green snake is probably the most arboreal of
all Texas serpents. Sometimes encountered in partially wooded
meadows, pastures, and even suburban gardens, this typically
brush- and tree-dwelling creature is found most frequently along
the edges of deciduous or evergreen woodland adjoining a lake,
pond, stream, marsh, swamp, or other open terrain. For example,

in central and eastern Oklahoma, Goldsmith (1984) found that among 98 sightings of this species, 84 were associated with a watercourse of some kind: 38 near lakeshores, 22 near creeks or dry creekbeds, 17 in upland ravines, and 7 along rivers. Of the rest, 10 were encountered on upland roads and 4 in wooded areas of somewhat higher elevation away from water.

Adult from Calhoun County. Photo by David Johnson.

At the western edge of its Texas range, the rough green snake has made its way into the easternmost parts of the arid Trans-Pecos region and the barren southern plains— both formidable barriers to the serpent's continued westward expansion—by clinging to the moist corridors of wooded gulches and canyons that transect these areas. Such vegetated corridors, according to Bailey (1905), occur near Kerrville and at Rocksprings, where the rough green snake is found in brush-covered gulches lined with stands of pecan, sycamore, elm, cherry, and oak. Nowhere does the snake appear to be attracted to any particular tree species, though it favors those with limbs growing more nearly horizontal than vertical, like willow and ironwood; apparently their boughs provide a more convenient perching angle than many of the others.

Even city parkland devoid of trees will support populations of this adaptable little serpent, as long as the area is not too dry and provided it contains plenty of leafy brush in which the snake can hide and forage. Similarly, Webb (1970) found that in the grasslands of Oklahoma, where trees are scarce or absent, it attains moderate perching heights by climbing into bushes. In such habitat he also discovered it hiding in animal burrows, with only its head protruding from the tunnel openings.

SMOOTH GREEN SNAKE
Opheodrys vernalis
blanchardi

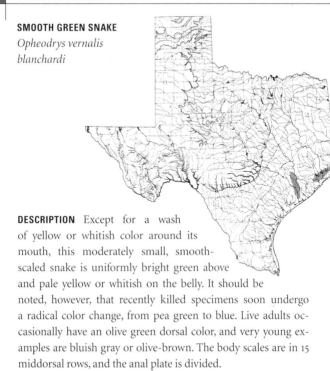

DESCRIPTION Except for a wash of yellow or whitish color around its mouth, this moderately small, smooth-scaled snake is uniformly bright green above and pale yellow or whitish on the belly. It should be noted, however, that recently killed specimens soon undergo a radical color change, from pea green to blue. Live adults occasionally have an olive green dorsal color, and very young examples are bluish gray or olive-brown. The body scales are in 15 middorsal rows, and the anal plate is divided.

COMPARABLE SNAKES The only Texas serpent closely resembling this remarkably distinct species is the rough green snake. It shares with its smaller cousin a similar, though slightly darker, shade of green on the back and sides and a whitish, yellow, or sometimes pale green underside—a hue that in both snakes extends as far up onto the snake's head as the upper lips. Its dorsal scales are prominently keeled and in 17 instead of 15 rows at midbody. Though most adult Mexican and eastern yellow-bellied racers are completely dark green or dull brown above, they are longer than green snakes and more heavy-bodied. Juvenile racers, though similar in size to young green snakes, are easily distinguished from them by their boldly blotched patterns.

SIZE Throughout its range, 14 to 20 inches (35.6–50.8 cm) is the usual adult length of this snake, although it is reported to reach a maximum length of 26 inches (66 cm). The largest Texas specimen found so far measured just over 15 inches (38.1 cm) long.

HABITAT In Texas this snake occurs as a relict population along the Gulf Coast. The few specimens discovered there, almost 500 miles from the nearest populations to the north and northwest,

have been found near sea level in habitats described as open shortgrass prairie or meadow. Known from fewer than 10 specimens, collected in Austin, Chambers, Harris, and Matagorda counties, it is one of our rarest serpents. Davis (1953) suggested that by moving along prairie corridors, such as those represented by

Adult from Arkansas.

the north-to-south-trending Blackland Prairie of Central Texas, this snake long ago made its way southward from the mainstream midwestern populations to the Texas Gulf Coast.

Elsewhere it is essentially a cool-climate, upland snake that sometimes ranges to elevations of more than 9,000 feet (2,743 m). It has also been reported from open country bordering forest edge and from pine barren clearings, especially those in which grass fills the spaces between the scattered rocks and boulders. In Indiana, Minton (1972) found it most often in both moist, sandy places and on muck prairie, though in more unusual circumstances he discovered two examples in dry, sandy oak woods. Even more out of the ordinary is its occurrence in relatively dry vacant lots on the outskirts of Chicago, Illinois, where Seibert (1950) found it in surprisingly large numbers; an estimated 185 snakes per hectare were taken in such urban habitats in the late 1940s. In nearby Missouri, however, this ordinarily abundant species is in danger of being exterminated. There, severe habitat destruction and the lavish use of agricultural pesticides have caused such a dramatic decline in its numbers that it is now regarded as one of that state's endangered reptiles.

SONORAN GOPHER SNAKE
Pituophis catenifer affinis

DESCRIPTION

This large yellow to cream-colored serpent closely resembles the bull snake, but the dorsal blotches on and near its tail are conspicuously darker than those on the forebody. The farther back on the trunk they are, the darker they become; on the tail they are nearly black. Below and alternating with the dorsal markings is a row of smaller dark spots, with yet another, even smaller series below them. In the pale areas between blotches, each scale may display a dark streak along its keel. The head markings, which consist of a dark bar across the head just forward of the eyes and another on each side of the head from the eye to the back of the mouthline, are like those of the bull snake, though ordinarily not as well defined. Black spots usually mark the snake's white or yellowish belly, particularly along the outer edges.

A distinctive feature of this and other Texas *Pituophis* is the usual presence on the forehead of four prefrontal scales instead of the two found in other native colubrid species. Typically arranged in 31 or 33 rows at midbody, the Sonoran gopher snake's dorsal scales, are strongly keeled, except for those on the lower rows. The anal plate is single.

COMPARABLE SNAKES The rostral plate of the bull snake is about twice as high as it is wide, standing out in bold relief above the adjacent scales; the same scale in the Sonoran gopher snake is barely higher than wide and not raised above its neighbors. (See the bull snake account.)

SIZE This subspecies is reported to reach a maximum length of 7 feet, 8 inches (233.7 cm), although the usual adult is from 4 $\frac{1}{2}$ to 5 $\frac{1}{2}$ feet (137.2–167.6 cm) long.

HABITAT The bull snake has managed to adapt to some extremely dry conditions at the lower end of its U.S. range, but it is the Sonoran gopher snake that often occupies the Southwest's most inhospitable desert habitats. Despite their tendency to inhabit dry environments, gopher snakes will nearly always choose irrigated farmlands over the adjacent deserts, no doubt attracted by the abundance of crop-eating rodents found there. Otherwise, gopher snakes are remarkably adaptable, occurring in nearly every type of major habitat encountered across the Southwest. In a census made by Klauber (1939) in southern California, for example, this subspecies was found in these diverse environments: cultivated fields (104 specimens), brushy desert (54), grass (42), rocky desert (17), orchards or vineyards (7), sandy desert (6), and barren desert (4). In the vicinity of Alamogordo, New Mexico, it was encountered in a variety of habitats including the mesquite plains association, the creosote association of the alluvial slopes, and the high pine-spruce forests at elevations exceeding 8,000 feet (2,438 m). In Texas it is generally restricted to the desert benches and sand dunes along the east side of the Rio Grande near El Paso, where the vegetation is primarily mesquite, creosote bush, and desert grasses.

Adult from Luna County, New Mexico. Photo by J. E. Werler.

BULL SNAKE
Pituophis catenifer sayi

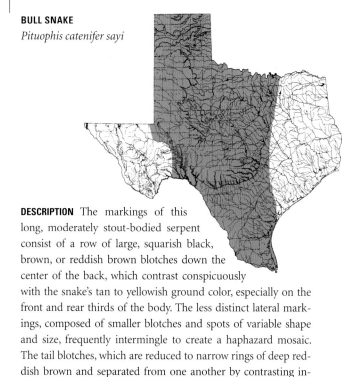

DESCRIPTION The markings of this long, moderately stout-bodied serpent consist of a row of large, squarish black, brown, or reddish brown blotches down the center of the back, which contrast conspicuously with the snake's tan to yellowish ground color, especially on the front and rear thirds of the body. The less distinct lateral markings, composed of smaller blotches and spots of variable shape and size, frequently intermingle to create a haphazard mosaic. The tail blotches, which are reduced to narrow rings of deep reddish brown and separated from one another by contrasting interspaces of tan or yellow, are the most prominent. Dark spots randomly mark the yellow belly, mostly along its outer edges. The snake's relatively small head is somewhat pointed at the snout, often lightly speckled with black above, and may have a dark-bordered pale band across the crown just ahead of the eyes. A dark band usually extends from each eye to the end of the mouthline.

Texas snakes of the genus *Pituophis* possess four prefrontal scales instead of the usual two, and the large scale on the end of the nose is vertically longer than in most other snakes. The dorsal scales, usually in 33 rows at midbody but ranging from 28 to 37, are strongly keeled, except for those in the first several rows on either side of the belly. The anal plate is single.

COMPARABLE SNAKES Only in the genus *Pituophis* do we normally find four prefrontal scales on the forehead; all other Texas snakes ordinarily have but two. In the adult Texas rat snake the top of the head is uniformly dark, and that of the Great Plains and southwestern rat snakes bears a forward-directed spearpoint marking. In addition, all of these look-alikes have a divided anal plate.

Despite certain physical features that characterize the western diamond-backed rattlesnake (a heavy body and the presence of rattles on the end of its tail), the bull snake is often mistaken for that venomous pit viper. Each snake in its own way is able to produce a loud, menacing sound, the rattler by vibrating its noise-making caudal appendage and the bull snake by expelling air forcefully past a modified epiglottis in the bottom of its mouth.

Adult from Atascosa County.

Probably the best way to recognize a diamond-backed rattlesnake (in addition to its characteristic rattle) is to look for a boldly black-and-white-banded tail, the hallmark of this species. The bull snake, on the other hand, has a long, pointed, yellowish tail bearing reddish brown, ringlike blotches.

SIZE This is one of Texas' longest snakes, reaching a maximum known length of nearly 9 feet (274 cm). Average size adults are usually between 4 and 5 feet (121.9–152.4 cm) long.

HABITAT This wide-ranging serpent typically inhabits sandy plains and prairies but is also abundant in other kinds of dry, open spaces, including the rocky, tree-studded country that dominates the Edwards Plateau, the gently rolling thorn scrub of the Rio Grande Plain, and the rocky hills and canyons of the Trans-Pecos, at both high and low elevations. In the Guadalupe Mountains, where some bull snakes live at exceptionally high elevations, a large specimen was captured in pine forest at an elevation of 9,000 feet (2,752 m) near the eastern rim of the plateau. Throughout its range, this serpent is decidedly partial to cultivated fields, where it finds an abundance of small mammals, its most important prey.

LOUISIANA PINE SNAKE
Pituophis ruthveni

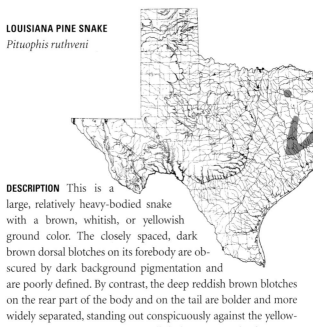

DESCRIPTION This is a large, relatively heavy-bodied snake with a brown, whitish, or yellowish ground color. The closely spaced, dark brown dorsal blotches on its forebody are obscured by dark background pigmentation and are poorly defined. By contrast, the deep reddish brown blotches on the rear part of the body and on the tail are bolder and more widely separated, standing out conspicuously against the yellowish ground color. Numerous small dark spots or splotches cover the crown. Marking the snake's belly are small, irregularly placed black splotches. And like all Texas snakes of the genus *Pituophis,* the Louisiana pine snake normally has four prefrontal scales on the forecrown. The dorsal scales are keeled and arranged in 27 to 33 rows at midbody. The anal plate is single.

COMPARABLE SNAKES The Texas rat snake, the only other large, blotched East Texas serpent, has a uniformly dark crown and a divided anal plate. The prairie king snake, which is covered with smooth scales, has a bold, dark longitudinal stripe behind each eye. In none of these look-alikes are there more than two prefrontal scales on the forecrown.

SIZE Adults of this subspecies ordinarily are 4 to 5 feet (121.9–152.4 cm) long, but a specimen of maximum length measured 70 ½ inches (179.1 cm) long.

HABITAT A forest-dwelling *Pituophis,* the Louisiana pine snake is restricted largely to open longleaf pine–oak sandhills interspersed with moist bottomlands. It is sometimes also encountered in adjacent blackjack oak woodlands and in sandy areas of shortleaf pine–post oak forest. Even before destruction of the serpent's prime habitat began in earnest during the 1920s, logging operations had already severely reduced significant portions of the original forests. What was happening in Louisiana was also occurring in Texas, where many areas of the native indigenous forest were being clear-cut and replaced with tree farms. Wherever such slash pine mono-culture is substituted for the original longleaf pine forest, the newly created environment is unsuitable pine snake habitat, in spite of its natural woodland appearance.

Adult from Angelina County.

Additional reasons for the pine snake's decline include the frequent torching of grasslands within the snake's habitat and the expanding human population, with its attendant increase in snake-killing episodes, especially those directed at large, conspicuous species such as this one. There is no doubt that the ever expanding vehicular traffic moving over more and more new highways and rural roads in East Texas is responsible as well for a reduction in pine snake numbers. Some alteration of the land, if it is not too severe, may actually improve the serpent's habitat. We know, for example, that the Louisiana pine snake prefers disturbed woodland over dense forest, for specimens have frequently been discovered in fields, farmland, and tracts of second-growth timber. Little else is known about its ecology.

The closely related northern pine snake, *P. melanoleucus,* whose ecology and behavior have been carefully studied by several herpetologists in the northernmost part of its geographic range, also exhibits a distinct preference for open woodlands. Although only 20 percent of the southern New Jersey study region examined by Zappalorti and Burger (1985) represented open, human-disturbed areas within the pine and pine-oak forests, a remarkable 88 percent of the Pine Barrens specimens were found there.

GRAHAM'S CRAYFISH SNAKE
Regina grahami

DESCRIPTION Featuring a relatively small head that is but little wider than its neck, this small to medium-sized snake is olive, dark brown, or yellowish brown above. The most prominent features of coloration are the broad cream or yellowish stripes, one on either side of the body near the abdomen. Occupying the three lowest rows of dorsal scales, each is margined below by a narrow, zigzag pinstripe where it and the outer edges of the belly scales meet and often by a threadlike upper margin as well. Sometimes also present along the midline of the back is a pale, often indistinct, dark-edged band. On the snake's cream or yellow abdomen may be a median row of very small black spots or, less often, none at all. When present, such spots sometimes unite to form a narrow, discontinuous, dark line. The top and sides of the head are the same dark hue as the upper body; the upper and lower lip scales and throat are the same color as the rest of the belly. The dorsal scales are keeled and in 19 rows at midbody; the anal plate is divided.

COMPARABLE SNAKES The Gulf crayfish snake has glossy instead of dull scales; a broad, light-colored band on each side of the body involving the first, or at most only the first and second, rows of dorsal scales above the belly; and a double row of large, dark, half-moon abdominal spots. The Gulf salt marsh snake, the only striped water snake of the genus *Nerodia* in Texas, is boldly patterned with a dark gray stripe on either side of the spine and another low on each side of the body. Furthermore, its dark-hued abdomen displays a central row of large, pale, oval spots that may be flanked by two rows of darker ones, the lip scales are dark-edged, and the body scales are in more than 19 rows at midbody. Garter, ribbon, and lined snakes are also longitudinally striped, but they have a distinct, narrow, median light stripe, no row of dark spots down the middle of the abdomen, and a single anal plate.

Pale adult from Liberty County on crayfish chimney.

SIZE Adults are usually between 18 and 28 inches (45.7–71 cm) long, but the species has a maximum known length of 47 inches (119.4 cm).

HABITAT Although generally distributed over much of Central and East Texas, this serpent occurs primarily in isolated colonies throughout its geographic range. It favors still or slow-moving bodies of water such as ponds, sluggish streams, lakes, wet meadows, prairie marshes, swamps, and the still backwaters of floodplains, especially those with muddy bottoms and abundant aquatic shoreline vegetation where embankments support sizable crayfish colonies. Exceptions are the Graham's crayfish snakes found by R. F. Clark (1949) in northern Louisiana in and near small, fast-moving streams.

Often prospering in the face of expanding human development, this adaptable serpent inhabits not only rice fields and freshwater canals but in the midst of large human populations also maintains its numbers by keeping to the natural shelter of sprawling urban parklands. One such concentration of crayfish snakes thrives to this day in Missouri's Forest Park, even though the park is encircled by extensive urban development. Another endures in San Antonio's Brackenridge Park, where the snake can still be found along that section of the San Antonio River and in one or two of the park's isolated ponds. Perhaps one reason the reptile so successfully avoids the throngs of visitors who constantly use its parkland habitat is the snake's secretive behavior.

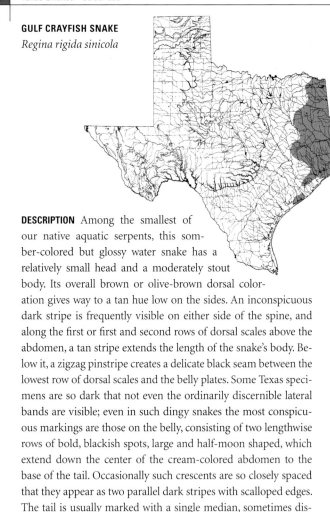

GULF CRAYFISH SNAKE
Regina rigida sinicola

DESCRIPTION Among the smallest of our native aquatic serpents, this somber-colored but glossy water snake has a relatively small head and a moderately stout body. Its overall brown or olive-brown dorsal coloration gives way to a tan hue low on the sides. An inconspicuous dark stripe is frequently visible on either side of the spine, and along the first or first and second rows of dorsal scales above the abdomen, a tan stripe extends the length of the snake's body. Below it, a zigzag pinstripe creates a delicate black seam between the lowest row of dorsal scales and the belly plates. Some Texas specimens are so dark that not even the ordinarily discernible lateral bands are visible; even in such dingy snakes the most conspicuous markings are those on the belly, consisting of two lengthwise rows of bold, blackish spots, large and half-moon shaped, which extend down the center of the cream-colored abdomen to the base of the tail. Occasionally such crescents are so closely spaced that they appear as two parallel dark stripes with scalloped edges. The tail is usually marked with a single median, sometimes discontinuous, narrow dark stripe. The top and sides of the head are the same dark tone as the body, but the upper and lower lip scales are yellowish and unmarked. The dorsal scales, of which all but the lowest rows are keeled, occur in 19 rows at midbody, and the anal plate is divided.

COMPARABLE SNAKES This species and Graham's crayfish snake look much alike. They are approximately the same size, with small

heads and a brownish dorsal coloration. Although both exhibit a
pale-colored stripe on either side of the body near the belly, that of
Graham's crayfish snake involves the first three scale rows above
the abdomen, whereas in the Gulf crayfish snake it covers only the
first or first and second
rows. The most conspicu-
ous difference between
them is in their belly
markings. In Graham's
crayfish snake the abdo-
men is either unspotted
or (most often) patterned
with a single median row
of small black spots. The
Gulf crayfish snake's
belly is marked with two
parallel rows of large

Adult from Harris County. Photo by J. E. Werler.

dark spots, usually half-moons, which extend down the length
of the abdomen. In the lengthwise-striped Gulf salt marsh snake,
a single median row of large, pale oval spots, often sandwiched
between two rows of darker ones, marks the length of the snake's
dark brown or reddish brown belly, and the dorsal scales are in
more than 19 rows at midbody. Garter, ribbon, and lined snakes,
although also longitudinally striped, have a distinct narrow pale
stripe along the spine, and their anal plate is single.

SIZE Adults of this subspecies are usually under 2 feet (61 cm) long.
The largest recorded specimen measured 31 ³/₈ inches (79.7 cm)
in length.

HABITAT One of Texas' most elusive and little-known serpents,
this highly aquatic reptile generally inhabits the margins of
swamps, marshes. Sometimes it even occupies canals, ditches,
and rice fields. In a departure from its usual preference for low-
lying habitats, specimens collected by R. F. Clark (1949) in north-
central Louisiana were found in small streams in upland sandjack
oak woodland. Kofron (1978), on the other hand, encountered it
in the following central Louisiana habitats: five in grasses, one in
a bayou canal, one in bottomland forest, and one in a miscellaneous unidentified habitat.

TEXAS LONG-NOSED SNAKE
Rhinocheilus lecontei
tessellatus

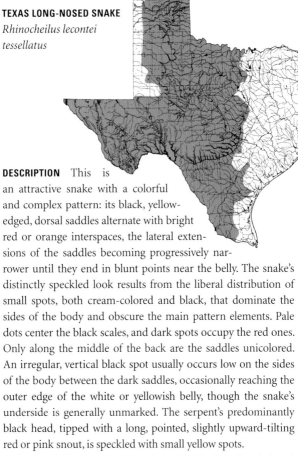

DESCRIPTION This is
an attractive snake with a colorful
and complex pattern: its black, yellow-
edged, dorsal saddles alternate with bright
red or orange interspaces, the lateral extensions of the saddles becoming progressively narrower until they end in blunt points near the belly. The snake's
distinctly speckled look results from the liberal distribution of
small spots, both cream-colored and black, that dominate the
sides of the body and obscure the main pattern elements. Pale
dots center the black scales, and dark spots occupy the red ones.
Only along the middle of the back are the saddles unicolored.
An irregular, vertical black spot usually occurs low on the sides
of the body between the dark saddles, occasionally reaching the
outer edge of the white or yellowish belly, though the snake's
underside is generally unmarked. The serpent's predominantly
black head, tipped with a long, pointed, slightly upward-tilting
red or pink snout, is speckled with small yellow spots.

In South Texas specimens both the black and red dorsal
markings generally take the form of squarish blotches that fail to
reach the heavily black-spotted, yellow lower sides of the body.

The smooth dorsal scales are arranged in 23 rows at midbody,
and the anal plate is single. Among Texas nonvenomous snakes,
this is the only species with most of its undertail scales in a single
row.

COMPARABLE SNAKES The coral snake can be distinguished from
the long-nosed snake by the extension of the well-defined dorsal

pattern across the belly, the solid black nose, the 15 rows of dorsal scales, and the divided anal plate. The Texas scarlet snake's red, black-edged saddles are essentially devoid of yellow speckling, as are the black rings of milk snakes. Finally, in none of these mimics are the scales on the underside of the tail mostly in a single row.

SIZE Although the snake's maximum known length is 41 inches (104.1 cm), the usual adult size is between 20 and 30 inches (50.8–76.2 cm) long.

HABITAT Found over the entire western two-thirds of Texas, this subspecies occupies a variety of dry

Adult. Photo by J. E. Werler.

habitats with sandy to gravelly soils in prairie grassland, thornbrush, or desert. It also occurs on rocky slopes at low to moderate elevations. Specific habitat descriptions include those of Fouquette and Lindsay (1955), who collected it from the area of deep sands in Hutchinson County (the northern Panhandle), in both the floodplain and rocky slopes, and above the rimrock in Dawson County (the southern Panhandle), where the dominant flora were mesquite, grama, and buffalo grass, plus some other small woody plant species. In Bexar and adjacent counties, Vermersch and Kuntz (1986) remarked that it generally occupies areas dominated by mesquite, acacia, prickly pear cactus, and low thornbrush. In an early survey of Stockton Plateau amphibians and reptiles, Milstead, Mecham, and McClintock (1950) described the snake's Terrell County habitat as the mesquite-creosote association. Jameson and Flury (1949) encountered it in southwestern Texas in the catclaw-grama and catclaw-tobosa associations within the Sierra Vieja Mountains of northwestern Presidio County.

Only occasionally is the long-nosed snake found in barren desert. Aside from its burrowing ability, it apparently is poorly equipped to survive in a harsh desert environment unless the land has first been made permeable by irrigation farming.

233

BIG BEND PATCH-NOSED SNAKE
Salvadora deserticola

DESCRIPTION

The most distinctive feature of a patch-nosed snake is its enlarged, laterally flared nose plate; its edges stand free from the adjacent scales, giving it a patchwork look, as though it had been attached as an afterthought. All snakes of this genus in the United States are longitudinally striped. In this species, a tan, yellowish, or brownish orange band about three scale rows wide extends down the center of the snake's back and is flanked by slightly narrower black or dark brown stripes on scale rows 6 and 7, whose upper and lower edges often form zigzag borders. Below these markings, where the body hue changes to light gray, a dark line, barely one scale wide, runs along the fourth scale row above the abdomen, at least at midbody. The belly, which may be plain off-white, is usually tinted with a pale orange blush, especially toward the tail. The dorsal scales are smooth and in 17 midbody rows. The anal plate is divided. Two or three small scales separate the rear pair of chin shields, and there are usually nine upper lip plates on either side of the head.

COMPARABLE SNAKES The mountain patch-nosed snake rarely has a thin dark line on each side of its body, but when such a stripe is present, it lies along the third row of dorsal scales and not the fourth. Its rear chin shields are separated by only a single small scale. Besides, the absence of an enlarged nose plate, all garter and ribbon snakes within the range of the Big Bend patch-nosed snake can be distinguished by their keeled body scales,

234

single anal plate, and greater number of dorsal scale rows (19 or 21). The Central Texas whipsnake has a dark instead of pale middorsal band (which is flanked by broken, pale stripes), a pale crossband or two pale blotches on the back of its head, and 15 (not 17) rows of dorsal scales at midbody. Furthermore, its nose scale is not enlarged.

SIZE Adults are usually between 24 and 32 inches (61–81.3 cm) in length. The largest known specimen measured 40 inches (101.6 cm) long.

HABITAT Essentially a serpent of desert scrub flatlands, desert valley hillsides, and the lower, rocky slopes of foothills and mesas, the Big Bend patch-nosed snake also commonly occupies the dry, mesquite-lined washes and rocky gorges that cut through such habitats at higher elevations. It is frequently encountered as well along terraces just above the Rio Grande. Jameson and Flury (1949), whose pioneer studies in Presidio County provided the first meaningful ecological picture of the reptile and amphibian fauna of the Sierra Vieja Mountains, collected this species mainly in the Plains belt, where one was taken from the catclaw-tobosa plant association, one from the tobosa-grama grassland community, and two from the creosote-catclaw-blackbrush association. Of two others found in the roughland belt, one was discovered in a streambed and the other in a huisache-lechuguilla plant community. Whatever the habitat, the snake occupies areas with sandy or gravelly soils.

Adult from Brewster County.

MOUNTAIN PATCH-NOSED SNAKE

Salvadora grahamiae grahamiae

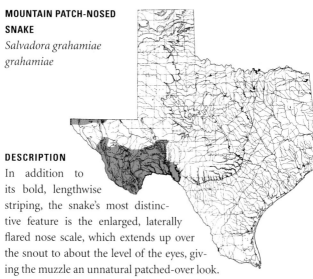

DESCRIPTION

In addition to its bold, lengthwise striping, the snake's most distinctive feature is the enlarged, laterally flared nose scale, which extends up over the snout to about the level of the eyes, giving the muzzle an unnatural patched-over look. Between two dark brown to nearly black stripes on either side of the spine (each two to three scales wide) lies a slightly broader pale gray to pale yellow vertebral band. Below the dark stripes the body is a bit darker, generally assuming a tan or olive hue. Only occasionally is a narrow dark line faintly indicated along the third row of scales above the belly plates. The head is usually pale gray, except for a brown mask behind each eye, which marks the beginning of each dark body stripe. The snake's underside is an immaculate white or yellow. The dorsal scales are smooth and arranged in 17 midbody rows, the anal plate is divided, there are usually eight upper lip scales, and the rearmost chin shields either touch one another or are separated by only a single scale.

COMPARABLE SNAKES The Big Bend patch-nosed snake has a narrow dark stripe, usually zigzag in outline, on the fourth row of scales above the belly, nine upper lip scales, and two or three small scales between the rearmost chin shields. The Central Texas whipsnake has a dark center stripe bordered on either side by broken white stripes, a white collar or two pale patches on the back of its head, and 15 midbody rows of dorsal scales, and it lacks an enlarged nose plate.

SIZE Adults of this subspecies normally are between 22 and 30 inches (55.9–76.2 cm) long. A record specimen measured 37 ¹/₂ inches (95.2 cm) in length.

HABITAT In Texas this snake inhabits the more humid, wooded mountain slopes and mesas of the Trans-Pecos region at eleva-

tions between 4,000 feet (1,219 m) and at least 6,000 feet (1,829 m). Although it may occasionally occupy the lower elevations of desert grassland, where it sometimes coexists with its cousin the Big Bend patch-nosed snake, it is more likely to be encountered in ever-

Adult from Brewster County.

green pine-juniper woodland, along the rocky slopes of canyons and hillsides, and in upland streambeds. At the Black Gap Wildlife Management Area in Brewster County, Axtell (1959) observed both species living side by side, finding one Big Bend patch-nosed snake at approximately 2,000 feet (610 m) and a specimen of the mountain patch-nosed snake on a nearby hillside no more than 300 feet (91 m) higher. Other examples of cohabitation of the two species are not rare where their geographic ranges overlap, but apparently the mountain species has an aversion to the low desert elevations inhabited by *S. deserticola,* for it seldom establishes permanent residence below 4,000 feet. It seems also to favor craggy mountain slopes and rock-laden ravines over the less severely tilted alluvial plains and lowland deserts. Within its Texas range it has been recorded from a variety of plant communities, including cedar-savannah and cedar-ocotillo associations on the Blackstone Ranch in Terrell County. In the Sierra Vieja Mountains of northwestern Presidio County, it has been reported by Jameson and Flury (1949) from the following plant communities: catclaw-cedar, lechuguilla-beargrass, catclaw-grama, and grama-bluestem.

**TEXAS PATCH-NOSED
SNAKE**
*Salvadora grahamiae
lineata*

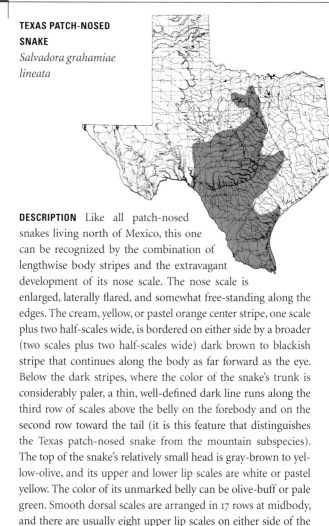

DESCRIPTION Like all patch-nosed
snakes living north of Mexico, this one
can be recognized by the combination of
lengthwise body stripes and the extravagant
development of its nose scale. The nose scale is
enlarged, laterally flared, and somewhat free-standing along the
edges. The cream, yellow, or pastel orange center stripe, one scale
plus two half-scales wide, is bordered on either side by a broader
(two scales plus two half-scales wide) dark brown to blackish
stripe that continues along the body as far forward as the eye.
Below the dark stripes, where the color of the snake's trunk is
considerably paler, a thin, well-defined dark line runs along the
third row of scales above the belly on the forebody and on the
second row toward the tail (it is this feature that distinguishes
the Texas patch-nosed snake from the mountain subspecies).
The top of the snake's relatively small head is gray-brown to yel-
low-olive, and its upper and lower lip scales are white or pastel
yellow. The color of its unmarked belly can be olive-buff or pale
green. Smooth dorsal scales are arranged in 17 rows at midbody,
and there are usually eight upper lip scales on either side of the
mouth, of which two touch the eye. The anal plate is divided.
COMPARABLE SNAKES The narrow, dark lateral stripe of the Big
Bend patch-nosed snake occupies the fourth scale row above the
belly, its rearmost chin shields are separated from one another
by two or three small scales, and typically nine upper lip scales

occur on either side of the mouth. Ribbon and garter snakes living within the range of the Texas patch-nosed snake lack its enlarged nose plate; they also possess keeled body scales, an undivided anal plate, and 19 or 21 rows of midbody dorsal scales. The modestly striped Schott's and Ruthven's whipsnakes both have a wide, dark center stripe, 15 rows of smooth dorsal scales at midbody, and a nose scale of average size.

SIZE Although this slender serpent is known to reach a maximum length of 47 inches (119.4 cm), the adults are usually between 26 and 40 inches (66–102 cm) long.

HABITAT Occupying a variety of habitats from sea level to nearly 2,000 feet (610 m) elevation, this snake is found as far north in the state as Throckmorton and Young counties and as far south as Brownsville. This region of Central Texas includes the northern prairies and Cross Timbers, the scrubby cedar-oak savannah of the Edwards Plateau, the brushland dominated by mesquite and prickly pear cactus on the Rio Grande Plain (including the intensely cultivated farmlands of the Valley), and to a limited extent the Blackland Prairie just east and northeast of San Antonio. It favors rocky hillsides, particularly those supporting rock ledges, but Vermersch and Kuntz (1986) noted that in south-central Texas it also frequents river and creek floodplains, replete with rotting logs and decaying plant debris.

Adult from Cameron County.

VARIABLE GROUND SNAKE
Sonora semiannulata
semiannulata

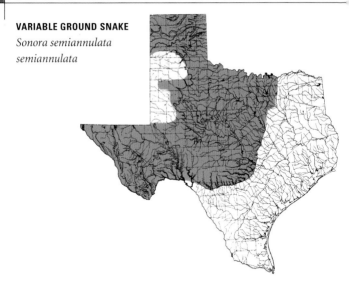

DESCRIPTION   So varied are the snake's background color and pattern—ranging from olive-brown to bright orange or reddish and from no markings to bold crossbands—that even specimens from the same locality can look like entirely different species, a circumstance responsible in part for the long-standing confusion over the snake's proper classification.

Based on an examination of more than 500 ground snakes from Texas, we believe there are two different subspecies of the variable ground snake in the state, each distinguished by the number of dorsal scale rows on its body. Generally, 15 midbody rows of scales occur in the variable ground snake, but if this number is only 14, then the number of rows near the anus is also 14. In the southern Texas ground snake, only 13 rows of scales normally are present at midbody. In the few instances in which this number is 14, then 13 rows occur near the anus. Moreover, the broad range of color and pattern variation displayed by the western ground snake is not duplicated in the southern Texas subspecies, which is essentially a unicolored serpent. In both races, a more or less distinct dark spot or horizontal dash usually occupies the forward or middle portion of each dorsal scale, giving the snake the appearance of being longitudinally striped with numerous thin, dotted lines.

The array of color and pattern variation displayed in the variable ground snake is enough to bewilder the novice, for not only does this subspecies come in collared, crossbanded, blotched, striped, and unicolored phases, but individual snakes can also exhibit any combination of such elements. Adding to the confusion is the possibility of finding specimens representing all of those pattern phases together in a single local community. Among the most colorful of all variable ground snakes are those inhabiting West Texas, where some individuals are both black-crossbanded and marked with a relatively wide red-orange stripe down the middle of the back. In others, either of these pattern elements is missing. Central Texas specimens, however, tend to have heads somewhat darker than the body, and their dorsal markings may consist of several dark crossbands, one, or none. There are also variable ground snakes whose only marking is an

Adult. Photo by J. R. Dixon.

abbreviated dark collar across the neck. Whatever the snake's upper body pattern, its underside is off-white to orange-yellow, usually unmarked but occasionally crossed by one or more of the dark dorsal crossbands, especially beneath the tail. The snake's small, blunt head, only a little wider than its neck, is followed by a relatively thick body. The dorsal scales are smooth, a loreal scale is present, and the anal plate is divided.

COMPARABLE SNAKES The lack of a loreal scale and the absence of crossbanding or longitudinal striping on the body distinguish flat-headed and black-headed snakes from this ground snake. Ring-necked snakes have bold black spots on a red-orange or yellowish belly, and the only dorsal marking, if present, is a pale neck ring. Both species of earth snakes possess at least some keeled dorsal scales, which are arranged in 17 rows at midbody. The Texas brown snake, also with 17 midbody rows of keeled dorsal scales, lacks a loreal scale and has a prominent dark spot on the lip scales directly below the eye. Blind snakes are much more slender than a ground snake, their sightless eyes are visible only as black dots beneath the overlying scales, and their belly scales are no larger than the dorsal scales.

SIZE Adults are generally 8 ½ to 12 inches (21.6–30.5 cm) in length. A record specimen measured 18 inches (45.7 cm) long.

HABITAT This snake has a wide distribution in Texas, including roughly the western two-thirds of the state, exclusive of the East Texas woodlands, the middle and upper coastal plain, and the South Texas thornbrush savanna. In such dry country, dominated by sandy or rocky terrain, it is most likely to be encountered in grassy plains, open desert grasslands, mesquite thickets, and oak-juniper savannahs, including those in the Guadalupe Mountains at slightly over 6,000 feet elevation (the greatest height at which this snake has been reported). In the Panhandle region of northwestern Texas, Fouquette and Lindsay (1955) found 52 of 55 Hutchinson County specimens on rocky limestone slopes where the primary vegetation was sparse bluestem, grama grass, and sumac. Two others were collected on sandy hillsides, and only 1 came from the floodplain. Along the southern edge of the subspecies' range in Bandera, Medina, Kendall, Comal, and Bexar counties, the majority of 38 specimens encountered by Vermersch and Kuntz (1986) came from rocky hillsides in oak-juniper habitat. Not far to the west, on the Stockton Plateau, a series of 21 variable ground snakes collected by Milstead, Mecham, and McClintock (1950) in northern Terrell County was taken in a variety of plant associations that included cedar-ocotillo (9), cedar-savannah (3), cedar-oak (3), persimmon–shin oak (2), mesquite-creosote (2), and walnut–desert willow (2). Like a number of other small snake species whose presence is not easily detected, this one is attracted to suburban environments where it can readily hide beneath the myriad of human-generated trash items that normally occur in such places.

**SOUTHERN TEXAS
GROUND SNAKE**
*Sonora semiannulata
taylori*

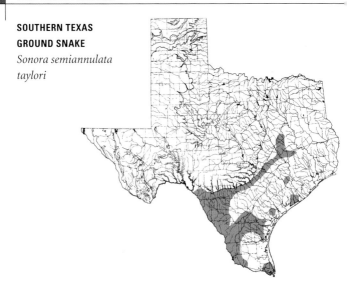

DESCRIPTION The overall color of this somewhat thick-bodied little snake is gray to medium brown above, usually with a more or less distinct dark spot or horizontal dash on the forward or middle part of each dorsal scale. Such markings, when viewed together, create the impression of numerous subtle, lengthwise stripes, giving the snake a delicately textured appearance. The extraordinary color and pattern variations of the Great Plains ground snake are not observed in this subspecies, an essentially unicolored serpent. In some specimens, all or part of the head is slightly darker than the rest of the body. The belly has a pale yellowish hue and is unmarked. The snake's small head is barely wider than its neck, and its body is relatively thick. The dorsal scales are smooth, a loreal scale is present, and the anal plate is divided.

A subspecies of the variable ground snake, it differs from that race in normally having only 13 (sometimes 14) midbody dorsal scale rows instead of the 15 (occasionally 14) that characterize the variable ground snake. Those with the unconventional 14 rows at midbody will have 13 rows near the anus (14 in *S. s. semiannulata*).

COMPARABLE SNAKES See Comparable Snakes account for the variable ground snake.

SIZE Adults are generally 10 to 16 inches (25.4–40.6 cm) long but are known to reach a maximum length of about 17 inches (43.2 cm).

HABITAT For the most part, this subspecies inhabits the South Texas thornbrush savannah, but is also found in the live oak and post oak savannahs to the northeast, where it has so far been reported in Austin, Bastrop, Brazos, Freestone, Harris, Robertson, and Wilson counties. Like other small, secretive snake species, it is sometimes encountered as often in the suburbs of towns and cities as in wilderness areas.

Gray adult from South Texas. Photo by J. R. Dixon.

MARSH BROWN SNAKE
Storeria dekayi limnetes

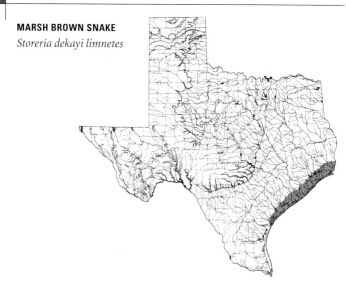

DESCRIPTION This drab little pale brown to grayish brown snake displays a broad, pale stripe down the middle of its back, which is margined along each outer edge by a row of widely spaced, often obscure, small black spots. Individual scales along the sides of the body are usually edged with horizontal white and black dashlike flecks that are most visible after the snake has eaten a large meal or when a female is heavy with young. The belly color can be yellowish tan to pastel pink, often with a row of dark dots along the outer edges of the ventral plates. The subspecies' most distinctive features are the horizontal black bar behind each eye and the absence of large, dark neck blotches and dark markings on the upper and lower lip scales. Unlike the adults, young marsh brown snakes have a yellowish tan collar across the neck and a dark dorsal coloration with virtually no markings. The dorsal scales are keeled and arranged in 17 midbody rows, a loreal scale is absent, and the anal plate is divided.

COMPARABLE SNAKES See Comparable Snakes account for the Texas brown snake.

SIZE Adults are generally 9 to 13 inches (22.9–33 cm) long, with a maximum known length of nearly 17 inches (43 cm), according to Boundy (1995).

HABITAT Confined chiefly to the narrow strip of coastal brackish and freshwater marshes and wet prairies between the Louisiana border and Eagle Lake in Texas, this snake also occurs in the region's scattered hardwood savannahs. Though it prefers a salt marsh habitat, a specimen from outside this zone was reported by Sabath and Sabath (1969); it was found on dry prairie in Colorado County 75 miles (121 km) inland from the nearest marsh.

Adult from Galveston County.

TEXAS BROWN SNAKE
Storeria dekayi texana

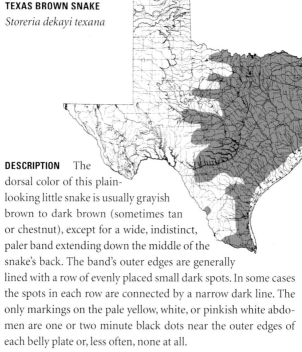

DESCRIPTION The dorsal color of this plain-looking little snake is usually grayish brown to dark brown (sometimes tan or chestnut), except for a wide, indistinct, paler band extending down the middle of the snake's back. The band's outer edges are generally lined with a row of evenly placed small dark spots. In some cases the spots in each row are connected by a narrow dark line. The only markings on the pale yellow, white, or pinkish white abdomen are one or two minute black dots near the outer edges of each belly plate or, less often, none at all.

A dark blotch of moderate to large size occurs on each side of the neck directly behind the head, often reaching down the sides as far as the belly line; another small, dark mark usually occupies the pale upper lip scales below each eye. The dorsal scales are keeled and arranged in 17 midbody rows, there are seven upper lip scales on each side of the face, a loreal scale is absent, and the anal plate is divided.

COMPARABLE SNAKES The Florida red-bellied snake has 15 rows of dorsal scales at midbody and a distinct white, circular patch below and behind each eye. The dorsal pattern of rough and western earth snakes, when present, is not clearly defined, and both serpents possess a long horizontal loreal scale. In ring-necked snakes, whose dorsal scales are smooth, the only upper body marking is a distinct pale collar (sometimes interrupted at the middle of the back), and the bright yellow or orange-red belly is punctuated with bold black spots. The lined snake and the several kinds of garter snakes coexisting with the Texas brown snake all have a single anal plate and a pale lateral stripe on each side of the body.

SIZE Adults, which are usually range 9 to 13 inches (22.9–33 cm) long, are known to reach a maximum length of 18 inches (45.7 cm).

HABITAT The Texas brown snake occupies a variety of environments ranging from mixed pine-oak woodland and pine forest to juniper brakes, grasslands, and thorn scrub. But regardless of habitat,

Adult from McLennan County.

it shows a preference for wet, shaded places that offer some ground cover and enough surface litter where hiding places, earthworms, and other favored prey abound. Such habitations include river and creek floodplains and their slopes, swamps, freshwater marshes, damp woods, and even water-filled ditches. Excluded, however, is the narrow coastal strip of mostly brackish marshland and prairie extending from the Louisiana border to Port Lavaca, where the Texas brown snake is replaced by its close relative, the marsh brown snake. Like several other kinds of small secretive serpents that thrive around human habitations, the Texas brown snake is abundant in large metropolitan areas. Klemens (1993) says of the northern brown snake in southern New England that it favors such disturbed sites over undisturbed habitats. To support this conclusion, he points out that approximately 93 percent of the specimens he collected in the region over 17 years came from the following modified natural areas: rural-agricultural 31 percent, suburban 13 percent, urban 18 percent, and radically disturbed 31 percent.

**FLORIDA RED-BELLIED
SNAKE**
*Storeria occipitomaculata
obscura*

DESCRIPTION The
upper body color
of this dark little
snake varies from slate
gray to some shade of brown, and
the underside of the body ordinarily is
tan, yellow, or pale orange, at least in Texas
specimens. Dorsal markings consist of two, or
sometimes four, longitudinal rows of ill-defined small
dark spots, one on either side of the spine, and occasionally a lateral row on each side.

Three pale-colored nuchal spots are often present; they may
be absent or may connect with one another to form a collar that
extends down either side of the neck to intercept the light color
of the belly. In some individuals, particularly those from Anderson County, the light nuchal markings are scarcely visible. The
snake's head, which normally is darker than the body, displays
one of the serpent's most distinctive markings, a white spot under the eye that involves all of the fifth upper lip scale and usually
the edge of the fourth. There are two preoculars, the keeled dorsal
scales are in 15 rows, and the anal plate is divided.

COMPARABLE SNAKES Brown snakes, in which the dorsal scale rows
are in 17 rows at midbody, either have dark markings on the upper lips or lack a single prominent light spot on the fifth upper lip
scale. Earth snakes possess a horizontal loreal scale that touches
the eye (the red-bellied snake lacks a loreal), and they have no
prominent pale spot on the fifth upper labial. The worm snake
is covered with 13 rows of smooth scales and is without a single
pale spot on the upper lips. Ring-necked snakes have small black

spots on the lips, a double row of bold black spots on the belly, and smooth body scales.

SIZE Adults are generally 8 to 10 inches (20.3–25.4 cm) long; the maximum known size for this species 16 inches (40.6 cm).

HABITAT Primarily an inhabitant of moist woodland containing plenty of logs and ample leaf litter, this serpent also occupies open places adjacent to such shaded forest, including bogs, swamp edge, old fields, and sometimes even roadside ditches. Although not common in the big thicket, it was found regularly during a study of seasonally flooded hardwood bottomlands.

Yellowish adult from Anderson County.

A good account of the snake's habitat preference is given by Semlitsch and Moran (1984), who found this subspecies to be moderately common within two natural aquatic depressions in the U.S. Department of Energy's Savannah River Plant along the Atlantic Coastal Plain below Aiken, South Carolina. Here, surrounded by relatively dry slash and loblolly pine plantations, prime red-bellied snake habitats contained sweet gum, black gum, water oak, and wax myrtle trees, as well as bulrush, rush, cattail, and spike rush plants. The snake was also discovered in fair numbers at an abandoned borrow pit covered with secondary plant growth not much different from that at the other two locations. The zoologists captured 137 red-bellied snakes at the first two sites in approximately four years and another 39 at the borrow pit in just two years. This is in sharp contrast to the several dozen specimens reported thus far from all of East Texas.

In Texas, as elsewhere, the Florida red-bellied snake shows a strong preference for damp situations. During drying conditions, it seems compelled to seek places of greater moisture.

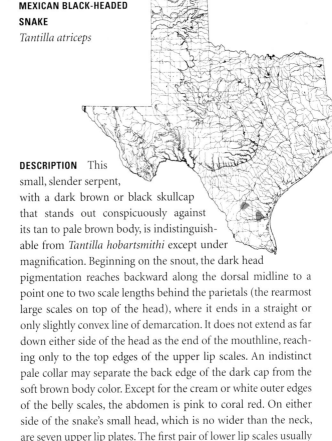

**MEXICAN BLACK-HEADED
SNAKE**
Tantilla atriceps

DESCRIPTION This
small, slender serpent,
with a dark brown or black skullcap
that stands out conspicuously against
its tan to pale brown body, is indistinguishable from *Tantilla hobartsmithi* except under
magnification. Beginning on the snout, the dark head
pigmentation reaches backward along the dorsal midline to a
point one to two scale lengths behind the parietals (the rearmost
large scales on top of the head), where it ends in a straight or
only slightly convex line of demarcation. It does not extend as far
down either side of the head as the end of the mouthline, reaching only to the top edges of the upper lip scales. An indistinct
pale collar may separate the back edge of the dark cap from the
soft brown body color. Except for the cream or white outer edges
of the belly scales, the abdomen is pink to coral red. On either
side of the snake's small head, which is no wider than the neck,
are seven upper lip plates. The first pair of lower lip scales usually
meets beneath the chin. The dorsal scales, all smooth, are in 15
midbody rows, and the anal plate is divided.

COMPARABLE SNAKES In color and pattern, as well as in nearly all
diagnostic features of scalation, the southwestern black-headed
snake is identical to *T. atriceps*. As far as we know, the two differ
with certainty solely in the structure of the male hemipenes. They
can therefore be distinguished only by carefully examining such
organs under magnification. Another is the arrangement of the
first pair of lower lip scales in relation to the mental shield on the
chin: the two lip scales of the Mexican black-headed snake ordi-

narily meet beneath the chin, whereas in the southwestern black-headed snake they are usually separated by the mental scale. The serpents also differ in the number of postocular scales directly behind each eye. There are usually two in the southwestern black-headed snake and normally but one in the Mexican black-headed snake. Like the previous-ly mentioned feature of scalation, however, this one is variable enough to make it unreliable. Because the geographic ranges are not known to overlap, the only prac-tical way to identify a specimen is to assign it to one species or the other based on its collecting locality.

Adult. Photo by P. Freed.

The plains black-headed snake has a longer cap, which extends backward three to five scale rows past the parietal plates; its rear margin is either convex or pointed. Its first pair of lower lip scales usually meet beneath the chin. The flat-headed snake's crown is normally only a bit darker than its body and it lacks a well-defined rear margin, but in the occasional specimen whose nearly solid cap is darker than usual, the back edge forms a distinct concave border. In addition, it has only six upper lip scales on each side of the head. Instead of a dark brown or black cap, ring-necked snakes have a pale collar on the neck (in the prairie ring-necked snake) or usually none at all (in the regal ring-necked snake), and distinct but random black spotting on the belly.

SIZE Adults are generally 5 to 8 inches (13–20.2 cm) long. They are known to reach a maximum length of 9 $^1/_8$ inches (23.2 cm).

HABITAT Primarily an inhabitant of the vast Chihuahuan Desert of north-central Mexico, this snake ranges northeast across the border into South Texas. There it has been found so far only in Duval and Kleberg counties, where the predominantly caliche and clay soils support mostly brushy plants and cactus. South of the border, according to Conant and Collins (1991), it is more liberal in its choice of environments, occupying not only desert flats and forested mountain canyons but other habitats in between.

TRANS-PECOS
BLACK-HEADED SNAKE
Tantilla cucullata

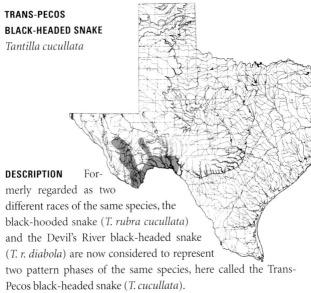

DESCRIPTION   Formerly regarded as two different races of the same species, the black-hooded snake (*T. rubra cucullata*) and the Devil's River black-headed snake (*T. r. diabola*) are now considered to represent two pattern phases of the same species, here called the Trans-Pecos black-headed snake (*T. cucullata*).

Three different types of head pattern are normally found in this seldom-encountered serpent. One is distinguished by its all-black head. The second resembles the former Devil's River black-headed snake, *T. rubra diabola,* in that it has a pale collar on the back of the head. The black on the rear of the head usually encroaches a short distance (one scale or less) onto the middle scale row of the pale collar. In the third pattern, the pale collar is completely interrupted by black along its dorsal midline, separating it into two whitish patches (Easterla 1995). Whatever the character of the head pattern, all of them have an unmarked pale brown or grayish brown upper body and a white abdomen. The dorsal scales, all smooth, are arranged in 15 rows at midbody, and the anal plate is divided.

COMPARABLE SNAKES The dark cap of the plains black-headed snake fails to reach the lower jaw, its rear edge is either convex or pointed, and it is not followed by a pale collar. It also has a pinkish to pink-red belly. The black skullcap of the southwestern black-headed snake is short, extending only one scale width behind the end of the parietal scales, and it does not reach as far down along the sides of the face as the end of the mouthline.

SIZE Most adults of this large *Tantilla* are 8 to 15 inches (20.3–38.1 cm) long. A record specimen was 25 ⁵/₈ inches (65.1 cm) long.

HABITAT The Trans-Pecos black-headed snake has so far been found only in western Texas, its known distribution extending for the most part along a north-south axis beginning at the Davis Mountains in the north and ending in the Chisos Mountains at Big Bend National Park, and from the Cuesta del Burro Mountains in the west to the vicinity of the Pecos and Devil's Rivers

Adult from Brewster County with interrupted white collar.

in the east and northeast. Most specimens have been encountered in steep-sided rocky canyons of Big Bend National Park at elevations between 5,400 and 5,600 feet (1,651–1,712 m), where the dominant vegetation consisted of pinyon pine, juniper, and oak. The lowest park-site record is for one specimen found near Volcanic Dike Overlook, outside the Chisos Mountains at only 3,871 feet (1,180 m). The first specimen to be discovered was not taken in Big Bend National Park but was found by Minton (1956) 6 miles (9.7 km) south-southeast of Alpine in hilly grassland at an altitude of about 5,000 feet (1,520 m), where the reddish lava soil supported scattered stands of juniper and cholla. The westernmost locality at which this snake has been found is the one in the Cuesta del Burro Mountains of Presidio County, where, at 5,115 feet (1,559 m), the low hills of arid grassland were vegetated chiefly with creosote bush, yucca, ocotillo, and agave. Curiously, all of the *T. cucullata* so far reported from northern Brewster, Jeff Davis, and Presidio counties have been of the black-hooded variety, whereas in the Chisos Mountains nearly half the specimens displayed white collars and the rest were marked with solid dark hoods that characterize the more northern and western populations.

All of the specimens (21) from the lower elevations of the Chihuahuan Desert east of the Pecos River (from Langtry to the Del Rio area) have a pale collar.

FLAT-HEADED SNAKE
Tantilla gracilis

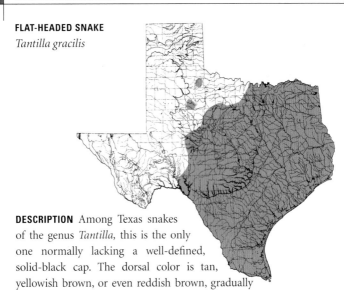

DESCRIPTION Among Texas snakes
of the genus *Tantilla*, this is the only
one normally lacking a well-defined,
solid-black cap. The dorsal color is tan,
yellowish brown, or even reddish brown, gradually
becoming a bit darker on the head. Only seldom is the crown
uniformly dark enough to have a clearly delineated rear border,
in which case the back edge of the cap is concave. The snake's
belly is usually whitish with a pale salmon pink to coral red hue
down its middle; the underside of its tail is colored like the abdomen, but more vividly. The moderately flattened head is about
the same width as the neck. On either side of the head are six
upper lip scales and one postocular, but there is no loreal scale.
The smooth dorsal scales are in 15 midbody rows, and the anal
plate is divided.
COMPARABLE SNAKES Native black-headed snakes share with the
flat-headed snake an unpatterned, brownish body but differ from
it in having a distinct black cap whose sharply delineated rear
margin may be convex, pointed, or straight, but never concave.
They normally possess seven instead of six upper lip scales on either side of the head. Earth snakes have a loreal scale; 17 midbody
rows of dorsal scales (at least some of which are keeled), and a
whitish instead of pinkish belly. Brown snakes, whose strongly
keeled body scales occur in 17 midbody rows, typically have a

pale, broad stripe down the middle of the back and one or more dark spots on each side of the head and neck. Some Florida red-bellied snakes possess a pale, reddish brown upper body, but their strongly keeled dorsal scales are arranged in 17 midbody

rows, and they have a prominent circular white spot on each side of the head directly below the eye. The more heavy-bodied ground snakes, which may or may not be patterned with black crossbands or a reddish stripe down the center of the back, ordinarily lack

Adult from Chase County, Kansas. Photo by Suzanne L. Collins, The Center for North American Herpetology.

a pink belly and usually have a loreal scale. The bright yellow or orange ring normally present on the nape of ring-necked snakes, together with their black-spotted bellies, will distinguish them from the flat-headed snake. The very slender blind snakes have tiny, blunt-snouted heads, degenerate scale-covered eyes, and belly plates no larger than the dorsal scales.

SIZE Most adults of this small, slender species are between 7 and 8 inches (17.8–20.3 cm) in length. The largest specimen on record measured 9 7/8 inches (25 cm) long.

HABITAT Widely distributed across the state, this snake inhabits every natural region in Texas except the High Plains and the Chihuahuan Desert region of the Trans-Pecos. It can be found in both the hardwood bottomlands and the pine-oak uplands of eastern Texas, the oak-hickory forests of the Cross Timbers, the oak-juniper brakes of the Edwards Plateau, the southeastern coastal prairies, and the South Texas thorn woodland. It has been reported to favor habitats with loose, damp soil, into which it can easily tunnel. Experiments performed by D. R. Clark (1967), however, revealed no preference for any particular soil type he investigated, probably because the flat-headed snake is only a modest burrower.

SOUTHWESTERN BLACK-HEADED SNAKE
Tantilla hobartsmithi

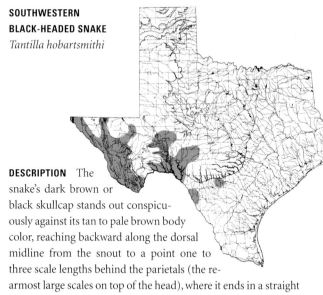

DESCRIPTION   The snake's dark brown or black skullcap stands out conspicuously against its tan to pale brown body color, reaching backward along the dorsal midline from the snout to a point one to three scale lengths behind the parietals (the rearmost large scales on top of the head), where it ends in a straight or only slightly convex line of demarcation. The dark pigment continues down either side of the head to the edges of the upper lip scales. A narrow, sometimes indistinct, pale collar often margins the back edge of the dark cap, with no dark pigment separating it from the soft brown body color. The abdomen is pink to coral red down the center, cream or white along the outer edges. On either side of the snake's small head are one preocular scale, usually two postocular scales, and seven upper lip scales, but no loreal scale. The dorsal scales, all smooth, are arranged in 15 midbody rows, and the anal plate is divided.

COMPARABLE SNAKES In color and pattern, as well as in nearly all diagnostic features of scalation, the Mexican black-headed snake is identical to the southwestern black-headed snake. As far as we know, the two differ solely in the structure of the male hemipenes.

The dark cap of the plains black-headed snake, which is longer than that of the southwestern black-headed snake, extends backward three to five scale rows beyond the parietal plates and is either convex or somewhat pointed along its rear margin. The head of the Trans-Pecos black-headed snake is entirely black as far back as the neck or is separated behind the parietal scales (the last pair of large plates on the crown) by a prominent white collar. Furthermore, its belly is uniformly white. The flat-headed snake's crown is typically only a bit darker than its body, and it lacks a well-defined rear margin. The flat-headed snake has only six upper lip scales on each side of the head.

Adult. Photo by J. E. Werler.

SIZE Adults usually measure 7 to 9 inches (17.8–22.9 cm) long. The record length for this species is 12 $^5/_{16}$ inches (31.3 cm).

HABITAT Although essentially a desert species, it usually lives in areas containing some source of moisture, such as along riverbeds, streams, and arroyos. It shows a strong preference for rocky situations but it occupies a wide variety of habitats ranging from low and midlevel desert grasslands to relatively moist mountain woodlands. In Presidio County's Sierra Vieja Mountains, Jameson and Flury (1949) found it in tobosa-grama grasslands. In southeastern Brewster County, Axtell (1959) collected it in the sotol-lechuguilla plant association. On the Stockton Plateau in northern Terrell County, Milstead, Mecham, and McClintock (1950) reported taking it in the following plant communities: cedar-ocotillo, persimmon–shin oak, mesquite-creosote, and the cedar savannah association. In the Chisos Mountains of Big Bend National Park, where it occurs at much higher elevations, at least to 6,000 feet (1,962 m), Degenhardt, Brown, and Easterla (1976) described it as common on the precipitous inclines and rocky gullies of Green Gulch.

PLAINS BLACK-HEADED SNAKE
Tantilla nigriceps

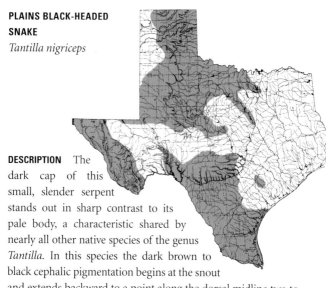

DESCRIPTION The dark cap of this small, slender serpent stands out in sharp contrast to its pale body, a characteristic shared by nearly all other native species of the genus *Tantilla*. In this species the dark brown to black cephalic pigmentation begins at the snout and extends backward to a point along the dorsal midline two to five scales behind the last pair of large plates on the crown, ending in a distinctly convex or even pointed line of demarcation where it meets the light brown to brownish gray body color. The dark cap is not followed by a pale collar. The abdomen is pink to reddish along the midline, whitish along the outer edges. On either side of the snake's small head, which is no wider than the neck, are seven upper lip scales. The first pair of lower lip scales normally meet beneath the chin. The dorsal scales, all smooth, are in 15 midbody rows, the loreal scale is absent, and the anal plate is divided.

COMPARABLE SNAKES The crown of the flat-headed snake, ordinarily just a bit darker than the serpent's upper body, is sometimes covered by a solid blackish cap, in which case its well-defined rear margin is *concave*. In both the Mexican and southwestern black-headed snakes, the dark cap is shorter than in the plains black-headed snake (usually ending one to three scales beyond the parietal plates), and its rear margin is normally straight across the nape and bordered behind by an indistinct pale collar. The Trans-Pecos black-headed snake's head and throat are completely black, or the black forecrown is followed by a distinct white collar, interrupted by a median black line or not, and then by a dark bar. It also has a sizable white spot on its snout and another below and behind each eye, and the black pigmentation on top of its head reaches down below the end of the mouthline. The variable ground snake has a loreal scale and lacks a distinct black cap.

SIZE Adults are generally 7 to 10 inches (17.8–25.4 cm) long. A record specimen measured 15 ¹/₁₆ inches (38.3 cm) in length.

HABITAT Primarily a resident of rocky grassland prairies and desert grassland, it also occurs in such diverse habitats as thorn scrub and open elevated woodlands, usually where

Adult from Cameron County.

there is at least a small amount of moisture. Despite the snake's broad distribution across the western two-thirds of the state, few accounts detail its habitat preferences.

One such habitat profile was reported by Fouquette and Lindsay (1955) for a northwestern Texas study site. Of 12 plains black-headed snakes the zoologists collected in Hutchinson County, 6 were discovered on sandy limestone slopes that rose rather abruptly from a nearby creekbed, where the vegetation was chiefly sparse bluestem, grama grasses, and sumac; on the hilltops it consisted of buffalo and grama grasses. Three others were found along the ordinarily dry, wide creekbed, in which water could be found only at night and following heavy rains. Three more were encountered in the deep, gradually rising sands above the creek, an area of rather dense vegetation consisting of a heavy growth of sage, scattered clumps of sumac, and a ground cover of grasses. Two specimens came from Wet Tobacco Creek, a floodplain location in Dawson County, where the soil was less sandy than in the previously described floodplain; the dominant plant growth was mesquite.

WESTERN BLACK-NECKED GARTER SNAKE

Thamnophis cyrtopsis cyrtopsis

DESCRIPTION

Like other Texas garter snakes, this one is marked with three pale lengthwise stripes on a dark body. In the western black-necked garter the center stripe is typically orange close to the head, fading to off-white or pale yellow on the rest of the trunk; each side stripe, generally positioned on scale rows 2 and 3 above the belly plates, is pale yellow at the front of the body but becomes whitish or pale brown farther back on the trunk. In addition, each lateral stripe is often flanked below by another, less distinct stripe of slightly darker hue, whose bottom edge may be lined with a continuous row of regularly spaced, small black spots. These spots are either singular or arranged in vertical pairs. Between the center stripe and each side stripe are two alternating rows of larger black spots, indistinct in some specimens, prominent in others (particularly on the forebody).

Another conspicuous hallmark is the pair of large, black blotches directly behind the snake's gray or bluish gray–topped head. Sometimes each blotch is preceded by an abbreviated white crescent near the end of the mouthline. Also prominent on the head are vertical black margins along some or all of the light-colored upper lip scales, a standard feature of all Texas garter snakes. The chin, throat, and belly normally are white, but in some specimens they have a greenish or bluish tint. The body scales are keeled and usually in 19 rows at midbody. The anal plate is single.

COMPARABLE SNAKES In the checkered garter snake, the white or yellowish crescent near the end of the mouthline is tall, reaching nearly to the top of the snake's head; each light side stripe occupies only the third row of scales above the belly, at least on the forebody (both second and third rows in the western black-necked garter snake); and the dorsal scales are in 21 rows at midbody. The arid land ribbon snake, which is more slender than the garter snake, has an unblotched dorsum and unmarked upper lip scales, and there are no large black blotches on its neck.

Adult from New Mexico. Photo by J. R. Dixon.

SIZE Adults are generally between 16 and 28 inches (40.6–71.1 cm) in length. A record specimen measured 42 ³/₁₆ inches (107.2 cm) long.

HABITAT Restricted to the Trans-Pecos region of the state, this serpent occupies a variety of habitats ranging from arid desert flats near sea level to the forested slopes of the Davis Mountains 5,700 feet (1,737 m) high, though it seems to prefer rocky canyon streams and small permanent bodies of water situated in foothills and on mountains. Of 15 specimens collected in the Black Gap region of southeastern Brewster County by Axtell (1959) and his colleagues during a five-week field study, 8 were discovered near limestone streambeds and their associated pools, and only 2 were found around the area's human-made earthen stock tanks. Some of its other haunts include desert grassland, chaparral woodland, talus slopes, oak forest, and pine-fir woodland.

Just how much this aridland serpent depends on moisture is revealed by Jameson and Flury (1949). Their field studies in the Sierra Vieja Mountains of southwestern Texas showed that of 102 specimens collected on the Miller Ranch in 1948, all but 3 came from the vicinity of streambeds, 1 was taken from a lake in the tobosa-grama association, and 2 others from the catclaw-cedar vegetation at the mouth of a canyon. Even more detailed is Mosauer's (1932) description of the snake's microhabitat in a portion of the Guadalupe Mountains. Three specimens he observed there routinely basked in the sunshine of a grassy streamside bank that was moistened by the spray from a nearby small riffle.

EASTERN BLACK-NECKED GARTER SNAKE
Thamnophis cyrtopsis ocellatus

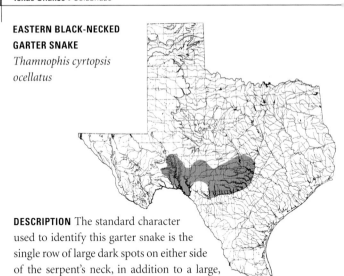

DESCRIPTION The standard character used to identify this garter snake is the single row of large dark spots on either side of the serpent's neck, in addition to a large, black blotch at the back of the head. In typical garter snake fashion, three light-colored stripes run the length of the body, one down the middle of the back and another low on either side. The one along the spine is orange or orange-yellow; the other two, located on scale rows 2 and 3 above the belly plates, are pale yellow or off-white. Farther back on the yellowish to olive green trunk, the lateral dark spots form a double row, the lowest series infringing onto the lateral stripe from above. This, together with a similar encroachment of smaller back spots from below, gives the stripe a distinctly wavy look. Toward the tail the two rows of larger black spots merge to form a broad black band that continues to the end of the tail.

The snake's gray or bluish gray crown is generally unmarked, but as in other Texas garter snakes, the whitish upper lip scales bear prominent black streaks along their vertical sutures. The chin, throat, and abdomen usually are white but in some individuals may have a greenish tint. The keeled dorsal scales are arranged in 19 rows at midbody, and the anal plate is single.

COMPARABLE SNAKES No other Texas garter snake species is marked with a single row of large, black spots on either side of its neck. In the checkered garter snake each of the pale side stripes involves only the third row of scales above the belly, at least on the forebody (both the second and third rows in the eastern black-necked garter snake), and the dorsal scale rows are in 21 rows at midbody. In the Texas garter snake, the bright orange center stripe is wider, occupying one full scale row plus half of each adjacent row, and each lateral stripe involves the third row of scales above the belly plates in addition to parts of rows 2 and 4. The red-striped ribbon snake is longer and more slender; it has an unblotched body and unmarked white upper lip scales. Patch-nosed snakes, which lack prominent head and neck markings, have smooth dorsal scales and a single anal plate.

SIZE The usual adult length is between 16 and 20 inches (40.6–50.8 cm); a specimen of record size measured 43 inches (109.2 cm) long.

HABITAT This snake occurs sporadically across the Edwards Plateau, one of the state's most arid natural regions. It exists in such a hostile environment by staying close to the countless springs, streams, and seeps that emanate from the plateau's vast underground aquifers, providing the moisture indispensable to the serpent's survival. Where natural watercourses are in short supply, it frequently resides near stock tanks, though rockier places are usually preferred. As a result, it is most likely to be found in rocky canyons, on stone-covered hillsides, and among limestone outcroppings.

Head of adult from Bexar County. Photo by R. A. Odum.

CHECKERED GARTER SNAKE
Thamnophis marcianus
marcianus

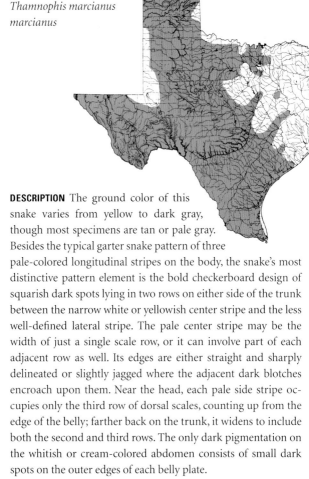

DESCRIPTION The ground color of this
snake varies from yellow to dark gray,
though most specimens are tan or pale gray.
Besides the typical garter snake pattern of three
pale-colored longitudinal stripes on the body, the snake's most
distinctive pattern element is the bold checkerboard design of
squarish dark spots lying in two rows on either side of the trunk
between the narrow white or yellowish center stripe and the less
well-defined lateral stripe. The pale center stripe may be the
width of just a single scale row, or it can involve part of each
adjacent row as well. Its edges are either straight and sharply
delineated or slightly jagged where the adjacent dark blotches
encroach upon them. Near the head, each pale side stripe occupies only the third row of dorsal scales, counting up from the
edge of the belly; farther back on the trunk, it widens to include
both the second and third rows. The only dark pigmentation on
the whitish or cream-colored abdomen consists of small dark
spots on the outer edges of each belly plate.

The head is somewhat wide at the back and distinct from the
neck. On top it is either uniformly olive (in olive-gray specimens) or light brown (in straw-colored individuals), except
for a pair of small, black-edged white or yellowish spots near
its center. The most distinctive cephalic markings, however, are

those on either side of the head, where a whitish or bright yellow crescent, preceded by a black border and followed by a large black collar, reaches upward onto the head from near the end of the mouthline. The color of the last two upper lip plates matches that of the crown, and the remaining labial scales above the mouth are off-white or vivid cream. Several are vertically edged in black, the lines bordering the back edges of the fifth and sixth upper lip scales being the most prominent. The last line, which is by far the longest, extends upward nearly to the top of the snake's head. The dorsal body scales are keeled and arranged in 21 rows at midbody. The anal plate is entire.

COMPARABLE SNAKES Among the several cohabiting garter snakes with which it may be confused, the eastern black-necked and western plains garter snakes most nearly resemble *T. m. marcianus*. The eastern black-necked garter has a single horizontal row of large black blotches on either side of its neck, a center stripe that frequently is orange, a wavy pale stripe low on each side, only 19 rows of midbody dorsal scales, and no well-defined yellowish crescent near the back of its head. Furthermore, the large black spots that dominate the body create the impression

Adult.

of an overall dark snake (the checkered garter is basically pale-toned). Likewise, in the western black-necked garter there is no clear-cut yellowish crescent at the back of the head; the center body stripe is generally orange, at least on the forebody; each side of the neck is marked with a large black blotch; and the dorsal scales are in 19 rows at midbody. Although the plains garter snake may have a yellow crescent behind the end of the mouthline and two lateral rows of alternating dark spots, it lacks a wide, dark collar. In addition, its dorsal stripe is usually orange, and each side stripe, at least on the forebody, occupies dorsal rows 3 and 4 above the belly. The Texas garter snake, whose overall dorsal ground color is much darker than that of the checkered garter, is marked along the spine by a wide orange center stripe. It has neither a yellow crescent on the side of its head nor a black collar; each of its yellowish side stripes is on the third dorsal scale row and on most of the second and fourth rows, at least on the forebody; and only 19 dorsal scale rows circle the trunk at midbody. The red-sided garter snake is adorned with red or orange bars along the sides of its body and lacks both the yellow crescent and the dark collar. In sharp contrast to the checkered garter snake, ribbon snakes are long, slender serpents with unblotched backs and unmarked upper lip scales; they have no dark collar and no yellowish crescent. The small lined snake, which has no distinctive marks on its head or neck, has two parallel rows of bold half-moons down the center of its belly. The lengthwise-striped patch-nosed snakes, which also lack bold head and neck markings, possess smooth dorsal scales and a divided anal plate.

SIZE The usual adult length varies from 18 to 24 inches (45.7–61 cm). At 42 $1/2$ inches (107.9 cm) long, the largest known specimen is a veritable giant for its kind.

HABITAT Better suited to a dry environment than most other Texas garter snakes, this abundant serpent is widely distributed across the arid and semiarid western three-quarters of the state. It occurs in a variety of habitats at low to midlevel elevations, extending from the dry grasslands of the Panhandle to the South

Texas thornbrush savannah. It avoids the higher mountain elevations, usually ascending no higher than about 3,000 feet (912 m). In the vicinity of the Guadalupe Mountains, for instance, Mecham (1979) says the checkered garter snake occurs along the lower eastern and northeastern slopes, staying close to permanent sources of water, just as in Big Bend National Park, according to Easterla (1989), it does not live high in the Chisos Mountains but remains close to fixed bodies of water, however large or small, along the Rio Grande floodplain and its principal tributaries, Tornillo and Terlingua creeks. Nevertheless, the snake is occasionally discovered a considerable distance from permanent water. A specimen collected in Hutchinson County by Fouquette and Lindsay (1955) was but 1,000 yards (917 m) from the nearest surface water. Where moisture is scarce, particularly in desert regions, the checkered garter snake is often attracted to temporary bodies of water that include mud puddles, roadside ditches, and flooded fields, and it can be unusually abundant along the permanent irrigation canals that have turned some of this barren landscape into productive farmland. Though it is sometimes found in open woodland, it prefers treeless terrain over heavily shaded habitats.

WESTERN RIBBON SNAKE
Thamnophis proximus proximus

DESCRIPTION This slender, medium-sized black or dark brown snake is longitudinally marked with three conspicuous light stripes. The one along the middle of the back is usually bright yellow or pale orange. The lateral stripe on each side of the body, which always occurs on the third and fourth scale rows above the belly, is pale yellow. Some northeastern Texas specimens are curiously different in displaying a peculiar overall bluish green hue that even pervades the serpent's pale-colored stripes.

The snake's head, which is distinctly wider than the neck, is black or dark brown on top, where it is marked only by a pair of small, prominent pale spots that closely adjoin one another or actually come together. The same dark pigmentation that occurs on the crown extends down each side of the head, stopping above the upper lip scales, which (together with the lower lips and chin) are an immaculate white, cream, or pale greenish color, as is the snake's belly. The other obvious facial marking is a pale vertical bar directly in front of each eye. The heavily keeled dorsal scales are arranged in 19 (rarely 21) rows at midbody, and the anal plate is single.

COMPARABLE SNAKES Although garter snakes are also longitudinally striped, they are stockier and have relatively shorter tails (occupying less than a quarter of the garter snake's total length but nearly a third in the ribbon snake). Distinct dark pigmentation marks their upper lip scales and the outer edges of their abdominal plates. Lined snakes, whose bodies also bear three longitudinal pale stripes, have small heads and a double row of bold, black spots down the middle of the abdomen. The bellies of crayfish snakes normally show some dark spotting, and their anal plates are divided.

SIZE Although their slim bodies appear longer than they really are, adult ribbon snakes are usually between 20 and 30 inches (50.8–76.2 cm) long. The maximum known size is nearly 42 inches (107 cm), according to Minton (1972).

HABITAT Although well adapted to a wide variety of habitats, this moisture-loving serpent typically lives along the brushy or

Adult.

grassy margins of still and moving bodies of water ranging from ditches, wallows, cattle tanks, and even water-filled vehicle tracks to marshes, damp meadows, swamps, sloughs, rice fields, ponds, lakes, springs, streams, and rivers. It sometimes invades the edges of soggy woodlands, but it is not considered a forest dweller. It may also inhabit areas disturbed by human development, provided such places are not continually occupied by people.

A notable example of such habitat is an abandoned 2-acre housing project in the post oak belt near Bryan, where D. R. Clark (1974) conducted a 31-month study of this subspecies. On this deserted tract, covered with old concrete building foundations, the ribbon snake was abundant, especially along several interconnecting drainage ditches that provided the only choice microhabitats within a ³/₄-mile radius of the study site. Minton (1972) pointed out that in Indiana, ribbon snakes are much more sensitive to drastic human-made alterations to their habitat than any of the local garter snakes, noting that disruptive activities such as land cultivation or the elimination of wet lowlands results in their speedy disappearance. Garter snakes, on the other hand, are so adaptable to human-modified habitats that they survive in many inner-city parks long after most other moderate- to large-sized snakes have been eliminated there.

ARID LAND RIBBON SNAKE
*Thamnophis proximus
diabolicus*

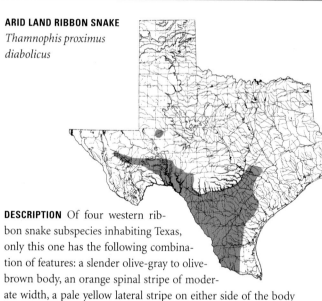

DESCRIPTION Of four western ribbon snake subspecies inhabiting Texas,
only this one has the following combination of features: a slender olive-gray to olive-
brown body, an orange spinal stripe of moder-
ate width, a pale yellow lateral stripe on either side of the body
that often narrows toward the tail and is frequently bordered
above by a line of discreet horizontal black dashes, and sometimes a narrow dark stripe along each side just above the belly.
Uncommonly dark specimens from tributaries of the Canadian
River in the northwestern part of the Texas Panhandle, although
geographically much closer to populations of the western ribbon
snake than to other arid land ribbon snake colonies far to the
south, are nevertheless considered *T. p. diabolicus.*

As in other ribbon snake subspecies, a pair of small, pale,
dashlike spots marks the top of the head, both the upper and
lower lip scales are pale-colored and immaculate, each yellowish
lateral stripe is on scale rows 3 and 4 above the belly, the keeled
dorsal scales are arranged in 19 rows at midbody, the pale abdomen displays no dark markings, and the anal plate is single.

COMPARABLE SNAKES Garter snakes are heavier-bodied and have
proportionately shorter tails (occupying less than a quarter of
the garter snake's total length but nearly a third in the ribbon
snake). In addition, they have black markings on the edges of

their upper lip scales and some dark pigmentation on the outer edges of their belly plates. Lined snakes have relatively small heads and a double row of bold, black spots down the middle of the abdomen. The dorsal scales of patch-nosed snakes are smooth, the anal plate is divided, and there is no pair of small, pale spots on top of the head.

SIZE While most arid land ribbon snakes are between 2 and 3 feet (61–91.4 cm) long. The largest known example measured 48 ¹/₂ inches (123.2 cm) in length.

HABITAT Across the dry Trans-Pecos region of Texas, in a land that once was more damp and where ribbon snakes no doubt were then more generously distributed, this semiaquatic reptile manages to survive the oppressive aridity by clinging to the margins of major waterways and their tributaries, to ponds and streams, springs and seeps, and even to permanent and semipermanent cattle tanks and irrigation canals. Water, in fact, is a primary environmental factor limiting the ribbon snake's distribution, for it sustains both the serpent's physiological and dietary needs. It is still unclear whether a separate population of this subspecies occurs about 250 miles (403 km) north of the Trans-Pecos along tributaries of the Canadian River system that wind through flat, shortgrass prairie in the northern Panhandle counties of Hartley and Oldham.

Adult from Terrell County.

GULF COAST RIBBON SNAKE
*Thamnophis proximus
orarius*

DESCRIPTION Of the four subspecies of the western ribbon snake in Texas, this one is characterized by an olive-brown dorsal coloration, a relatively broad stripe of pale gold along its spine, and the absence of a dark stripe below each of its yellowish lateral stripes. The upper lip scales normally are pale yellowish green, except for the first three, which are tan. The belly, also pale green down the middle, is usually faded orange along the outer edges. In common with the other subspecies of *T. proximus,* the Gulf Coast ribbon snake displays a pair of small, pale spots on top of the head, pale upper and lower lip scales devoid of dark pigmentation, and an unmarked abdomen. Like them, it always has the side stripes on scale rows 3 and 4 above the belly, the keeled dorsal scales in 19 midbody rows, and a single anal plate.

Rossman (1963) mentioned specimens from southeastern Texas (including the Channelview area) and from Refugio, San Patricio, and Victoria counties whose usually all-brown dorsal scales contained varying amounts of black pigmentation. He believed some of them to be intergrades between the Gulf Coast and western ribbon snake subspecies.

COMPARABLE SNAKES Garter snakes are heavier-bodied and have relatively shorter tails (occupying less than a quarter of the snake's total length but nearly a third in the ribbon snake); some distinct, dark pigmentation marks the upper lip scales and the outer edges of the belly scales. Graham's crayfish snake usually has a row of small, often indistinct dark spots down the middle of its abdomen; the closely related Gulf crayfish snake has the length of its belly punctuated by a double row of prominent black crescents.

SIZE The usual adult length for the species is 20 to 30 inches (50.8–76.2 cm), and the record length is 48 ¹/₂ inches (123.2 cm). It is likely, however, that this subspecies does not attain as great a length as the others.

HABITAT Although this snake occurs abundantly along the entire coastal plain of Texas and Louisiana, little detailed information is available about its ecology. The most comprehensive field study of its habitat

Adult.

and life history is the 13-month study conducted by Tinkle (1957) at Tulane University's Sarpy Wildlife Refuge, a swampy region in the Mississippi Delta near Lake Ponchartrain, Louisiana. The area, supporting a diversity of ideal microhabitats, harbored a sizable population of ribbon snakes; 221 specimens were encountered there during the study, along with only 73 cottonmouths, 60 broad-banded water snakes, 18 speckled king snakes, 16 eastern yellow-bellied racers, 5 western mud snakes, 4 Texas rat snakes, 3 rough green snakes, and 2 delta crayfish snakes. The others together represented less than the number of *T. p. orarius*.

Situated in a cypress-gum swamp, the area's basic habitats were described as (1) the swamp itself, where less waterlogged expanses supported an abundant palmetto growth, (2) the dry ridges, where predominant plants were willow, maple, and buckrush, (3) the permanent deep pools, and (4) the extensive shallow-water flats that fluctuated seasonally between being wet and dry. Areas harboring the most ribbon snakes were the main ridge and the shoulders of roadside ditches in the flats.

In Texas, where it is abundant along the Gulf coastal plain from the Louisiana border to Brownsville, the snake occupies a broad range of wet, open habitats including lakes, ponds, streams, marshes, swamps, wet meadows, rice fields, cattle tanks, and ditches. In the southeastern corner of the state, Guidry (1953) found it in a wide variety of terrain, including suburban areas.

RED-STRIPED RIBBON SNAKE

Thamnophis proximus rubrilineatus

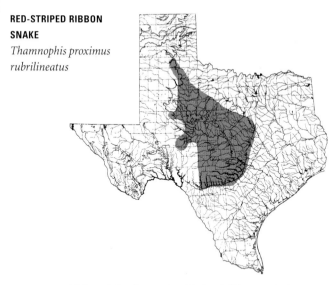

DESCRIPTION This and the three other kinds of ribbon snake inhabiting Texas are all races of a single species, differing only in details of coloration. In the red-striped ribbon snake the overall coloration varies from olive-brown to olive-gray. The relatively narrow stripe along the middle of the back normally is bright red (rarely orange), while a pale-colored lateral stripe occupies each side of the body. In some specimens a narrow dark line occurs below each side stripe. As in all other Texas ribbon snakes, a pair of small whitish spots marks the top of the head, the upper and lower lip scales are pale-hued and immaculate. The lateral stripes are always on scale rows three and four above the belly. The keeled dorsal scales occur in 19 midbody rows, the belly is without markings, and the anal plate is single.

COMPARABLE SNAKES Several kinds of garter snakes occur within the red-striped ribbon's range; they are stouter than *T. p. rubrilineatus* and possess relatively shorter tails. In addition, they have some dark pigmentation on their upper lip scales and along the outer edges of their belly plates. Lined snakes possess small heads and a double row of prominent black spots down the middle of the abdomen. The Texas patch-nosed snake's spinal stripe is wide, its dorsal scales smooth, and its anal plate divided. Graham's crayfish snake, although displaying a faintly striped pattern, has no distinct, light middorsal stripe, and its abdomen is marked with bold, black spots. Its anal plate is divided.

SIZE The usual adult length is between 20 and 30 inches (50.8–76.2 cm). The largest known specimen measured 48 inches (121.9 cm) long.

HABITAT This locally abundant ribbon snake, which occupies the Edwards Plateau and some of the surrounding regions, normally is restricted to the margins of watercourses, particularly those with open, grassy borders. Included in this category are streams, ponds, rivers, marshes, and cattle tanks. Davenport (1943) noted that in Bexar County the greatest numbers occurred near clear, spring-fed rivers; in certain remote wooded canyons, the serpent's presence was attributed to the permanent springs or seeps that provided the reptiles with moisture and amphibian prey.

Adult from Bexar County.

**WESTERN PLAINS GARTER
SNAKE**
Thamnophis radix haydeni

DESCRIPTION This
moderate-sized,
greenish gray to olive-
brown garter snake is marked with
a distinct bright yellow or orange stripe
down the middle of its back, a pale yellow
or greenish stripe on either side of the trunk
along scale rows 3 and 4, and two alternating rows
of squarish black spots between the middorsal and lateral stripes.
Another row of black spots is located below each side stripe, and
a row of prominent but smaller black spots, sometimes crescent-
shaped, occurs on the outer edges of the whitish to greenish belly
scales. An overall darkening of the snake's ground color, which
occurs in some older individuals, may obscure the dorsal markings and make such snakes difficult to identify. The lips are boldly marked with vertical black bars. The dorsal scales are keeled
and in 19 or 21 rows at midbody. The anal plate is single.

COMPARABLE SNAKES All native garter snakes except the checkered garter snake and this one possess fewer than 19 middorsal
scale rows, but the checkered garter snake's center stripe is narrower than that of the western plains subspecies and its lower
stripes never occupy the fourth row of scales. Since there is evidence that hybrids between checkered and plains garter snakes
occur in Hutchinson County, certain specimens there may not
be clearly assignable to either species. Like some western plains
garter snakes, the Texas garter snake has a broad, pale-orange
center stripe and lateral stripes that reach the fourth row of body
scales, but there is no double row of black spots between them.
Ribbon snakes are more slender and longer-tailed than garter

snakes and have no black markings on their lips or abdomen.

SIZE Adult specimens are generally 22 to 28 inches (55.9–71.1 cm) long. The maximum reported length is 42 ³/₅ inches (108.2 cm).

HABITAT Although surprisingly abundant over much of its broad geographic range, this is one of Texas' rarest garter snakes, entering the state only along the northern edge of the Panhandle. Typical habitats include grassy plains, prairies, and farmlands, where it usually lives along the vegetated margins of streams, rivers, ponds, lakes, sloughs, and marshes. In Ohio, Reichenbach

Adult from Oklahoma.

and Dalrymple (1986) described one such habitat as an area of prairie slough ponds in poorly drained clay soils surrounded by grasses. According to Webb (1970), garter snakes from Cimarron County, Oklahoma (close to the Texas border), were captured in and near a shallow pond bordered with sunflowers, grasses, and other herbaceous plants.

Despite the snake's fondness for water, it does not entirely restrict itself to wet environments. Elsewhere it has been seen occasionally in cultivated fields. At one time it could also be found in and near large metropolitan areas, sometimes in surprisingly large numbers. Until at least the late 1960s, its close relative the eastern plains garter snake was common in parks, gardens, and vacant lots of Chicago's populated suburbs, sometimes even hibernating beneath inner-city sidewalks. Because of expanding land development and perhaps also as a result of long-term pesticide use, some of these urban populations have been severely reduced and others have been completely eliminated. That populations of even greater density occurred in natural open prairie environments was illustrated by Seibert (1950), who concluded that at least 845 plains garter snakes occupied a single hectare of prime habitat at his Illinois field study site, and by Reichenbach and Dalrymple, who estimated a density of at least 114 garter snakes per hectare at their Ohio study location.

EASTERN GARTER SNAKE

Thamnophis sirtalis sirtalis

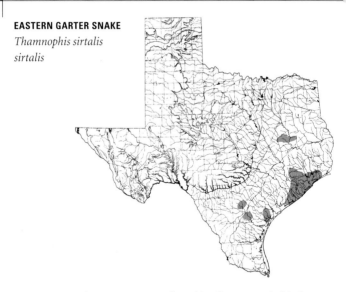

DESCRIPTION Like most garter snakes, this olive to nearly black subspecies is marked by three pale stripes extending from the neck to nearly the end of the tail. The straw-colored stripe that traces the spine is the most conspicuous, being the width of one complete scale row plus half of an adjacent row on either side. Less clearly defined are the lateral stripes, one on either side of the body, which ordinarily occur only on dorsal scale rows 2 and 3 above the belly plates but may occasionally involve the edge of row 1 as well. Between the upper and lower stripes are two alternating rows of rectangular or oval black spots, with yet another row of vertical black marks situated below the lateral stripe. The skin of most eastern garter snakes (usually concealed by the body's overlapping scales) normally is greenish or some shade of olive, yet in the majority of specimens we have seen from the southeastern part of the state, it was reddish or reddish orange, as were the edges of some dorsal scales. Also present on the skin are pairs of small, white, nearly horizontal dashlike marks, best seen when the body is distended, as when the snake is heavy with food or young or when it flattens itself in a threat posture. Its whitish abdomen is marked only with one or two rows of small black spots along the outer edge of each belly plate. The head is dark on top and pale greenish white on the cheeks and underside of the jaw. Prominent dark vertical bars edge the upper lip scales, and a parallel pair of tiny white or yellowish dashlike spots marks the top of the crown. The dorsal scales are keeled and arranged in 19 rows at midbody. The anal plate is single.

COMPARABLE SNAKES On the checkered garter snake each lateral stripe is narrower and situated just on the third row of dorsal scales (except on the forebody, where it may occupy the fourth row as well), but the dorsal scales are arranged in 21 rows at midbody, and a large black mark on each side of the neck directly behind the head is preceded by a cream-colored crescent. The more slender ribbon snakes lack prominent dark spots between the longitudinal stripes, and they have neither vertical black sutures on the lips nor distinct dark markings on the outer edges of

Reddish adult from Harris County.

the abdomen. Lined snakes closely resemble garter snakes, but their bellies and the underside of their tails are decorated with two longitudinal rows of prominent, dark, half-moons. Brown snakes have 17 rows of dorsal scales at midbody and a divided anal plate. The Gulf salt marsh snake has no black spots along its sides, its belly is vividly marked with a central row of large yellowish oval spots on a dark abdomen, its midbody dorsal scales are in 21 to 25 rows, and its anal plate is divided. Both Graham's and Gulf crayfish snakes (which lack a distinct, light middorsal stripe) have either one indistinct or two prominent rows of dark oval-shaped spots down the center of the belly, and their anal plates are divided.

SIZE Although the eastern garter snake is reported by Froom (1972) to reach an extreme length of 54 inches (137 cm), its usual adult length is 18 to 26 inches (45.7–66 cm). The largest specimen reported from Texas is one from Harris County that measured 32 $1/2$ inches (82.6 cm) long.

HABITAT Although abundant over much of its vast geographic range, which includes the eastern third of the United States as well as parts of central and eastern Canada, this snake is infrequently encountered in Texas. In some midwestern and northeastern states it often occurs in such large numbers close to urban centers that it has been referred to as the sparrow of the snake world. At one site in Wyandot County, Ohio, for example, Reichenbach and Dalrymple (1986) counted 45 to 89 specimens per hectare.

A moisture-loving serpent, it can be found in almost any area containing damp soil and some natural or human-made debris under which it can find shelter. Such habitats include the vicinity of streams and ponds, meadows, marshes, wet grasslands, drainage ditches, and even the suburbs of large cities where it occupies seldom-disturbed vacant lots, gardens, and parklands. Being decidedly partial to more open spaces, it is unlikely to inhabit dense woodland.

Most specimens we observed in the past were encountered in moist, grassy areas within the city limits of Houston, where scattered weeds and shrubs were the dominant plants and ground debris was abundant. From the 1950s through the early 1970s, the garter snake was frequently encountered in and around Mac-Gregor Park not far from downtown Houston, where it could be found crawling along the boggy edges of small, sluggish canals or hidden beneath debris near some source of moisture. We also observed individuals sunning along the banks of drainage canals in Freeport. Today, because of commercial and residential development around the park, it appears to have been eliminated from the area, for no specimens have been reported from this part of the city in at least 25 years. Despite its disappearance from various parks and previously undeveloped areas in and around the city, probably due in part to the long-term use of agricultural and industrial chemicals, the snake has been collected recently in western Harris County and near several Galveston County communities including Alta Loma, Arcadia, Webster, and La Marque. One specimen was collected along the edge of a salt marsh near Sargent in Matagorda County.

TEXAS GARTER SNAKE
Thamnophis sirtalis annectens

DESCRIPTION

The Texas garter snake is similar to the eastern garter snake in coloration and pattern. It has a wide deep-orange instead of slightly narrower yellowish stripe along the spine, and the distinct light-hued lateral stripe on each side of its body involves not only the third row of scales above the belly plates but also the adjacent parts of rows 2 and 4, at least on the forward third of the trunk. Between the upper and lower stripes on either side of the grayish brown trunk are two alternating rows of squarish dark spots, which in some individuals are obscured by an overall darkening of the ground color. The white or light-greenish abdomen is unmarked except for the encroachment of some dark dorsal ground color onto the outer edges of the belly plates. The top of the head is the same dark hue as the ground color of the body, its only markings being a pair of small, side-by-side, yellowish dashlike spots near the back of the crown. The dorsal scales are keeled and arranged in 19 rows at midbody. The anal plate is undivided.

COMPARABLE SNAKES No other native *Thamnophis* has the pale lateral stripes on the second, third, and fourth rows of scales above the belly plates. The western plains garter snake, whose middle stripe may also be orange, at least on the forebody, is patterned with a row of distinct large black spots below its light lateral stripe. The eastern black-necked garter snake has a *single* row of large, black, roundish spots on each side of its neck and a curved black mark behind the end of the mouthline. In addition to its three light stripes, the pale body of the checkered garter snake is adorned with a bold pattern of dark checkerboard spots and a pale crescent behind the end of the mouthline, which is followed by an even larger dark blotch.

SIZE Adults of this subspecies range from 15 to 28 inches (38–71 cm) long. A record specimen is said to have measured 42 ³/₄ inches (108.6 cm) in length.

HABITAT Uncommon throughout most of its Central Texas range, the Texas garter snake is seldom encountered in large numbers. Most specimens that formed the basis

Adult from Dallas County.

for B. C. Brown's (1950) original description of this subspecies were collected along a small tributary of Boggy Creek, about a mile east of Austin (21 snakes) and from Waco and vicinity (10 specimens). Eleven others came from various scattered localities throughout the reptile's range, with no more than 2 specimens represented from any single location.

Like most other garter snakes, this one is found in a wide range of habitats, though nearly always in the vicinity of moisture, whether along the margins of streams, rivers, ponds, lakes, or marshes or around damp soil some distance from such bodies of water. Although even drainage ditches and irrigation canals relatively free of plant life sometimes attract this moisture-dependent serpent, its most typical haunts include a ground cover of grass, weeds, or other brushy streamside vegetation. The Dallas County specimens collected by Curtis (1949) were encountered along small creeks in the hilly southwestern part of the county, though one was discovered at the south end of White Rock Lake near a fish hatchery pond. In many years of local collecting, Tim Jones (pers. com.) encountered only three specimens in the Waco area, none of which was found near a permanent source of surface water.

RED-SIDED GARTER SNAKE
Thamnophis sirtalis parietalis

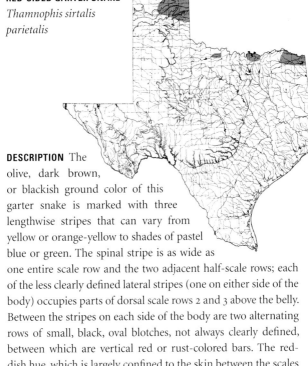

DESCRIPTION The olive, dark brown, or blackish ground color of this garter snake is marked with three lengthwise stripes that can vary from yellow or orange-yellow to shades of pastel blue or green. The spinal stripe is as wide as one entire scale row and the two adjacent half-scale rows; each of the less clearly defined lateral stripes (one on either side of the body) occupies parts of dorsal scale rows 2 and 3 above the belly. Between the stripes on each side of the body are two alternating rows of small, black, oval blotches, not always clearly defined, between which are vertical red or rust-colored bars. The reddish hue, which is largely confined to the skin between the scales but may also be present on the scale edges, is most conspicuous when the dorsal scutes are separated, as when the snake flattens its body in threat or when the skin is stretched after the snake has swallowed a large meal. Also visible on the skin at such times are numerous pale, dashlike marks. The dark spots below the lateral stripes may or may not extend onto the belly. Narrow, dark vertical bars usually margin some or all of the pale upper lip scales. The dorsal scales are keeled and in 19 rows at midbody. The anal plate is single.

COMPARABLE SNAKES Besides lacking vertical red bars on the sides of the body, other Texas garter snakes living within the range of *T. s. parietalis* can be distinguished as follows: in the checkered garter snake the lateral stripe is narrow and occupies only the third scale row above the abdomen (on the forebody it may also occupy the fourth), and its dorsal scales are in 21 rows at midbody. In addition, a large black blotch occurs on each side of the neck immediately behind the snake's head and is preceded by a pale crescent. In the western plains garter snake the lateral stripe in-

volves the fourth row of scales above the belly, and the dorsal scales are arranged in 21 midbody rows. Ribbon snakes are more slender, have neither red color nor dark spots between the lengthwise stripes, lack vertical dark sutures on the upper lips, and have no obvious dark markings on the abdomen.

Adult from Polk County, Iowa. Photo by R. W. Van Devender.

The lined snake, which also lacks any red coloration, displays a double row of bold, dark half-moons on the belly.

SIZE Sixteen to 20 inches (40.6–66 cm) is considered the usual adult length for this subspecies. The largest known specimen was 48 ⅞ inches (124.2 cm) long.

HABITAT No other snake lives as far north on our continent as this one. With a vast north-south geographic range that extends 1,700 miles (2,742 km), this cold-tolerant subspecies is found from the southern end of great Slave Lake in Canada's Northwest Territories (approximately 400 airline miles south of the Arctic Circle) to extreme northern Texas. As expected in such a broad-ranging reptile, it occupies a wide variety of habitats, most of them near moisture. In spring and summer it is likely to be found in brushy or grassy areas close to moist or aquatic environments, including lakes, ponds, rivers, streams, wet ditches, swamps, and prairie swales, although it sometimes inhabits relatively dry places such as arid fields, vacant suburban lots, rocky slopes, and upland prairies.

TEXAS LYRE SNAKE
Trimorphodon vilkinsoni

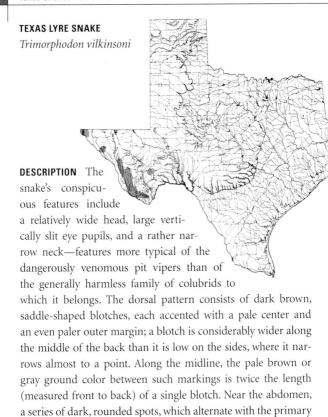

DESCRIPTION The snake's conspicuous features include a relatively wide head, large vertically slit eye pupils, and a rather narrow neck—features more typical of the dangerously venomous pit vipers than of the generally harmless family of colubrids to which it belongs. The dorsal pattern consists of dark brown, saddle-shaped blotches, each accented with a pale center and an even paler outer margin; a blotch is considerably wider along the middle of the back than it is low on the sides, where it narrows almost to a point. Along the midline, the pale brown or gray ground color between such markings is twice the length (measured front to back) of a single blotch. Near the abdomen, a series of dark, rounded spots, which alternate with the primary markings or are aligned with them, intrudes onto the outer edges of the belly. Otherwise, the pale abdomen is immaculate.

A scale called the lorilabial, on the side of the snake's head between the loreal and the upper lip scales, is found in no other Texas serpent. The dorsal scales are smooth and usually arranged in 23 rows at midbody; the anal plate is divided.

COMPARABLE SNAKES Gray-banded king snakes from the Big Bend region resemble to some extent the Texas lyre snake, even to their relatively large eyes, but the king snake's pupils are round, and its anal plate is single. The small night snake, whose elliptical pupils resemble those of the Texas lyre snake, is spotted dorsally and has distinct large, dark blotches on the top and sides of its neck.

SIZE Most adults of this rather slender snake are 18 to 30 inches

(45.7–76.2 cm) in length. A record specimen measured 41 inches (104.1 cm) long.

HABITAT The Texas lyre snake is probably more abundant than the few published records of its capture suggest. McCrystal (1991) found 35 to 40 specimens of this species each year in the Big Bend Region of Texas. It is intimately associated with rock piles, rock outcroppings, and talus slopes in which it finds an endless network of underground hiding places.

Most Texas specimens have been discovered in El Paso County's Franklin Mountains, where from 1961 through 1975, Banicki and Webb (1982) found 22 examples of this elusive serpent, primarily along Trans-Mountain Road. According to the zoologists, the Franklin mountain range is approximately 15 miles long and 3 miles wide, with the greatest elevation represented by 7,192-foot (2,199 m) North Franklin Peak. The highest point in these mountains at which they found a lyre snake was along the summit of Trans-

Pale adult.

Mountain Road at an elevation of 5,280 feet (1,615 m). Another specimen was collected by Medica (1962) at 5,500 feet (1,682 m), near the base of the Organ Mountains, a site 30 miles (48 km) north of the Franklins and not far from Las Cruces, New Mexico. According to Banicki and Webb, the snake's preferred habitat in the arid Franklin Mountains contains a variety of desert plants; the dominant species include ocotillo, catclaw mimosa, white thorn, Torrey yucca, lechuguilla, prickly pear cactus, cholla, and grasses. The snake is sometimes also encountered on desert flats where creosote bush is the dominant large plant and in the area's shallow canyons where the prevailing tree is mesquite. In Big Bend National Park, the lyre snake has been collected in the Grapevine Hills at 3,135 feet (859 m) elevation and in the Chisos Mountains as high as 5,940 feet (1,856 m).

LINED SNAKE
Tropidoclonion lineatum

DESCRIPTION Except
for its small, pointed
head, thick neck, and the double
row of bold, black, half-moons down
the middle of its belly, the little lined
snake closely resembles a small garter snake.
It has the same dark trunk, ranging in hue from
gray-brown to olive-brown, and three narrow, longitudinal
stripes on its body. The stripe along the midline of the back is
whitish, pale gray, or yellow and usually flanked on either side by
a row of minute black spots. Below it, along each side of the body
on scale rows 2 and 3 above the belly, lies another light stripe, often less conspicuous than the first and edged above and below by
a horizontal row of small black spots. Two parallel rows of rather
large black spots adorn the snake's white or yellowish abdomen,
one pair on each belly plate. To a greater or lesser extent, dark
flecks cover the top of its head. The upper and lower lip scales are
pale and immaculate. The keeled body scales are arranged in 19
rows at midbody, and the anal plate is single.

COMPARABLE SNAKES In color and markings, garter snakes bear a
strong resemblance to the lined snake, although their black belly
spots, when present at all, are neither large half-moons nor arranged in a uniform double row down the middle of the belly.
Besides, a garter snake's large head, which is followed by its much
narrower neck, stands out prominently compared to that of the
lined snake. The abdomen of the Gulf crayfish snake, like that of
the lined snake, is boldly patterned with two rows of black half-
moons down its middle, but the lengthwise stripes on its back and

sides are dark and obscure, and its anal plate is divided. Besides its distinct dark mark on the upper lip below the eye and another just back of the head, the Texas brown snake differs from the lined snake in having only 17 rows of dorsal scales at midbody, and a divided anal plate.

SIZE Although the record length for this snake is 21 ¹/₂ inches (54.6 cm), most adults measure between 8 ³/₄ and 15 inches (22–38.1 cm).

HABITAT Essentially a snake of open grassland prairie and sparsely wooded flatlands where

Pale adult from Val Verde County.

the limestone substrate and its decomposing surface debris provide an abundance of sheltering rock, this species generally avoids dense woods. It also shuns constantly wet places. Writing about the lined snake in the Waco area, Strecker (1926) commented that during the many years he collected reptiles near the old lagoon along Waco's railroad tracks and in the Brazos River bottoms, he found only two specimens of this species, both from the dry part of Gurley Park, about ¹/₂ mile from the river.

To many Texans living within its range, this little garden snake is a familiar sight, for apparently it is encountered more often in some urban neighborhoods than in many remote areas. This adaptable little creature survives within some of the state's largest metropolitan areas, where it can be found by poking around litter-strewn vacant lots, flower beds, and abandoned wooden buildings or by looking under trash and leaf piles, rocks, boards, fallen tree limbs, tin, paper, and other surface debris. Strecker, for example, collected 15 lined snakes from under loose paving stones near an old house. The lined snake is found in greatest numbers along open, rock-strewn prairies and hillsides where surface shelter is plentiful. For instance, in one day alone Taggart (1992) captured 47 specimens of this species from under rocks scattered over a single hillside in Hodgeman, Kansas, and in just three hours he collected another 72 from under flat rocks in Ellis County, Kansas.

ROUGH EARTH SNAKE
Virginia striatula

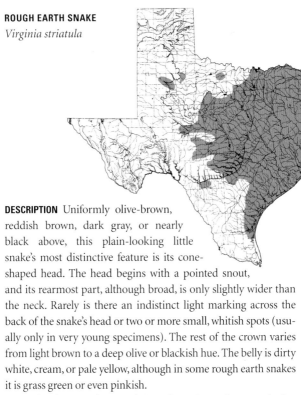

DESCRIPTION Uniformly olive-brown, reddish brown, dark gray, or nearly black above, this plain-looking little snake's most distinctive feature is its cone-shaped head. The head begins with a pointed snout, and its rearmost part, although broad, is only slightly wider than the neck. Rarely is there an indistinct light marking across the back of the snake's head or two or more small, whitish spots (usually only in very young specimens). The rest of the crown varies from light brown to a deep olive or blackish hue. The belly is dirty white, cream, or pale yellow, although in some rough earth snakes it is grass green or even pinkish.

In the absence of any explicit and consistent features of color or markings, the identification can best be confirmed by examining certain details of scale arrangement, a task accomplished on such a small snake only under magnification. Beginning at the head, they include a single internasal scale, an elongated horizontal loreal plate that touches the eye, one postocular scale, and five upper lip scales on either side of the face. The body scales, arranged in 17 middorsal rows, are keeled only along the upper back part of the trunk. The anal plate is nearly always divided.

COMPARABLE SNAKES The earthy color of *V. striatula* is so like that of several other similar-sized local snakes that its pointed, cone-shaped snout is an important item of distinction. The western earth snake typically has a more reddish upper body, smooth dorsal scales (a few weakly keeled on the rear part of the trunk), two internasal scales, and usually six upper lip scales on either side of the head. The flat-headed snake has a lighter-hued upper trunk, smooth dorsal scales in only 15 rows at midbody, and no a loreal scale. The brown snake, which is somewhat thicker in body than the rough earth snake, typically possesses a pale band down the middle of the back, on either side of which is a row of discrete small black spots. In addition to having two internasal plates and seven scales lining each side of the upper lip, it lacks a loreal scale. The Florida red-bellied snake, rare in Texas, likewise lacks a

Adult from Brazos County. Photo by T. J. Hibbitts.

loreal scale; it can be distinguished by the presence of six upper lip scales on each side of the mouth and by the prominent circle of pale pigment on the upper lip below and behind each eye. Another potentially confusing species is the western worm snake, a smooth-scaled serpent whose deep-pink belly color extends up along the sides of the body to the third row of dorsal scales.

SIZE Among the smallest of Texas serpents, adult rough earth snakes are generally 7 to 10 inches (17.8–25.4 cm) in length. A record specimen measured 12 $^3/_4$ inches (32 cm) long.

HABITAT This abundant reptile inhabits the eastern half of the state, where it is likely to be encountered in almost any region with damp soil and debris for concealment. Suitable habitat includes pine woods, hardwood forest, sparsely wooded rocky hillsides, swamp edge, and grasslands. It usually avoids desert or semidesert habitats, invading such regions only along the wooded margins of rivers and streams that flow through them. A testament to the snake's adaptability is its continued abundance well within the borders of large metropolitan areas, where, despite disruption by human activity, it continues to prosper. It seem to fare well along the foundation of houses, piles of leaf litter, any debris from gardening, and is frequently found in loose soil associated with buildings and yards.

WESTERN EARTH SNAKE
Virginia valeriae elegans

DESCRIPTION

This ordinary-looking gray, medium brown, yellowish brown, or reddish brown little snake has no conspicuous markings by which it can be easily identified. Some specimens are plain-colored above; others have an obscure light stripe down the middle of the back. The color of the belly typically is off-white, dull gray, or pale yellow, but in some individuals it is cream, pastel green, or subdued pink. Except for the small brown dots on the outer edges of the ventral plates in a few specimens, the snake's underside is unmarked. Its small, narrow head is only a bit wider than the neck and bluntly pointed. Its crown, generally a little darker than the upper body, often displays irregular dark speckling, as sometimes do the pale pink to coral pink upper lip scales.

Since the western earth snake displays considerable variation in its overall appearance and also closely resembles several other diminutive serpents living within its geographic range, trying to identify this nondescript little snake may be difficult. In *V. v. elegans,* most of the dorsal scales are smooth, although some on the upper rear of the body may be weakly keeled. These dorsal scales are arranged in 17 rows at midbody. On the head there are two internasal scales, six upper lip scales on each side of the mouth, one elongated loreal scale in front of each eye (with no preoculars), and two scales directly behind each eye. The anal plate is divided.

COMPARABLE SNAKES The closely related rough earth snake has a more cone-shaped head, distinctly keeled dorsal scales on much of its body, a single internasal scale, only five upper lip plates on either side of its mouth, and a single scale immediately behind each eye. Ground snakes, whose 13 to 15 rows of middorsal scales are smooth over the entire body, have the appearance of being striped longitudinally with many thin dotted lines, and they have a preocular scale separating the eye from the loreal plate. Brown snakes, which also lack a loreal scale, possess seven upper lip scales on each side of the mouth. The Florida red-bellied snake lacks a loreal scale, its upper lip plates number six on either side of

Pale adult from Arkansas. Photo by Suzanne L. Collins, The Center for North American Herpetology.

the mouth, there is a distinct pale collar (or three separate spots) on its neck, and a conspicuous whitish patch on the upper lip below and behind each eye. Ring-necked snakes are easily distinguished by their pale nuchal collars (sometimes interrupted at the middle of the back) and the bold black spotting on their yellowish bellies. The western worm snake possesses only 13 midbody rows of dorsal scales, and the deep-pink color of its belly continues up the sides of its body to the third such row.

SIZE Adults of this subspecies generally measure between 7 and 10 inches (17.8–25.4 cm) long. Their maximum length according to Laposha and Powell (1982) is 15 inches (38 cm).

HABITAT This uncommon snake prefers moist, heavily shaded woodland, such as that found along creek and river floodplains, where the ground surface is covered with a bed of leaf litter and an abundance of rotting logs, though it also occurs in less densely timbered habitats and along woodland edges. In south-central Texas, according to Vermersch and Kuntz (1986), it occupies mixed oak, juniper, cedar elm, and hackberry woodlands and sometimes even wet lowland marshes. It has also been collected in dry deciduous forest, along the slopes of well-drained, partly wooded hillsides, and in abandoned fields, especially those adjoining woodlands. It occurs with reasonable frequency near human habitations and in areas disturbed by humans, particularly those supporting residual stands of timber or brush.

TEXAS POISONOUS SNAKES

Family Elapidae
CORAL SNAKES AND THEIR ALLIES

TEXAS CORAL SNAKE
Micrurus tener

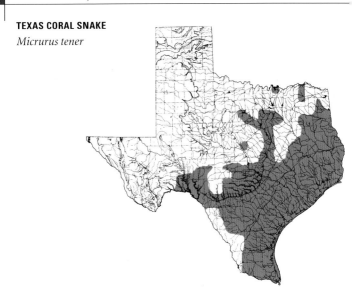

DESCRIPTION   By far the most colorful of our venomous serpents, the Texas coral snake is also the most distinctively shaped. Its blunt head is barely wider than the neck, and its shiny, slender trunk, ordinarily only as thick as a ballpoint pen, maintains approximately the same diameter for much of its entire length. Narrow, sulphur yellow rings separate the broad, alternating red and black body rings; the red rings are mottled unevenly with black. Yet there is no trace of red on the snake's head or tail, only black and yellow. From the snout to just behind the eye, the head is black, followed by a broad yellow band across the back of the crown. Thereafter, the pattern follows the typical North American coral snake color sequence of black-yellow-red-yellow, black-yellow-red-yellow, etc. The red and yellow rings always in direct contact with each other. These rings continue uninterrupted across the belly. The round pupils of the snake's small, black eyes are not easy to make out, for they are nearly as dark as the rest of the eye. The smooth, glossy dorsal scales are in 15 rows throughout the length of the body, and the scales under the tail are arranged in a double row, just as in most nonvenomous snakes. The loreal scale is absent, and the anal plate is divided.

COMPARABLE SNAKES Some kinds of harmless native snakes possess the same red, yellow (or whitish), and black colors in banded or seemingly banded patterns that mark the coral snake. A careful examination of these mimics shows, however, that their black bands invariably separate the red and yellow ones, whereas in the coral snake's sequence of colors the red and yellow are always in contact. Hence, the time-tested rhyme, "Red touch yellow, kill a fellow; red touch black, venom lack," remains the simplest way to separate them. Another way to remember the coral's color code is to visualize a traffic control signal with its red light always located next to the caution yellow, the same color arrangement as in the coral snake. Another distinction between the Texas coral snake and its harmless look-alikes concerns their dorsal markings. Those of the coral snake continue uninterrupted across the snake's belly, but the mark-

Adult from Harris County.

ings of some of the harmless mimics never reach the abdomen (scarlet and long-nosed snakes), or they are interrupted there (milk snakes). To the extent that it is marked with red, yellow, and black, the long-nosed snake also bears a resemblance to the coral, although its overall speckled appearance contrasts strikingly with the coral snake's bold, clear-cut pattern. Very young long-nosed snakes, however, show little, if any, such spotting. Unlike *Micrurus,* long-nosed snakes of all ages possess an immaculate belly or one marked with just a few small dark spots; a red, pinkish, or pale-colored snout; and an undivided anal plate. In addition, the scales under its tail are arranged mostly in a single row.

SIZE Most adult Texas coral snakes are about 2 feet (61 cm) long, specimens up to 3 feet (91.4 cm) in length are occasionally found. An unusually large one, 46¹/₂ inches (118.1 cm) long, was collected by Don Mascarelli in Colorado County, and a record individual of 47³/₄ inches (121.3 cm) is said to have been taken in Brazoria County (Tennant 1984).

HABITAT Wherever it occurs—whether in the mixed hardwood and pine forests of East Texas, the tallgrass prairie and deciduous woodlands of north-central Texas, or the small parcels of remnant subtropical forest below Brownsville—the coral snake prefers partially wooded sites containing organic ground litter.

Even in Terrell and Pecos counties, where the westernmost extension of its range crosses into the Chihuahuan Desert, the coral generally restricts itself to isolated stands of live oaks growing in or near moist canyons.

It also occurs with moderate frequency in and around some of our major Texas cities, living successfully in such populated areas by taking refuge in the vegetative debris of gardens, wooded lots, and undeveloped parklands. Also plentiful there are several kinds of small terrestrial snakes that constitute its most important prey species. Just how plentiful the coral snake was in at least one of our large urban areas is revealed in a three-month survey by A. C. Stimson in the early 1960s (pers. com.). Aimed at determining the snake's abundance in the immediate Houston area, the study produced 113 verified coral snake sightings within a 12-mile radius of city hall, a surprisingly large number even for that time. Like most reptilian species, the coral snake is not nearly as common around the Houston metropolitan area today as it was then.

Family Viperidae
VIPERS

UTHERN COPPERHEAD
Agkistrodon contortrix contortrix

DESCRIPTION

This pale race of the copperhead is distinguished from the two other Texas subspecies by the distinctly hourglass configuration of its dark crossbands; each one, although wide and rounded at the base, is very narrow at the middle of the back, where it may occasionally divide and form two separate triangular markings, one on either side of the body. The crossbands are usually a lighter shade of brown at their centers than along their outer margins. The snake's ground color is pale brown or light tan, often with a pinkish cast. The large, oval, dark brown spots that mark the outer edges of the belly may extend upward between the crossbands onto the first one or two dorsal scale rows. The dorsal scales, arranged in 23 or 25 rows at midbody, are weakly keeled, and the anal plate is single. Most scales under the tail are arranged in a single row, except those near the end of the tail, which are paired.

COMPARABLE SNAKES The eastern hog-nosed snake, especially in its copper or reddish color phases, bears a superficial resemblance to the southern copperhead. The similarity is particularly evident in the juvenile hog-nosed snake, which, at least in southeastern Texas, frequently is pale orange on the head and forebody. The snake's markings, when present, are oval, rectangular, or irregular in shape, not hourglass-shaped and never continuous across the snake's back from one side of the belly to the other. Its neck is not distinctly narrower than its head, its snout is upturned and pointed, its pupils are round instead of elliptical, and it lacks the facial cavities characteristic of the pit vipers. The light and dark crossbanded pattern of the infant cottonmouth closely resembles that of the copperhead, but the dark bands are jagged along the edges instead of smooth and nearly as wide at the middle of the back as along the sides. In both the juvenile and adult cottonmouth, a wide, dark mask runs back-ward from the eye.

Adult from Liberty County.

SIZE Adults are gener-ally between 24 and 36 inches (61–91 cm) long, but a specimen of record length measured 52 inches (132.1 cm).

HABITAT Generally distrib-uted over the moist eastern third of the state, the south-ern copperhead inhabits primarily the wooded low-lands, most often in the vicinity of river bottoms, streams, and swamps, but it also ranges inland across the hilly northeastern part of the state to the Red River. Although it occurs in heavily shaded forest, the southern copperhead seems to prefer partially wooded areas where some sunlight filters through the trees to the forest floor. In such places it finds shelter under logs and boards, beneath the loose bark of fallen dead trees, within the decaying interiors of logs and stumps, and even in the accumulated leaf litter carpeting the forest floor.

Although we have no precise information about the southern copperhead's population density in Texas, there is no doubt that in the wooded eastern third of the state it usually outnumbers all other venomous species. Ford, Cobb, and Stout (1991) found the copperhead to be the most abundant snake in Sheff's Wood, a relatively undisturbed second-growth forest of lowland flood-plain, upland deciduous woodland, and upland pine forest in Smith County. It was Guidry (1953) who encountered one of the largest nonhibernating concentrations of southern copperheads yet reported in southeastern Texas. In several hours of nighttime collecting, he captured 35 specimens in a small area of woodland in Newton County.

BROAD-BANDED COPPERHEAD

Agkistrodon contortrix laticinctus

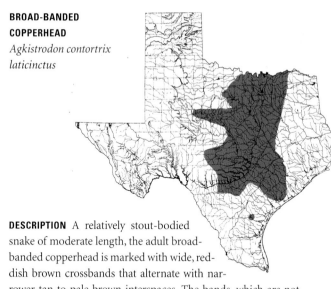

DESCRIPTION A relatively stout-bodied snake of moderate length, the adult broad-banded copperhead is marked with wide, reddish brown crossbands that alternate with narrower tan to pale brown interspaces. The bands, which are not much wider on the sides of the body than along the spine, may be finely edged in white; the terminal portion of the tail is greenish gray, often crossed with subtle, thin white lines. A narrow, dark brown V lies along each side of the head, its apex located near the end of the mouthline, with one arm terminating behind the eye and the other tracing the lower lip. Very young specimens are clad in shades of gray instead of brown, and their tail tips are bright yellow. The snake's body scales are only weakly keeled and usually in 23 middorsal rows. Most scales under the tail are arranged in a single row, except those near the end of the tail, which are paired. The anal plate is single.

COMPARABLE SNAKES Among our native serpents, the infant western cottonmouth most closely resembles the broad-banded copperhead. Although the two snakes share a similar dorsal pattern of wide, dark body crossbands and pale interspaces, the cottonmouth's head is mostly dusky and bears a broad, horizontal, mahogany cheek stripe behind each eye. In addition, its dorsal scales are in 25 rows at midbody. Both the eastern and dusty hognosed snakes are sometimes mistaken for the copperhead, but except for occasional unmarked specimens of the eastern species, their dorsal patterns consist of spots or blotches. Other distinguishing features of hog-nosed snakes are their sharply upturned snouts, round pupils, absence of heat-sensing facial pits, and divided anal plates. Although the wide, dark crossbands and yellow to reddish interspaces of the broad-banded water snake somewhat resemble those of the copperhead, they are seldom clearly defined. The water snake, which lacks facial pits, has a wide dark band extending backward from the eye to the end of the mouthline, round pupils, and a divided anal plate.

Adult from McLennan County.

SIZE The usual length of adults is 22 to 30 inches (56–76.2 cm). The maximum length reported as 37 $^1/_4$ inches (95 cm).

HABITAT This Central Texas subspecies of the copperhead is most commonly associated with wooded areas extending from the Red River in the north to the Balcones Escarpment in the south, except that to the southwest its range continues to Frio County and to the southeast to Victoria County. The region encompasses primarily the post oak woodlands of the Cross Timbers and the live oak–cedar association of the Edwards Plateau, although the broad-banded copperhead occurs as well in the generally inhospitable Blackland Prairie, where it is confined to the margins of woodland streams that flow through the area. According to Gehlbach (in Gloyd and Conant 1990), the largest concentrations of copperheads found in the Waco area occur in the deciduous woodlands, containing primarily cedar elm and sugarberry but including some American elm, bur oak, and pecan. Elsewhere throughout its range it frequently occurs near some form of surface water such as streams, ponds, or lakes, often in the vicinity of ridges and rocky ledges and usually where the sandy or gravelly soils are blanketed with accumulations of leaf litter.

TRANS-PECOS COPPERHEAD
Agkistrodon contortrix pictigaster

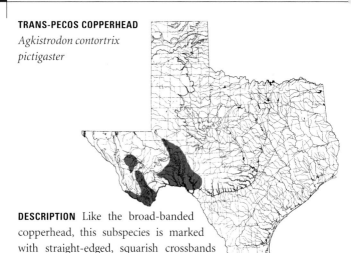

DESCRIPTION Like the broad-banded
copperhead, this subspecies is marked
with straight-edged, squarish crossbands
that are nearly as wide along the spine as they
are on the sides, but it differs from that subspecies by
its heavily mottled belly pattern of deep chestnut (sometimes
almost solid black) and the pale inverted U at the base of each
crossband. The chestnut brown, cinnamon, or dark seal brown
crossbands, which are distinctly darker along their outer margins
and also finely edged in white, are separated from one another by
spaces of pale hazel brown or an even paler, almost off-white col-
or. The crossbands of some specimens contain a few small, dark
spots. The dorsal scales, arranged in 21 or 23 rows at midbody, are
only lightly keeled, and the anal plate is single. Most scales under
the tail are in a single row, except those near the end of the tail,
which are paired.

COMPARABLE SNAKES The grayish Texas lyre snake is more slender than a copper-head, has a pale belly, and possesses a divided
anal plate.

SIZE Slightly smaller on average than the other races of copperhead, adults of this subspecies are 20 to 30 inches (51–76 cm)
long. The maximum known length is 32 ⁷/₈ inches (38.5 cm).

HABITAT An inhabitant of the arid Trans-Pecos region of Texas,
this copperhead occupies a variety of sites ranging from moist,
tree-dominated mountain canyons to dry desert flats, which in
some cases appear to be devoid of surface water. In his study

of the copperhead's natural history, Fitch (1960) described the Trans-Pecos copperhead's typical Chisos Mountain habitat as the mouth of a canyon encompassing an area roughly 100 yards (91.2 m) long and 20 to 110 feet (6.1–33.5 m) wide, where the plant life consists of willow, walnut, hackberry, Mexican buckeye, persimmon, fragrant sumac, and grape. The largest trees in this sheltered canyon grove have trunks about 2 feet (61 cm) in diameter, and the ground beneath them is mostly bare and rocky, but with scattered accumulations of leaf litter. When he gave this description, Fitch estimated that less than 1 square mile

Adult from Val Verde County.

(2.59 km²) of such suitable habitat still existed in all of the Chisos Mountains, although he painted a more optimistic picture for the Davis Mountains, where, he suggested, the remaining groves of live oak totaled at least several square miles.

In more arid circumstances, Trans-Pecos copperheads have been collected in arroyos lined with igneous boulders, and some in dense stands of river cane, a habitat that can harbor unusually large numbers of the serpents. William G. Degenhardt and his wife, Paula, encountered a plethora of serpents on July 8, 1961, in a cane thicket growing along a trail leading into Santa Elena Canyon in Big Bend National Park. (Gloyd and Conant 1990).

Although the largest concentrations of Trans-Pecos copperheads have been reported in moist wooded canyons such as the one described by Milstead, Mecham, and McClintock (1950), where 90 specimens were collected in one month near Independence Creek on the Stockton Plateau, more recent reports show that the subspecies is widely distributed in some remarkably dry habitats far removed from surface water and trees, including the most arid creosote bush and chaparral flats in Terrell and Brewster counties.

WESTERN COTTONMOUTH
Agkistrodon piscivorus leucostoma

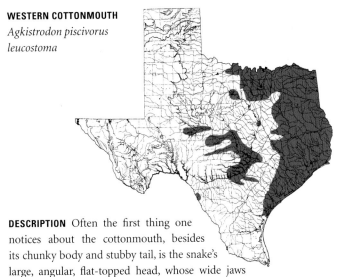

DESCRIPTION Often the first thing one notices about the cottonmouth, besides its chunky body and stubby tail, is the snake's large, angular, flat-topped head, whose wide jaws stand out prominently against the relatively narrow neck. The head markings are not conspicuous in the adult snake, except for a broad, dark cheek stripe narrowly trimmed in white. Below this mask, which stretches from the eye to the back of the mouthline, is an area of yellowish brown that is often suffused with darker brown.

The overall appearance of this stout-bodied serpent is typically dark and lackluster, with little noticeable distinction between the snake's obscure markings and its dull ground color. As a rule, the adult pattern consists of broad, ill-defined crossbands of grayish brown, dark brown, or black, each band light-centered, dark-edged, and sometimes also narrowly trimmed in white on its jagged outer margins, especially along the sides. This pattern generally darkens with age, disappearing altogether in most older individuals. Patternless young snakes are also occasionally found throughout the snake's range; such solid black or dark brown cottonmouths occur with the greatest frequency among Gulf Coast populations.

The newborn cottonmouth bears little resemblance to its parents. For the first year of its life, the boldly patterned juvenile looks remarkably like a young copperhead, its tan body marked with broad, jagged, mahogany crossbands, each containing a light brown, vertical inner core. Both the crossbands and the paler interspaces bear prominent, widely scattered dark spots. Equally pronounced are the white horizontal pinstripes bordering the dark mask and the narrow, pale-colored ones that edge the lower lip scales. The tail tip, like that of the baby copperhead, is sulphur yellow.

Because of considerable color and pattern variation among individual western cottonmouths, the most useful diagnostic features are those found in the less conspicuous but more reliable details of scalation. Among the most important of these is the arrangement of the scales under the tail, called subcaudals, which in this species typically occur in a single row, except for a few divided ones near the end of the tail. The weakly keeled dorsal scales are arranged in 25 rows at midbody, and the anal plate is single.

COMPARABLE SNAKES Several harmless water snakes of the genus *Nerodia* resemble the cottonmouth by virtue of their relatively

Adult from Liberty County.

313

thick-set bodies, somewhat large, wide heads, and dark bodies. Unlike the cottonmouth, however, they have round pupils, no facial pits, a divided anal plate, and two rows of scales under the tail. But such details are helpful only when the snake is examined close up. A safer though perhaps less conclusive way to recognize a water snake is to observe its behavior in the water. In contrast to the cottonmouth, which swims with much of its body visible above the waterline and its head raised fully out of the water and held nearly parallel to the surface, a water snake moves with its head barely out of the water, its submerged body trailing behind, largely unseen.

There is also a close similarity between the very young cottonmouth and the juvenile copperhead; a notable difference between them is seen in their head markings. The pale cheek of the copperhead is bordered above by a narrow, dark line that extends rearward from the eye and curves around the end of the mouthline, whereas in the young cottonmouth the side of the head is dominated by a broad, dark mask thinly margined with white, both above and below.

SIZE Although the western cottonmouth is known to reach a maximum length of slightly more than 5 feet (152 cm), most Texas specimens are 24 to 36 inches (61–91.4 cm) long. Several particularly large adults, measuring just over 4 feet (122 cm) long, were captured in the coastal marshes of Hall's Bayou along the upper Texas coast. As a rule, western cottonmouths inhabiting the inland forests of East Texas do not grow as large as those found elsewhere.

HABITAT The ubiquitous cottonmouth occurs over the entire eastern half of the state, occupying nearly every kind of stable aquatic habitat from brackish coastal marshes to cool, clear upland streams, and from sea level sites to elevations as high as 2,300 feet (703 m). It is especially abundant in the lowland swamps, marshes, and slow-moving streams of southeastern Texas as far down the coast as Corpus Christi but is surprisingly absent from the lower Rio Grande Valley, where much of the coastal environment seems equally suitable for its survival. That it also occurs on Texas' offshore barrier islands is well documented. One

2 ¹/₂-foot specimen was discovered under a clump of prickly pear cactus growing in sand dunes on the mainland side of San Jose Island, an unlikely microhabitat for this moisture-loving serpent. Despite its propensity for wet environments, this snake is occasionally found some distance from water. A few individuals have been observed at localities a mile or more from any permanent source of moisture.

Occasionally, portentous weather conditions cause larger concentrations of the western cottonmouth in Texas, although such aggregations are exceptional and generally of short duration. For example, when a major hurricane churns inland across the upper Texas coast, creating powerful storm surges, heavy downpours, and extensive flooding, cottonmouths are among the vertebrates most frequently observed seeking refuge from the rising waters. At such times, large numbers of the displaced pit vipers, along with other snakes and a variety of small mammals, gather on isolated patches of high ground.

In the East Texas pine and pine-oak forests, the cottonmouth confines itself mostly to large and small ponds scattered throughout the region, to palmetto and cypress swamps, and to broad river bottoms and their attendant sloughs. Farther inland in Texas, where aquatic environments are less prevalent, it is usually restricted to the woodland borders of sizable rivers and their tributaries and to lakes and ponds with shoreline vegetation. It has also managed to follow the Colorado and Brazos river systems westward across the semiarid and essentially inhospitable (to an aquatic serpent) Edwards Plateau to Crockett and Irion counties. In this austere land, where creeks and rivers cut through stone canyons and flow over solid bedrock, the cottonmouth is most apt to be found near cool, shallow springs a short distance from the main waterways. Despite its affinity for natural wetlands, it sometimes also inhabits wet agricultural and suburban areas, particularly those supporting an abundant food supply. Such places can include rice fields, artificial fish ponds, and drainage ditches. This venomous serpent has even been found within the borders of some of the state's largest cities, but it is seldom encountered there.

WESTERN DIAMOND-BACKED RATTLESNAKE
Crotalus atrox

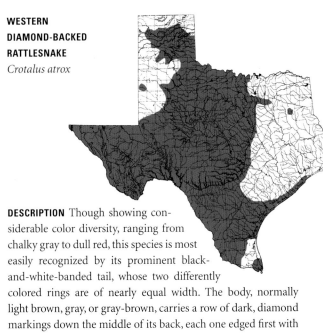

DESCRIPTION Though showing considerable color diversity, ranging from chalky gray to dull red, this species is most easily recognized by its prominent black-and-white-banded tail, whose two differently colored rings are of nearly equal width. The body, normally light brown, gray, or gray-brown, carries a row of dark, diamond markings down the middle of its back, each one edged first with black, then white. This pattern is not always conspicuous, since it may be obscured by the minute flecks and dots, both light and dark, that liberally cover the snake's body and give it an overall dusty appearance. In some specimens, particularly those from the Rio Grande Valley, the black diamonds contrast sharply with the yellowish ground color to create a bold, clearly defined pattern, whereas diamond-backed rattlesnakes from extreme southwestern Texas may be pinkish, with indistinct diamonds.

The lateral head markings of this species are also definitive. They consist of two parallel pale stripes on each side of the face, one of which passes diagonally downward from in front of the eye to the middle of the upper lip. The other extends from behind the eye to a point just preceding the end of the mouthline. The strongly keeled scales are in 25 or 27 midbody rows, and the anal plate is single.

COMPARABLE SNAKES The snake most likely to be mistaken for *C. atrox* is the Mohave rattler, whose diamondlike dorsal markings are similar to those of the diamond-backed rattlesnake but usually better defined. This species also has a black-and-white-banded tail, but its dark caudal rings are significantly narrower than its pale ones. The pale line extending downward diagonally from behind the eye does not intersect the mouthline but passes above and behind it. In addition, most of the pale scales that margin the dorsal markings are unicolored, and no more than three rows of scales lie between its supraoculars. The massasaugas and prairie rattlesnakes also show some resemblance to the western diamond-backed rattlesnake, but their rounded, nearly uniformly colored dorsal markings are unlike the angular, polychromatic diamonds of *C. atrox,* nor do they display the diamondback's boldly ringed, black-and-white-banded tail. The series of large plates on top of the massasauga's head differs from the mostly small scales that cover the diamondback's crown. The black-tailed rattlesnake is uniquely marked with a combination

Adult from Atascosa County.

of an all-black forecrown and a uniformly black tail (indistinctly banded in juveniles). The harmless bull snake may not precisely resemble the western diamond-backed rattlesnake, but the two snakes share enough physical features to cause them to be confused with one another. Moreover, both species respond in a similar way when threatened.

SIZE Among U.S. serpents, the western diamond-backed rattlesnake is exceeded in size only by the slightly heavier and longer eastern diamond-backed rattlesnake, *Crotalus adamanteus,* which inhabits the coastal lowlands of the southeastern states. On average, adult western diamond-backed rattlesnakes are between 3 and 4 feet (91.4–121.9 cm) long.

Historically, the largest *C. atrox* have come from Hidalgo and Starr counties in the lower Rio Grande Valley. Before the 1960s, specimens 6 feet (182.9 cm) long were frequently captured there. Such large rattlesnakes are seldom encountered today. The most generally accepted maximum recorded length for this species is an imposing 7 feet, 4 inches (223.5 cm).

HABITAT This snake is by far the most abundant and widespread venomous serpent in Texas. Nevertheless, it avoids the extensive pine and pine-hardwood forests covering the eastern quarter of the state, just as it does most densely wooded habitats within its range, for this is essentially a snake of sparsely vegetated, arid and semiarid terrain. It also occurs more commonly in the lowlands than at higher elevations, although in the moderately elevated hills and plateaus that spread out north and west of Austin, the western diamond-backed rattlesnake is locally plentiful. In the Chisos Mountains of Texas, the western diamond-backed rattler wanders up the slopes of Green Gulch to 4,500 feet (1,371 m). Although one was collected on the Marine Ranch in the Eagle Mountains at 5,500 feet (1,672 m), in Texas it probably reaches its maximum elevation (approaching 6,000 feet [1,829 m]) on the slopes and canyons of the Davis Mountains in Jeff Davis County.

Within those limits, it lives in a wide variety of habitats, including desert flats, brush-covered plains, mesquite- and creosote-covered intermesa valleys, rolling hills, cedar-covered mesa tops, thorny thickets, rocky canyons, sandstone outcroppings, river bluffs, rocky mountain foothills, and plant-covered sand dunes, to mention just a few. Despite the snake's propensity for dry habitats, it frequently chooses to live near watercourses and dry arroyos that sometimes contain water. As every Texas rancher knows, this precocious reptile is frequently seen around abandoned wooden buildings and trash heaps near human habitations.

One of our more familiar Texas stereotypes—the angry rattlesnake coiled defiantly in a prickly pear cactus thicket—is really not that far off the mark, in the South Texas brush country where the diamond-backed rattlesnake undoubtedly reaches its greatest population density. Here, in the open mesquite-cactus-chaparral environment of the Rio Grande Plain, it is encountered most frequently in or near the impenetrable stands of prickly pear cactus that dot the gently rolling landscape.

On the low offshore islands the rattlesnakes take refuge in the cactus and saltgrass that grow behind the sand dunes. They are also plentiful in the scrubby vegetation, cactus, and saltgrass clumps on the adjacent mainland, just as they are among the elevated piles of driftwood that line the more isolated beaches from Galveston to Brownsville.

CANEBRAKE RATTLESNAKE
Crotalus horridus
atricaudatus

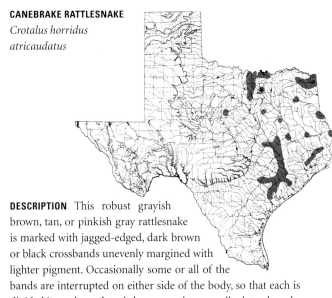

DESCRIPTION This robust grayish brown, tan, or pinkish gray rattlesnake is marked with jagged-edged, dark brown or black crossbands unevenly margined with lighter pigment. Occasionally some or all of the bands are interrupted on either side of the body, so that each is divided into a large dorsal chevron and two smaller lateral markings. Whatever the pattern, the ground color always darkens toward the rear of the body, becoming uniformly black on the tail. In addition, a dull, reddish brown stripe extends along the spine, at least on the forward part of the body. On either side of the snake's sharply triangular head, a wide dark brown or brownish yellow band extends obliquely across the cheek from the eye to well behind the end of the mouthline. The strongly keeled dorsal scales occur in 23 or 25 rows at midbody, and the anal plate is divided.

COMPARABLE SNAKES The western diamond-backed rattlesnake, which is unlikely to invade the canebrake's moist woodland habitat, has diamond markings, a light-bordered dark band behind each eye, and a distinctly black-and-white-banded tail. Both the western pygmy rattler and western massasauga can be recognized by the group of large scales and prominent black markings on their crowns, in contrast to the small scales and the absence of markings on top of the canebrake's head. Both possess oval

dorsal markings instead of zigzag crossbands, and their tails have
dark banding.

SIZE Among Texas rattlesnakes, the canebrake, with a maximum
known length of 74 $\frac{1}{2}$ inches (189.1 cm), ranks second in size only
to the western diamond-backed rattler. Adults of this subspecies
are generally between 40
and 60 inches (101.6–152.4
cm) long.

HABITAT Primarily a snake
of moist lowland forest
and hilly woodland near
rivers, streams, and lakes,
the canebrake ranges
across the eastern third
of the state from the Red
River to the Gulf Coast.
Although nowhere abun-
dant, it is evidently as
plentiful along the lower

Adult from Polk County.

reaches of the Trinity, Neches, and Angelina rivers and their numerous tributaries as in any other part of its Texas range. Nearly
all of the 35 to 40 canebrake rattlers donated to the Houston Zoo
over the last 30 years have come from this region of pine and
mixed pine-hardwood forest; most were found less than a mile
from some source of permanent water. A number of such specimens came from the river bottoms themselves, others from nearby sandy ridges. According to Gordon Henley (pers. com.), a few
were observed in large crevices of sedimentary rock formations
that sometimes occur in the otherwise rock-free environment of
Angelina County. Canebrake rattlesnakes also inhabit palmetto-
covered lowlands and cane thickets, as well as abandoned, brush-
covered fields and woodland clearings littered with decaying logs
and tree stumps.

During 20 years of field work in extreme southeastern Texas,
Ed Guidry (1953), an ardent amateur herpetologist from Port Arthur, observed only two canebrake rattlesnakes.

MOTTLED ROCK RATTLESNAKE
Crotalus lepidus lepidus

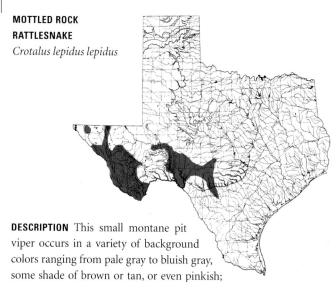

DESCRIPTION This small montane pit viper occurs in a variety of background colors ranging from pale gray to bluish gray, some shade of brown or tan, or even pinkish; the dorsal pattern consists of widely separated narrow, dark, serrated crossbands, which on the forebody are often indistinct and blotch-shaped. As the result of small, dark spots and blotches scattered between the crossbands, most specimens have a speckled or dusty appearance, and in some snakes such ancillary markings unite to form smaller, secondary crossbars between the primary series. Widely spaced narrow dark bands cross the tail. There is usually a dark stripe from each eye to near the end of the mouthline, which is distinct in most snakes, vague or absent in others. The infants are flecked more heavily with dark spots than the adults, their black crossbands are often indistinct or absent, and their tails are yellowish. The dorsal scales are keeled and in 23 rows at midbody; the anal plate is single.

In southwestern Texas, Vincent (1982) identified two distinctly different and geographically separate populations of this subspecies, each displaying its own colors to match the dominant soils and rock formations of its particular habitat. Not only do they occupy different geographic areas, but they are also separated by significant expanses of lowland desert. The easternmost population, occupying the elevated parts of the Edwards and Stockton plateaus where the limestone rock is predominantly gray and the soils mostly light colored, consists primarily of matching light gray or bluish gray snakes. In these individuals, the anterior body blotches are mostly faded; some light-toned examples displaying a nearly chalk white coloration with scarcely a trace of crossbanding on the forward third of the trunk. Mottled rock rattlesnakes inhabiting the Davis, Chinati, Sierra Vieja, and Wylie mountains, as well as those living in the upland zones of the Big Bend region, have a strikingly different appearance. Their primary markings are usually more conspicuous and sometimes fairly prominent across the entire length of the snake's body, but in keeping with the dark volcanic soils and rocks that characterize these areas of southwestern Texas, their background colors consist of reddish, pinkish, or buff tones instead of pale gray.

COMPARABLE SNAKES No other southwestern Texas rattlesnake species has a dorsal pattern whose primary markings consist of widely spaced, narrow dark crossbands with jagged edges, although the spaces between the bands are often heavily speckled and may even contain smaller secondary bands. This is the only native rattlesnake species in which the preocular scale is vertically divided.

Adult.

SIZE Although the largest known specimen measured 30 $\frac{1}{2}$ inches (77.5 cm) long, adults are less than 2 feet (61 cm) in length.

HABITAT Primarily an inhabitant of craggy ridges, rocky gorges, talus slides, and boulder fields in semiarid to arid environments, this mountain-dwelling rattlesnake usually occurs at elevations ranging from 2,500 feet (762 m) along the eastern portions of its Texas range to 6,800 feet (2,073 m) on Mount Locke in the Davis Mountains and approximately 7,000 feet (2,134 m) in the Chisos Mountains of the Big Bend. Although it normally occupies relatively moist evergreen woodland slopes at higher elevations, it can also be found, often in moderate numbers, along the Pecos and Devil's rivers and their boulder-strewn, tree- and brush-filled tributary canyons, some of the lowest elevations at which it is found. At the eastern end of the snake's geographic range, not far from the small town of Leaky, in Real County, the mottled rock rattler occurs in rugged limestone hills dominated by stands of oak, scrub black walnut, and juniper, along with scattered thickets of mountain laurel and intermittent patches of needle grass. Farther west, in Terrell County, Milstead, Mecham, and Mc-Clintock (1950) found mottled rock rattlesnakes in persimmon and shin oak plant associations, mostly along steep rimrock or at the edges of limestone outcroppings. In the Sierra Vieja mountain range of southwestern Texas, in Presidio County, Jameson and Flury (1949) collected two specimens in the catclaw-grama association and two more in streambeds. Axtell (1959) captured two and saw others in the basalt rubble habitat of the Black Gap area in Brewster County, though none were seen in the nearby limestone formations. According to Michael Forstner (pers. com.), the subspecies prefers habitats in far West Texas that consist of extensive monolithic ledge systems with crevice caves below them, limestone outcroppings containing large fissured areas of rock, and boulder scree slopes.

Beaupre (1995) studied the snake's ecology at two distinctly different sites within Big Bend National Park. The first location, containing a series of limestone gorges emptying into Boquillas Canyon at 1,837 feet (556 m), marked one of the lowest known elevations for this subspecies in Texas. The at Grapevine Hills site, at an elevation of 3,398 feet (1,036 m), consisted of an exposed volcanic extrusion associated with several large boulder fields. In spite of similar desert vegetation at both locations (primarily lechuguilla, creosote, and cactus), the Grapevine Hills area contained greater plant cover, experienced more rainfall, and had a lower average monthly air temperature than the Boquillas site. As expected, the background colors of the two snake populations closely matched those of their respective habitats: the Boquillas Canyon serpents possessed an overall gray tone, whereas the Grapevine Hills snakes were rust red.

BANDED ROCK
RATTLESNAKE
Crotalus lepidus klauberi

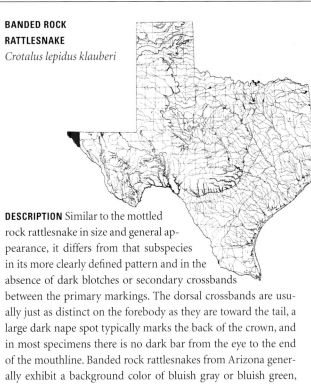

DESCRIPTION Similar to the mottled rock rattlesnake in size and general appearance, it differs from that subspecies in its more clearly defined pattern and in the absence of dark blotches or secondary crossbands between the primary markings. The dorsal crossbands are usually just as distinct on the forebody as they are toward the tail, a large dark nape spot typically marks the back of the crown, and in most specimens there is no dark bar from the eye to the end of the mouthline. Banded rock rattlesnakes from Arizona generally exhibit a background color of bluish gray or bluish green, but those from El Paso County, Texas, and adjacent counties of New Mexico represent some of the most stunning examples of this subspecies to be found within the snake's range, their dark dorsal crossbands set boldly against a ground color of tan or light brown. Perhaps even more spectacular are specimens from the Franklin Mountains in Texas, whose jagged, deep black cross-bars stand out in vivid contrast to an unblemished dorsal hue of pearl gray. Whatever the background color of such snakes, the dark cheek stripe, usually present in the mottled subspecies, is normally absent or indistinct in the adult banded race; conspicuous only in the infant, it nearly always disappears before the snake reaches maturity. The dorsal scales are keeled and in 23 rows at midbody; the anal plate is single.

COMPARABLE SNAKES Among Texas rattlesnakes, only the two subspecies of *C. lepidus* possess widely spaced, narrow dark crossbars along the back and a vertically divided preocular scale on either side of the head.

SIZE Most adults of this moderately small rattlesnake are less than 2 feet (61 cm) long. The largest known specimen measured 32 ⁵/₈

Adult from Franklin Mountains, El Paso County.

inches (82.9 cm) in length.

HABITAT This snake ordinarily inhabits fissured rock ledges, rock-strewn canyons, and precipitous talus slides in upland scrub forest or pine-oak woodland at relatively high elevations, preferring open spaces where a gap in the canopy permits sunlight to reach the ground. Elsewhere most banded rock rattlesnake populations inhabit moist forests, but those living in the Franklin Mountains of far West Texas occupy rather sparsely vegetated arid terrain. Although rocks are an essential component of the snake's habitat over of its range, in Arizona it may be found in grassy meadows some distance from any sizable surface rock formations.

NORTHERN BLACK-TAILED RATTLESNAKE

Crotalus molossus molossus

DESCRIPTION

Texas specimens are olive green, olive-brown, or gray above and greenish on the sides; those from the higher elevations of the Davis and Chisos mountains are somewhat darker in color than black-tailed rattlesnakes from other parts of the state. The snake can easily be identified by the unique pigmentation of its upper body scales. In the dorsal markings of most other rattlesnakes, two colors often cut randomly across a single scute, producing bicolored scales. In the black-tailed rattlesnake's upper markings, most individual scales are pigmented entirely with a single, solid hue.

Dark vertical bars with uneven edges extend downward from the lateral tips of each blotch nearly to the belly. The blotches, separated dorsally by sizable patches of cream to whitish scales, are most distinct near midbody, becoming narrower posteriorly and gradually more faded.

Also characteristic are the head markings. The blackish coloration on top of the snout and over the forward third of the crown is followed by clusters of dark spots scattered across the light rear part. Conspicuous, too, is a broad, dark brown mask that emanates from the blackish forecrown and runs obliquely downward behind the eye, narrowing gradually to a point near the mouthline.

The dorsal scales, usually in 27 midbody rows but ranging from 25 to 29, are keeled, and the anal plate is single.

SIZE Although a 52-inch (132.1 cm) black-tailed rattlesnake recently was reported from Kerr County, Texas (Tennant 1984), we believe the most credible record length for Texas is 49 ¹/₂ inches (125.7 cm). A specimen measuring 52 $^2/_5$ inches (133.1 cm) in length, collected in Cochise County, Arizona, and reported by Hardy and Greene (1995), represents the largest known specimen for the subspecies. The average adult is between 2 $^1/_2$ and 3 $^1/_2$ feet (76.2–106.7 cm) long.

COMPARABLE SNAKES Among Texas rattlesnakes, only the black-tailed rattlesnake has the combination of a black forecrown, a dark neck stripe containing patches of pale spots, paired groups of whitish scales in the dark dorsal markings, and a black tail that contrasts sharply against the paler body.

HABITAT In Texas the black-tailed rattlesnake inhabits wooded hills and mountains

Adult from Brewster County.

containing myriad rock crevices and stony ridges. At the eastern end of its range it inhabits the rugged central Hill Country, a nearly unbroken continuum of steep-sided sylvan canyons between wooded limestone hills and ridges. In arid habitat, specimens have been taken in Terrell County from thickets of persimmon–shin oak and stands of cedar-oak; each environment supported sufficient vegetative cover to guarantee the snakes a measure of shade from the hot sun. Scattered records show the black-tailed rattlesnake's Texas distribution extending from the Hill Country southwestward to Big Bend National Park, where it is the most common rattlesnake species. In the park itself, it reaches its greatest abundance in the foothills and mountains of the Chisos range at elevations above 4,000 feet (1,219 m), even ascending the slopes of Emory Peak to the rock slides at 7,400 feet (2,428 m), barely 145 yards (2,255 m) from the top. In the narrow stone canyons and gulches of the Guadalupe Mountains, where it frequents rock slides and dry, rocky streambeds, as well as the leaf-covered floors of pine-oak forest, it makes its way up the mountain slopes to an altitude of at least 8,200 feet (2,499 m).

MOHAVE RATTLESNAKE
*Crotalus scutulatus
scutulatus*

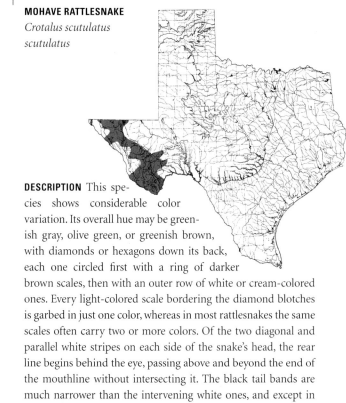

DESCRIPTION This spe-
cies shows considerable color
variation. Its overall hue may be greenish gray, olive green, or greenish brown,
with diamonds or hexagons down its back,
each one circled first with a ring of darker
brown scales, then with an outer row of white or cream-colored
ones. Every light-colored scale bordering the diamond blotches
is garbed in just one color, whereas in most rattlesnakes the same
scales often carry two or more colors. Of the two diagonal and
parallel white stripes on each side of the snake's head, the rear
line begins behind the eye, passing above and beyond the end of
the mouthline without intersecting it. The black tail bands are
much narrower than the intervening white ones, and except in
very young snakes, the bottom half of the base rattle segment is
pale yellow and of a lighter hue than the dark brown upper portion. The presence of only two enlarged scales on top of the head
between the large plates over the eyes also characterizes this species. The keeled dorsal scales are in 25 rows at midbody, and the
anal plate is single.

COMPARABLE SNAKES The western diamond-backed rattlesnake
closely resembles the Mohave, but its diamond dorsal markings
are not as clearly defined, the black rings on its tail are about the
same width as the white ones, the whitish stripe slanting diagonally downward from behind the eye intersects the mouthline,
the base rattle segment consists of one color, and on top of the
snake's head more than three rows of small scales occupy the

space between the enlarged eye plates. In contrast to the angular body blotches of the Mohave, those of both the desert massasauga and prairie rattlesnake are rounded, and each of the white scales bordering them is apt to be intersected by two or more colors (in the Mohave they are nearly always monochromatic). In these snakes the tail lacks the bold black-and-white banding of the Mohave.

SIZE A rattlesnake of moderate length and girth, it is generally between 2 and 3 feet (61–91.4 cm) in length. A 51-inch (129.5 cm) specimen represents Pale adult from Brewster County.

the most reliable record of maximum size for this species.

HABITAT Although the Mohave rattlesnake occurs in sparsely vegetated arid lowlands, grass-covered flatlands, and less often along the lower mountain slopes below 4,000 feet (1,219 m), it prefers high, barren desertland dotted with creosote bush, mesquite and cactus. Gehlbach (1981), who has had extensive field experience with our southwestern desert fauna, says it favors both the shortest grass and the fewest shrubs in regions with the lowest elevations. One such place, the area around Big Bend's Terlingua Flats, supports a sizable population of Mohave rattlers. On Mexico's northern plateau it sometimes ranges to unusually high elevations; it was reported by Armstrong and Murphy (1979) from grassland and juniper plains in central Durango at an elevation of approximately 8,000 feet (2,625 m). In California, Bryant and Miller (in Klauber 1956) found it on moderately sloping alluvial fans where soils, intersected by shallow washes, were coarse and rather tightly packed. Whatever the habitat, this rattlesnake tends to avoid severely uneven, rocky terrain and areas of dense vegetation. South and west of Marfa, Texas, it occurs in open grassland at 4,650 feet (1,417 m).

GREEN PRAIRIE RATTLESNAKE
Crotalus viridis viridis

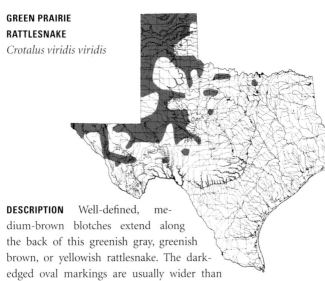

DESCRIPTION Well-defined, medium-brown blotches extend along the back of this greenish gray, greenish brown, or yellowish rattlesnake. The dark-edged oval markings are usually wider than long, often indented at front and back, and generally enclosed by a narrow white border. They become faded, narrow crossbands on the rear of the body, where they merge with the smaller, more discrete lateral blotches. Distinct narrow, dark rings circle the tail; the last one or two rings frequently are black. The lateral head markings provide an additional means of identification. In particular, a narrow white or yellowish stripe on the side of the head runs obliquely downward from in front of the eye to intersect the mouthline; another, nearly parallel to the first, extends from behind the eye to above the end of the mouthline. In the arrangement of scales on top of the snout, the prairie rattler is unique among Texas rattlesnakes. Only in this species do more than two internasal scales touch the rostral plate.

COMPARABLE SNAKES The dark tail rings of both Mohave and western diamond-backed rattlesnakes are black or nearly so, and they contrast strongly with the white spaces that separate them. In addition, the oblique, narrow light line behind the diamondback's eye intersects the mouthline, but that of the prairie rattler passes behind it. Where the prairie rattlesnake's crown is covered by numerous small scales, the massasauga has nine large plates. Among

Texas rattlesnakes, only the prairie has more than two internasal scales touching the rostral plate. The plains and dusty hog-nosed snakes, because of their stout bodies and dark dorsal markings,

are the nonvenomous snakes most likely to be confused with the prairie rattler, but they are easily identified by their broad necks, sharply upturned snouts, considerable black belly pigment, sharply pointed tails, and absence of rattles.

Adult.

SIZE A rattlesnake of moderate length, the adult usually ranges between 35 and 40 inches (88.9–114 cm) long. The maximum recorded length is 57 inches (144.8 cm).

HABITAT Although the prairie rattlesnake typically inhabits high grassy plains and associated canyons throughout most of its Texas range, it also occurs sparingly in the more arid southwestern part of the state. It exists, for example, in scattered localities across the sparsely vegetated limestone hills and plateaus marking the southeastern limits of its geographic range, and it extends westward from there across the northern edge of the Chihuahuan Desert, where it usually occupies transitional mesquite-grassland habitat and may even be found in dry creosote bush scrubland.

Despite its continued survival in such depauperate country, it is absent from Big Bend National Park, where it probably lived before humans' influence seriously depleted the area's native grasses and with them the prairie rattler's prime habitat, for this is essentially a grassland snake. In other parts of southwestern Texas it frequently ascends the rocky hills and bluffs of the lower mountain slopes to elevations above 5,000 feet (1,520 m). Wherever it is found, the prairie rattler inhabits sandy to rocky soils, generally avoiding areas of constant wetness such as marshy pond edges, soggy meadows, and damp river valleys.

DESERT MASSASAUGA
Sistrurus catenatus edwardsi

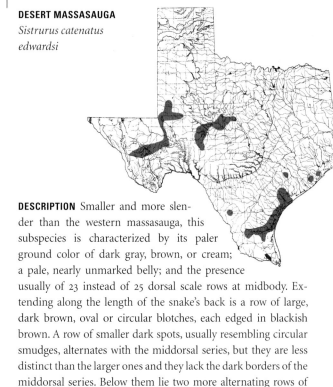

DESCRIPTION Smaller and more slender than the western massasauga, this subspecies is characterized by its paler ground color of dark gray, brown, or cream; a pale, nearly unmarked belly; and the presence usually of 23 instead of 25 dorsal scale rows at midbody. Extending along the length of the snake's back is a row of large, dark brown, oval or circular blotches, each edged in blackish brown. A row of smaller dark spots, usually resembling circular smudges, alternates with the middorsal series, but they are less distinct than the larger ones and they lack the dark borders of the middorsal series. Below them lie two more alternating rows of even smaller dark spots. On top of the head, two somewhat wavy dark brown stripes extend backward from near the eyes to the neck, although in some snakes such markings may be reduced to a pair of large nuchal spots. On either side of the head, a wide, dark brown mask, typically margined above and below by distinct white lines, extends rearward from the eye onto the neck. The dorsal scales are keeled, and the anal plate is single.

COMPARABLE SNAKES In addition to certain features of pattern and coloration, all other Texas rattlesnake species living within the range of the desert massasauga can be distinguished by the mostly small scales covering the top of the head. Mohave and western diamond-backed rattlesnakes also have diamond dorsal markings and distinctly black-and-white-banded tails. The prairie rattler, which lacks a bold, dark mask on either side of the head, has 25 or more midbody dorsal scale rows and more than two internasal scales in contact with the rostral plate. The dark crossbands of the black-tailed rattlesnake continue down the sides of its body to the snake's belly, and its tail is uniformly black. Hog-nosed snakes (particularly the races of the western species) are the nonvenomous serpents most likely to be confused with the desert massasauga. They do not have facial pits, elliptical pupils, or rattles. Moreover, they possess a uniquely flared and upturned snout, a neck fully as large in diameter as the head, and a divided anal plate.

Adult. Photo by R. A. Odum.

SIZE Among Texas' smallest rattlesnakes, the adults of this subspecies are generally less than 18 inches (45.7 cm) in length. A specimen of record size measured 21 $^1/_5$ inches (53.8 cm) long.

HABITAT This wide-ranging inhabitant of desert grassland and shortgrass prairie has a curiously discontinuous Texas distribution that includes the west-central part of the state on the one hand and extreme South Texas on the other. In between lie the Stockton and Edwards plateaus and a large stretch of northern Rio Grande Plain thornbrush, from which, despite many years of herpetological exploration, no massasaugas have been collected. This region extends from Sutton County in the north to Webb County in the south.

Although in Texas the desert massasauga is primarily a grassland and thornbrush dweller, like the other races of *S. catenatus* it often favors moist areas, such as those near streams, riverbeds, lakes, ponds, and water holes. Along the South Texas coast it can frequently be found in and near grass- and brush-covered sand dunes and grassy meadows.

WESTERN MASSASAUGA

Sistrurus catenatus
tergeminus

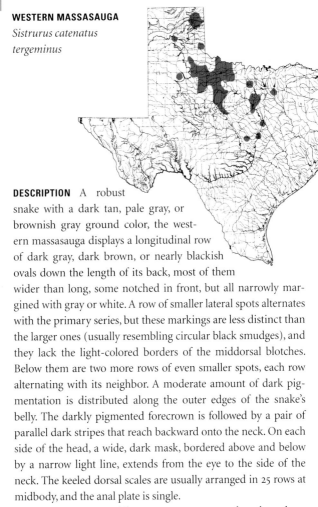

DESCRIPTION A robust
snake with a dark tan, pale gray, or
brownish gray ground color, the western massasauga displays a longitudinal row
of dark gray, dark brown, or nearly blackish
ovals down the length of its back, most of them
wider than long, some notched in front, but all narrowly margined with gray or white. A row of smaller lateral spots alternates
with the primary series, but these markings are less distinct than
the larger ones (usually resembling circular black smudges), and
they lack the light-colored borders of the middorsal blotches.
Below them are two more rows of even smaller spots, each row
alternating with its neighbor. A moderate amount of dark pigmentation is distributed along the outer edges of the snake's
belly. The darkly pigmented forecrown is followed by a pair of
parallel dark stripes that reach backward onto the neck. On each
side of the head, a wide, dark mask, bordered above and below
by a narrow light line, extends from the eye to the side of the
neck. The keeled dorsal scales are usually arranged in 25 rows at
midbody, and the anal plate is single.

COMPARABLE SNAKES The western pygmy rattlesnake, whose
crown is covered like that of the western massasauga mostly with
large plates, is distinguished by its smaller, more widely spaced
middorsal blotches, a pale orange stripe down the middle of its
back, and an unusually small rattle. All other Texas rattlesnakes
have primarily small scales on top of the head. In the prairie
rattlesnake there is no bold dark mask; and in the western

diamond-backed rattler the dorsal markings consist of angular diamonds.

SIZE Averaging only about 18 to 24 inches (46–61 cm) in length, this is one of our smallest native rattlesnakes. The largest known specimen measured 34 ³/₄ inches (88.3 cm) long.

HABITAT The snake's Texas distribution includes the gently rolling plains and prairies of the northwestern part of the state from the Caprock Escarpment in the west to the Blackland Prairie in the east, then continues southeastward to Bell and Lampasas counties. Over most of this region it is encountered in both shortgrass and tallgrass prairie. All of the 92 specimens collected by Greene and Oliver (1965) in eastern Parker and western Tarrant counties came from rolling tallgrass prairie, although Wright and Wright (1957) described the species' habitat throughout its range as lowlands, moist areas near rivers and streams, damp sandy places, swampy regions, and meadows. There is ample evidence that until recently, it was quite common in some parts of the state. On the evening of May 14, 1960, for example, Knopf and Tinkle (1961) collected 15 specimens in Throckmorton County on the road between the towns of Throckmorton and Woodson, a distance of just 16 miles. During nighttime collecting activities, Greene and Oliver found this to be the most abundant serpent on roadways in western Tarrant and eastern Parker counties.

In Texas, as elsewhere within the snake's geographic range, continued alteration of the reptile's open habitat for farmland and suburban housing development has caused a significant decline in the snake's numbers.

Adult from McLennan County.

WESTERN PYGMY RATTLESNAKE
Sistrurus miliarius streckeri

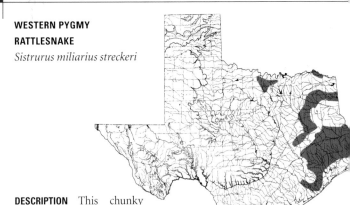

DESCRIPTION This chunky little pale gray or grayish brown rattlesnake bears a row of small, blackish spots down the middle of its back. The markings are often irregularly shaped, usually wider than long across the spine, and sometimes finely edged in white. They are often flanked on either side by a second row of similarly colored spots, more circular than the first, and below them is a third row of alternating dark spots, each of which extends onto the outer edges of the abdomen. In most specimens a pale orange wash occurs between the dorsal blotches without crossing them, giving the impression of an orange stripe running down the center of the snake's back. The head is conspicuously marked by a pair of slightly wavy, parallel black lines on the crown that extend from between the eyes onto the neck and a black band that runs along each side of the face from the eye to the back of the mouthline. The tail is indistinctly banded and ends in a tiny rattle. The dorsal scales, usually arranged in 21 (sometimes 23) rows at midbody, are strongly keeled, and the anal plate is single. As in all *Sistrurus*, the top of the head is covered with nine large plates.

COMPARABLE SNAKES Hog-nosed snakes, which have a distinctly upturned snout, lack both a rattle and the heat-sensing facial cavities of the western pygmy rattler. In addition, they have round instead of elliptical pupils. The much larger dorsal blotches of the western massasauga are closely spaced, and its dorsal scales are arranged in 25 rows at midbody. Both the western diamond-backed and canebrake rattlers can be distinguished by their larger dorsal markings, by the absence of a distinct pattern on their crowns, and by the presence of numerous small scales instead of large plates on top of their heads. The diamondback's tail is boldly banded with black and white; that of the canebrake is all black.

SIZE The adults of this subspecies are usually between 15 and 20 inches (38.1–50.8 cm) long. They have long been known to reach a maximum size of 25 $1/8$ inches (63.8 cm).

HABITAT Restricted primarily to the partially wooded or open lowlands of the upper Texas coast and to the hilly second-growth forests of East Texas, this uncommon snake occurs on sandy in-

Adult from Polk County. Photo by J. E. Werler.

land soils and on some of the less permeable coastal substrates, but nearly always close to standing water, which can include river bottoms, lakes, ponds, swamps, marshes, wet pastures, and even rice-field canals and roadside ditches. Of the numerous pygmy rattlesnakes donated to the Houston Zoo over the last 35 years, by far the greatest number have come from near towns and cities scattered throughout the pine-hardwood forest along U.S. Highway 59, from Lake Houston to Nacogdoches. This sporadically distributed serpent is infrequently encountered in Texas, even by professional collectors, and then usually only a specimen at a time. Judging by the observations of Percy Viosca (in Dundee and Rossman 1989), it may actually be more common than we believe, for in neighboring Louisiana he collected 103 western pygmy rattlesnakes from levees on Delacroix Island, where they had been driven after 12 days of severe flooding.

GLOSSARY

ANAL PLATE The rearmost belly scale, usually larger than the preceding abdominal scales, which covers the anal opening and marks the separation of the snake's body from its tail.

ANTERIOR Pertaining to the forward or head end of an animal.

CAUDAL Pertaining to the tail.

CLOACA In amphibians and reptiles, the common chamber into which the digestive, urinary, and reproductive tracts discharge their contents (= vent).

COLD-BLOODED Refers to an animal without a constant body temperature, one whose body heat is regulated not by its own metabolism but by exposing itself to certain external sources. It may increase its body temperature by basking or lower it by seeking shade. To avoid prolonged subfreezing temperatures in winter, it must hibernate.

DEPAUPERATE Impoverished or destitute.

DORSAL Referring to an organism's back; in the cases of a snake, its upper body surface.

DORSUM The entire upper surface or back of an organism.

ECCHYMOSIS The oozing of blood into the tissues, causing skin discoloration.

ECOSYSTEM In a given environment, a system of interaction among plants and animals with one another and with their surroundings.

ELAPID Referring to the family Elapidae, which includes coral snakes, cobras, mambas, and sea snakes, among others.

ENDEMIC Restricted to a limited geographic region.

ENVENOMATION The introduction of venom into an animal, which in snakes is typically accomplished through grooved or hollow fangs.

EPIDERMIS The thin, nonvascular outer layer of skin, which in snakes is periodically shed.

GENETICS The study of heredity and the transmission of characteristics.

GENUS A group of closely related species.

GROUND COLOR The overall background color of a snake, on which its markings appear to lie.

HEMIPENIS Either of the paired copulatory organs of male snakes and lizards.

HERPETOFAUNA Collectively, the species of amphibians and reptiles inhabiting a specific region.

HERPETOLOGY The study of amphibians and reptiles.

HOME RANGE The area within which an organism usually travels during its normal activities.

HYBRID The offspring of a mating between two different species.

HYPOTENSION Abnormally low blood pressure.

INTERGRADE An intermediate individual that shares the characteristics of two closely related subspecies of the same species.

INTERSPACE The ground color between a snake's primary markings of blotches, bands, or rings.

KEEL A ridge running lengthwise along the center of a scale.

LATERAL Referring to the side of an organism.

LONGITUDINAL Extending lengthwise.

MEDIAN In or of the middle.

MELANISTIC Having an unusual predominance of black pigmentation.

MICROHABITAT A small piece of an animal's habitat.

MIDDORSAL The area down the center of the back.

MIMIC A species whose form, color, or behavior imitates to its own advantage that of another species; in snakes, a harmless serpent that resembles a venomous species.

MORPHOLOGY The study of the form and structure of plants and animals, especially their outward appearance.

MOTTLED Irregularly marked with spots and blotches of various shapes, sizes, or colors.

MOUTHLINE The seam formed by the juncture of a snake's upper and lower lips, which extends from one side of the mouth to the other.

NECROSIS The death or decay of tissue.

NEUROTOXIC Referring to components in snake venom that damage the nervous system, often causing paralysis.

NOMINATE SUBSPECIES An organism whose species and subspecies names are the same.

NUCHAL Referring to the back of the neck.

OPHIDIAN Pertaining to snakes.

ORBIT The bony cavity within which the eye fits.

PERMEABLE Referring to tissues that are easily penetrated by liquids.

POPULATION A group of organisms of a single species or subspecies living together in the same geographic area.

POSTERIOR Pertaining to the rear portion of the body.

RACE Subspecies.

RELICT POPULATION The surviving remnant of a once more widespread population that is now confined to an isolated geographic area.

ROSTRAL Pertaining to the snout or to the scale covering the snout.

SCUTE A large scale.

STEREOTYPE A fixed pattern of behavior.

SUBSTRATE The surface covering of the ground.

TALUS A pile of rock fragments at the base of a slope or cliff.

TOXIC Poisonous.

TAXONOMY The science of identifying and classifying plants and animals.

TRANSLUCENT Transmitting but diffusing light.

TRANSVERSE Extending across the body or limb as opposed to being disposed lengthwise.

VENT In reptiles and amphibians, the external orifice of the cloaca.

VENTRAL Pertaining to the underside of an animal.

VERTEBRAL Lying lengthwise along the midline of the back.

VOUCHER SPECIMEN A specimen of an organism preserved in a permanent scientific collection to verify the species' presence at a particular geographic location.

REFERENCES

Allen, E. R., and D. Swindell. 1948. Cottonmouth moccasin of Florida. Herpetologica (suppl. 1):1–16.

Amaral, A. do. 1927. The antisnake-bite campaign in Texas and in the subtropical United States. Bull. Antivenin Inst. Amer. 1:77–85.

Armstrong, B. L., and J. B. Murphy. 1979. The natural history of Mexican rattlesnakes. Univ. Kansas Mus. Nat. Hist. Spec. Publ. 5:1–88.

Axtell, R. W. 1959. Amphibians and reptiles of the Black Gap Wildlife Management Area, Brewster County, Texas. Southwest. Nat. 4(2):88–109.

———. 1969. Another *Ficimia streckeri* from southern Texas. Tex. J. Sci. 20(4):381.

Bailey, V. 1905. Biological Survey of Texas. North American Fauna 25.

Banicki, L. H., and R. G. Webb. 1982. Morphological variation of the Texas lyre snake (*Trimorphodon biscutatus vilkinsoni*) from the Franklin Mountains, West Texas. Southwest. Nat. 27(3):321–324.

Beaupre, S. J. 1995. Comparative ecology of the mottled rock rattlesnake, *Crotalus lepidus,* in Big Bend National Park. Herpetologica 51(1):45–56.

Bechtel, H. B. 1995. Reptile and Amphibian Variants. Krieger Publishing, Malabar, Fla.

Betz, T. 1963. The gross ovarian morphology of the diamond-backed water snake, *Natrix rhombifer,* during the reproductive cycle. Copeia 1963(4): 692–697.

Blaney, R. M. 1977. Systematics of the common kingsnake, *Lampropeltis getulus* (Linnaeus). Tulane Stud. Zool. Bot. 19: 47–103.

Boundy, J. 1995. Maximum lengths of North American snakes. Bull. Chicago Herpetol. Soc. 30:109–122.

Brown, B. C. 1950. An annotated checklist of the reptiles and amphibians of Texas. Baylor University Studies, Waco, Tex.

Burbrink, F. T. 2002. Phylogeographic analysis of the cornsnake (*Elaphe guttata*) complex as inferred from maximum likelihood and Bayesian analysis. Molecular Phylo. Evol. 25:465–476.

Burt, C. E., and W. L. Hoyle. 1935. Additional records of the reptiles of the central prairie region of the United States. Trans. Kansas Acad. Sci. 37: 193–216.

Clark, D. R., Jr. 1967. Experiments into selection of soil type, soil moisture level, and temperature by five species of small snakes. Trans. Kansas Acad. Sci. 70(4):490–496.

———. 1970. Age-specific "reproductive efforts" in the worm snake *Carphophis vermis* (Kennicott). Trans. Kansas Acad. Sci. 73:20–24.

———. 1974. The western ribbon snake (*Thamnophis proximus*): Ecology of a Texas population. Herpetologica 30(4): 372–379.

Clark, R. F. 1949. Snakes of the hill parishes of Louisiana. J. Tennessee Acad. Sci. 24: 244–261.

Collins, J. T., and T. W. Taggart. 2002. Standard common and current scientific names for North American amphibians, turtles, reptiles, and crocodilians. Center No. Amer. Herpetol., 44 pp.

Conant, R. 1955. Notes on three Texas reptiles, including an addition to the fauna of the state. Amer. Mus. Novitates 1726:1–6.

Conant, R., and J. T. Collins. 1991. A Field Guide to the Reptiles and Amphibians of Eastern and Central North America. 3rd ed. Houghton Mifflin, Boston.

Crother, B. I., et al. 2000. Scientific and standard English names of amphibians and reptiles of North America north of Mexico, with comments regarding confidence in our understanding. Soc. Stud. Amph. Rept., Herpetological Circular 29:1–82.

Crother, B. I., et al. 2003. Scientific and standard English names of amphibians and reptiles of North America north of Mexico: Update. Herpetol. Rev. 34(3):196–203.

Curtis, L. 1949. The snakes of Dallas County, Texas. Field and Lab. 17(1):1–13.

Davenport, J. W. 1943. Fieldbook of the Snakes of Bexar County, Texas, and Vicinity. Witte Memorial Mus., San Antonio, Tex.

Davis, W. B. 1953. Another record of the smooth green snake in Texas. Herpetologica 9(2):165.

Degenhardt, W. G., T. L. Brown, and D. A. Easterla. 1976. The taxonomic status of *Tantilla cucullata* and *Tantilla diabola*. Texas J. Sci. 27(1):226–234.

Diener, R. A. 1957. An anatomical study of the plain-bellied water snake. Herpetologica 13:203–211.

Dixon, J. R., B. D. Greene, and J. M. Mueller. 1988. 1988 Annual Report, Concho Water Snake Natural History Study, for the Colorado River Municipal Water District, Big Springs, Tex., 36 pp.

———. 1989. 1989 Annual Report, Concho Water Snake Natural History Study, for the Colorado River Municipal Water District, Big Springs, Tex., 66 pp.

Dixon, J. R., B. D. Greene, and M. J. Whiting. 1990. 1990 Annual Report, Concho Water Snake Natural History Study, for the Colorado River Municipal Water District, Big Springs, Tex., 69 pp.

Dundee, H. A., and D. A. Rossman. 1989. The Amphibians and Reptiles of Louisiana. Louisiana State Univ. Press, Baton Rouge.

Easterla, D. A. 1975. Reproductive and ecological observations on *Tantilla cucullata* from Big Bend National Park, Texas (Serpentes, Colubridae). Herpetologica 31(2):234–236.

———. 1989. Amphibians and reptiles checklist, Big Bend National Park, Rio Grande wild and scenic river. Big Bend Nat. Hist. Assoc. leaflet.

Ferguson, G. W. 1965. Verification of a population of *Ficimia cana* in north-central Texas. Herpetologica 21(2): 156–157.

Fitch. H. S. 1960. Autecology of the copperhead. Univ. Kansas Publ. Mus. Nat. Hist. 13: 85–288.

———. 1963. Natural history of the racer *Coluber constrictor*. Univ. Kansas Publ. Mus. Nat. Hist. 15(8):351–468.

———. 1975. A demographic study of the ringneck snake (*Diadophis punctatus*) in Kansas. Univ. Kansas Mus. Nat. Hist. Misc. Publ. 62:1–53.

———. 1978. A field study of the prairie kingsnake (*Lampropeltis calligaster*). Trans. Kansas Acad. Sci. 81:354–362.

Fitch, H. S., and R. R. Fleet. 1970. Natural history of the milk snake (*Lampropeltis triangulum*) in northeastern Kansas. Herpetologica 26(4):387–396.

Fix, J. D., and S. A. Minton, Jr. 1976. Venom extraction and yields from the North American coral snake, *Micrurus fulvius*. Toxicon 14:143–145.

Ford, N. B., V. A. Cobb, and J. Stout. 1991. Species diversity and seasonal abundance of snakes in a mixed pine-hardwood forest of east Texas. Southwest. Nat. 36(2):171–177.

Fouquette, M. J., Jr., and H. L. Lindsay, Jr. 1955. An ecological survey of reptiles in parts of northwestern Texas. Texas J. Sci. 7(4):402–421.

Fowlie, J. A. 1965. The Snakes of Arizona. Azul Quinta Press, Fallbrook, Calif.

Froom, B. 1972. The Snakes of Canada. McClelland and Stewart, Ontario.

Gehlbach, F. R. 1974. Evolutionary relationships of southwestern ringneck snakes (*Diadophis punctatus*). Herpetologica 30(2):140–148.

———. 1981. Mountain Islands and Desert Seas: A Natural History of the U.S.-Mexican Borderlands. Texas A&M Univ. Press, College Station, Tex.

Glenn, J. L., and R. C. Straight. 1978. Mohave rattlesnake, *Crotalus scutulatus,* venom: Variation in toxicity with geographical origin. Toxicon 16(1):81–84.

———. 1982. The rattlesnakes and their venom yield and lethal toxicity. Pp. 3–119 *in* Rattlesnake Venoms: Their Actions and Treatment, A. T. Tu, ed. Marcel Dekker, New York.

Gloyd, H. K. 1938. A case of poisoning from the bite of a black coral snake. Herpetologica 1(5):121–124.

Gloyd, H. K., and R. Conant. 1990. Snakes of the *Agkistrodon* complex: A monographic review. Soc. Stud. Amph. Rept., Contrib. Herpetol. no. 6.

Goldsmith, S. K. 1984. Aspects of the natural history of the rough green snake, *Opheodrys aestivus* (Colubridae). Southwest. Nat. 29(4):445–452.

Greene, B. D. 1993. Life history and ecology of the Concho water snake, *Nerodia harteri paucimaculata.* Ph.D. diss., Texas A&M Univ., College Station, 134 pp.

Greene, B. D., et al. 1994. Feeding ecology of the Concho water snake, *Nerodia harteri pauci-maculata*. J. Herpetology 28(2):165–172.

Greene, H. W., and G. V. Oliver, Jr. 1965. Notes on the natural history of the western massasauga. Herpetologica 21(3): 225–228.

Guidry, E. V. 1953. Herpetological notes from southeastern Texas. Herpetologica 9(1):49–56.

Hardy, D. L. 1992. A review of first aid measures for pitviper bite in North America with an appraisal of extractor suction and stungun electroshock. Pp. 405–414 *in* Biology of the Pitvipers, Campbell and Brodie, eds. Selva, Tyler, Tex.

Hardy, D. L., and H. W. Greene. 1995. Natural history notes: *Crotalus molossus molossus* (blacktail rattlesnake), maximum length. Herpetol. Rev. 26(2):101.

Hardy, D. L., M. Jeter, and J. J. Corrigan, Jr. 1982. Envenomation by the northern blacktail rattlesnake (*Crotalus molossus molossus*): Report of two cases and the *in vitro* effects of the venom on fibrinolysis and platelet aggregation. Toxicon 20(2):487–493.

Jameson, D. L., and A. G. Flury. 1949. Reptiles and amphibians of the Sierra Vieja. Texas J. Sci. 1(2):54–79.

Kitchens, C. S., S. Hunter, and L. H. S. Van Mierop. 1987. Severe myonecrosis in a fatal case of envenomation by the canebrake rattlesnake (*Crotalus horridus atricaudatus*). Toxicon 25:455–458.

Klauber, L. M. 1939. Studies of reptile life in the arid southwest, 1: Night collecting on the desert with ecological statistics. Bull. Zool. Soc. San Diego 14(1):6–64.

———. 1940. The worm snakes of the genus *Leptotyphlops* in the United States and northern Mexico. Trans. San Diego Soc. Nat. Hist. 9(18):87–162.

———. 1956. Rattlesnakes: Their Habits, Life Histories, and Influence on Mankind. 2 vols. Univ. California Press, Berkeley.

Klemens, M. W. 1993. Amphibians and reptiles of Connecticut and adjacent regions. State Geolog. Nat. Hist. Survey Connecticut, Bull. 112.

Knopf, G. N., and D. W. Tinkle. 1961. The distribution and habits of *Sistrurus catenatus* in northwest Texas. Herpetologica 17(2):126–131.

Kofron, C. P. 1978. Foods and habitats of aquatic snakes (Reptilia, Serpentes) in a Louisiana swamp. J. Herpetol. 12(4):543–554.

Laposha, N., and R. Powell. 1982. Life history, *Virginia valeriae*. Herpetol. Rev. 13:97.

Lawson, R., and C. S. Lieb. 1990. Variation and hybridization in *Elaphe bairdi* (Serpentes:

Colubridae). J. Herpetol. 24(3):280–292.

McCrystal, H. K. 1991. The herpetofauna of the Big Bend region. Sonoran Herpetologist 4(4):137–141.

Mecham, J. S. 1979. The biogeographical relationships of the amphibians and reptiles of the Guadalupe Mountains. Natl. Park Serv. Trans. Proc. Ser. 4:169–179.

Medica, P. A. 1962. The Texas lyre snake, *Trimorphodon vilkinsonii*, in New Mexico. Herpetologica 18(1):65.

Miller, D. 1979. A life history study of the gray-banded kingsnake, *Lampropeltis mexicana alterna*, in Texas. Chihuahuan Desert Res. Inst. Contrib. 87:1–48.

Milstead, W. W., J. S. Mecham, and H. McClintock. 1950. The amphibians and reptiles of the Stockton Plateau in northern Terrell County, Texas. Texas J. Sci. 2(4):543–562.

Minton, S. A., Jr. 1956. A new snake of the genus *Tantilla* from west Texas. Fieldiana Zoology 34:449–452.

———. 1957. Variation in yield and toxicity of venom from a rattlesnake (*Crotalus atrox*). Copeia 1957(4):265–268.

———. 1959. Observations on amphibians and reptiles of the Big Bend region of Texas. Southwest. Nat. 3(1–4):28–54.

———. 1967. Observations on toxicity and antigenic make-up of venoms from juvenile snakes. Toxicon 4:294.

———. 1972. Amphibians and reptiles of Indiana. Indiana Acad. Sci. Mongr. 3:1–346.

Minton, S. A., Jr., and M. R. Minton. 1969. Venomous Reptiles. Charles Scribner's Sons, New York.

Minton, S. A., Jr., and S. A. Weinstein. 1986. Geographic and ontogenetic variation in venom of the western diamondback rattlesnake (*Crotalus atrox*). Toxicon 24:71–80.

Mount, R. M. 1975. The Reptiles and Amphibians of Alabama. Agr. Exp. Sta., Auburn University, Auburn, Ala.

Mueller, J. M. 1990. Population dynamics of the Concho water snake. M.S. thesis, Texas A&M Univ., College Station, 52 pp.

Mulaik, S., and D. Mulaik. 1943. Observations on *Ficimia streckeri* Taylor. Amer. Midl. Nat. 29(3):796–797.

Murray, L. T. 1939. Annotated list of amphibians and reptiles from the Chisos Mountains. Contr. Baylor Univ. Mus. 24:4–16.

Mushinsky, H. R., and J. J. Hebrard. 1977. Food partitioning by five species of water snakes in Louisiana. Herpetologica 33:127–129.

Mushinsky, H. R., J. J. Hebrard, and M. G. Walley. 1980. The role of temperature on the behavioral and ecological associations of sympatric water snakes. Copeia 1980(4): 744–754.

Nelson, D. H., and J. W. Gibbons. 1972. Ecology, abundance, and seasonal activity of the scarlet snake, *Cemophora coccinea.* Copeia 1972(3):582–584.

Olson, R. E. 1977. Evidence for the species status of Baird's ratsnake. Texas J. Sci. 29(1): 79–84.

Painter, C. W., P. W. Hyder, and G. Swinford. 1992. Three species new to the herpetofauna of New Mexico. Herpetol. Rev. 24(4):155–156.

Parrish, H. M. 1964. Texas snakebite statistics. Texas State J. Med. 60:592–598.

Parrish, H. M., and R. E. Thompson. 1958. Human envenomation from bites of recently milked rattlesnakes: A report of three cases. Copeia 1958(2): 83–86.

Pettus, D. 1958. Water relationships in *Natrix sipedon.* Copeia 1958:207–211.

———. 1963. Salinity and subspecies in *Natrix sipedon.* Copeia 1963(3):499–504.

Rael, E. D., J. D. Johnson, O. Molina, and H. K. McCrystal. 1992. Distribution of a Mohave-like protein in rock rattlesnake (*Crotalus lepidus*) venom. Pp. 163–168 *in* Biology of the Pitvipers, Campbell and Brodie, eds. Selva, Tyler, Tex.

Reichenbach, N. G., and G. H. Dalrymple. 1986. Energy use, life histories, and the evaluation of potential competition of two species of garter snake. J. Herpetol. 20(2):133–153.

Rossman, D. A. 1963. The colubrid snake genus *Thamnophis:* A revision of the *sauritus* group. Bull. Florida St. Mus. Biol. Sci. 7:99–178.

Rundquist, E. M., E. Stegall, D. Grow, and P. Gray. 1978. New herpetological records from Kansas. Trans. Kansas Acad. Sci. 81(1):73–77.

Russell, F. E. 1960. Snake venom poisoning in southern California. California Med. 93: 347–350.

———. 1980. Snake Venom Poisoning. Scholium International, Great Neck, N.Y.

Russell, F. E., C. Gans, and S. A. Minton, Jr. 1978. Poisonous snakes. Clinical Med. 85(2): 13–30.

Russell, F. E., and H. W. Puffer. 1971. Pharmacology of snake venoms. *In* Snake Venoms and Envenomation. Marcel Dekker, New York.

Sabath, M. C., and L. E. Sabath. 1969. Morphological intergradation in Gulf coastal brown snakes, *Storeria dekayi* and *Storeria tropica.* Amer. Midl. Nat. 81(2):148–155.

Scott, N. J., et al. 1989. Distribution, habitat, and future of Harter's water snake, *Nerodia harteri,* in Texas. J. Herpetol. 23(4):373–389.

Seibert, H. C. 1950. Population density of snakes in an area near Chicago. Copeia 1950: 229–230.

Semlitsch, R. D., and G. B. Moran. 1984. Ecology of the redbelly snake (*Storeria occipitomaculata*) using mesic habitats in South Carolina. Amer. Midl. Nat. 111(1):33–40.

Strecker, J. K. 1926. On the habits of some southern snakes. Contr. Baylor Univ. Mus. 4: 3–10.

Taggart, T. W. 1992. Observations on Kansas amphibians and reptiles. Kansas Herpetol. Soc. Nwsl. 88:13–15.

Tanner, W. W. 1985. Snakes of western Chihuahua. Great Basin Nat. 45(4):615–676.

Tennant, A. 1984. The Snakes of Texas. Texas Monthly Press, Austin.

Theakston, R. D. G., and H. A. Reid. 1978. Changes in the biological properties of venom from *Crotalus atrox* with aging. Period. Biol. 80 (suppl. 1):123–133.

Tinkle, D. W. 1957. Ecology, maturation, and reproduction of *Thamnophis sauritus proximus.* Ecology 38:69–77.

True, F. W. 1883. On the bite of the North American coral snakes (genus *Elaps*). Amer. Nat. 17:26–31.

Vaughan, R. K., J. R. Dixon, and R. A. Thomas. 1996. A reevaluation of populations of the corn snake *Elaphe guttata* (Reptilia: Serpentes: Colubridae) in Texas. Texas J. Sci. 48(3):175–190.

Vermersch, T. G., and R. E. Kuntz. 1986. Snakes of South-central Texas. Eakin Press, Austin, Tex.

Vick, V. A. 1971. Symptomology of experimental and clinical envenomation. Pp. 71–86 *in* Neuropoisons: Their Pathophysiological Actions, vol. 1, L. L. Simpson, ed. Plenum, New York.

Vincent, J. W. 1982. Color pattern variation in *Crotalus lepidus* (Viperidae) in southwestern Texas. Southwest. Nat. 27(3): 263–272.

Webb, R. G. 1970. Reptiles of Oklahoma. Univ. Oklahoma Press, Norman.

Werler, J. E., and J. R. Dixon. 2000. Texas Snakes: Identification, Distribution, and Natural History. Univ. Texas Press, Austin.

Whiting, M. J. 1993. Population ecology of the Concho water snake, *Nerodia harteri paucimaculata,* in artificial habitats. M.S. thesis, Texas A&M University, College Station, 137 pp.

Williams, N. R. 1969. Population ecology of *Natrix harteri.*

M.S. thesis, Texas Tech Univ., Lubbock, 51 pp.

Wilson, L. D. 1970. The coachwhip snake, *Masticophis flagellum* (Shaw): taxonomy and distribution. Tulane Stud. Zool. Bot. 16:31–99.

Wilson, P. 1908. Snake poisoning in the United States: A study based on an analysis of 740 cases. Arch. Int. Med. 1(5): 516–570.

Wingert, W. A., et al. 1980. Distribution and pathology of copperhead (*Agkistrodon contortrix*) venom. Toxicon 18:591–601.

Wright, A. H., and A. A. Wright. 1957. Handbook of Snakes of the United States and Canada. 2 vols. Comstock Publishing, Ithaca, N.Y.

Yancey, F. D. 1997. Maximum size: *Hypsiglena torquata jani* (Texas night snake). Herpetol. Rev. 28:205.

Zappalorti, R. T., and J. Burger. 1985. On the importance of disturbed sites to habitat selection by pine snakes in the Pine Barrens of New Jersey. Environ. Conserv. 12(4): 358–361.

INDEX OF COMMON NAMES

Italic numbers indicate detailed discussion.

INDEX OF SCIENTIFIC NAMES

Italic numbers indicate detailed discussion.